NGO Leadership and Human Rights

NGO Leadership and Human Rights

Richard K. Ghere

Foreword by
H. George Frederickson

Kumarian Press
An Imprint of Stylus Publishing

NGO Leadership and Human Rights

COPYRIGHT © 2013 by Kumarian Press, an imprint of STYLUS PUBLISHING, LLC.

Published by Stylus Publishing, LLC
22883 Quicksilver Drive
Sterling, Virginia 20166-2102

Library of Congress Cataloging-in-Publication Data

Ghere, Richard K., 1945-
NGO leadership and human rights / Richard Ghere. — 1st ed.
      p.   cm.
  Includes bibliographical references and index.
  ISBN 978-1-56549-419-0 (cloth : alk. paper) — ISBN 978-1-56549-418-3 (pbk. : alk.
    paper) — ISBN 978-1-56549-420-6 (library networkable e-edition) — ISBN
    978-1-56549-421-3 (consumer e-edition)
  1. Non-governmental organizations—Management. 2. Human rights. 3. Community
    development. I. Title.
  HD62.6.G473   2012
  658—dc23

                                                                    2012006921

13-digit ISBN: 978-1-56549-419-0 (cloth)
13-digit ISBN: 978-1-56549-418-3 (paper)
13-digit ISBN: 978-1-56549-420-6 (library networkable e-edition)
13-digit ISBN: 978-1-56549-421-3 (consumer e-edition)

Printed in the United States of America

All first editions printed on acid free paper that meets the American National Standards Institute Z39-48 Standard.

Bulk Purchases: Quantity discounts are available for use in workshops and for staff development. Call 1-800-232-0223

First Edition, 2013
10   9   8   7   6   5   4   3   2   1

Contents

Foreword

In the past twenty-five years the public service has changed significantly. We have witnessed "the end of the government-centered public service and the rise of a multisectored service to replace it."[1] The federal government has relentlessly pushed responsibilities down to the states and localities. States continue to push responsibilities and financing down to their localities. States and localities, in turn, push responsibilities out to nonprofits and other nongovernmental organizations (NGOs). Federal, state, and local governments, in the endless drive to wish to appear small and to claim to have downsized, continue to contract out more and more public work. The most conservative estimate for just the federal government is that there are at least eight contract or grant employees being paid with government funds for every one actual government employee.[2] Add state and local government contract and grant employees, and nonprofit and NGO employees paid from foundation and philanthropic grants, and one sees, however unclearly, a vast "shadow bureaucracy." In the past "the public service" was thought to refer to those working for government. No longer. We now see more clearly the distinctions between the government and the public. There are many more people working for nonprofits and NGOs engaged in public service than there are government employees.

The new public service has changed the language of public policy and administration and the metaphors used to explain and understand it. The phrase "shadow bureaucracy" paints a word picture that helps one see the potential vastness of the new public service. The phrases "extended state" and "hollow state" help describe how government can appear stable or even smaller while public services can be growing and expanding. A friendly phrase, "public-private partnerships," is widely used to positively describe contract or grant arrangements between governments and NGO public service providers. But, the word most often used to describe the new public service is "governance." A nonprofit or an NGO engaged in public service may not be governmental but is certainly public and could be said to be engaged in governance.[3]

As the new public service has become less government-centered, young people preparing for careers have changed. Fewer and fewer want to work for government and more and more want to "help people," or "work with people," and look to nonprofit organizations and NGOs as the places where they might find satisfying careers.[4] After a slow start, American schools of public policy and administration have adapted their degree curricula in response to the sharply increased interest of graduate students in nonprofit and NGO careers. Also, after a slow start, there is a growing body of literature, both theoretical and empirical, having to do with public service in nonprofits and NGOs. This brings us to Richard K. Ghere's contribution, *NGO Leadership and Human Rights*.

Ghere takes on a three-part challenge—describing NGOs, particularly NGOs dedicated to matters of human rights; explaining what a human rights or "rights-based" approach to organization and management might mean; and unpacking the nature of leadership in such organizations. Ghere points out that there are distinctions between NGOs and nonprofits, and he is right. However, anyone working for or contemplating a career in a nonprofit or a nongovernmental organization might consider these distinctions but will soon recognize that the problems and challenges faced by them are very similar, as are the suggestions for dealing with these problems and challenges. To explain his perspective Ghere reduces the range of his consideration to those NGOs working on human rights. In the abstract it would seem that human rights is both too broad and too hopelessly idealistic. In fact, the NGOs Ghere considers are working on the most applied forms of human rights—right to bodily health and integrity, right of affiliation, right of practical reason, right to learn, and so forth. Again, while his examples have to do with human rights NGOs, Ghere's messages regarding the cultural, funding, and organizational challenges faced by human rights NGOs can be easily and readily applied to most other types of nonprofits and NGOs.

While it is axiomatic in all organizations that leadership matters, in many organizations, particularly governmental organizations, leaders matter in terms of productivity or effectiveness. In the NGO world leadership often determines organizational survival. In his treatment of human rights NGO leadership Ghere deftly uses contemporary institutional theory. The "sense making" logic of institutional theory is the thread that weaves through considerations of NGO organization and management, performance measurement and other forms of stake holder accountability, organizational learning and knowledge management, issues of gender, and human resources management. In this logic of leadership there is a particularly thoughtful treatment of the place of leadership rhetoric suited to the place and purposes of human rights NGOs. At the risk of being repetitive, while these leadership subjects have more or less to do with human rights NGOs, the lessons in them are broadly applicable to leadership and management in the full range of nonprofit organizations.

Ghere's *NGO Leadership and Human Rights* is an important contribution to the improving literature on the new public service.

H. George Frederickson

Notes

1. Light, Paul C. 1999. *The New Public Service*. Washington, DC: The Brookings Institution, p. 1.

2. Light, Paul C. 1999. *The True Size of Government*. Washington, DC: The Brookings Institution.

3. Frederickson, H. George. 2005. "Whatever Happened to Public Administration: Governance, Governance Everywhere." In *The Oxford Handbook of Public Management*, edited by Ewan Farlie, Lawrence E. Lynn Jr., and Christopher Pollitt, 282–304. Oxford: Oxford University Press.

4. Light, 1999. *The New Public Service*.

Preface

At an academic conference a few years ago, a colleague whom I have known for quite a while asked me to join him for refreshments. In response to a paper I had presented an hour or so earlier, he remarked, "You write about stuff I would be afraid to touch." At first, I took this as somewhat of a compliment, but upon further reflection it set in that he was likely referring to my tendency to tread fearlessly in strange places. Fortunately, I am privileged to work among friends who welcome such treading, at least in leveraging my teaching background in public administration to focus as well on nongovernmental organization (NGO) leadership. Specifically, the University of Dayton has instituted an interdisciplinary human rights studies undergraduate major intended on one hand to prepare some students for human-rights-related vocations but on the other to articulate what it means to be human and to advocate for human dignity in *any* chosen career. A next step is to add a human rights concentration to the Master of Public Administration Program that will allow career-oriented human rights students to earn both degrees. So in large part, this book is a child of curricular necessity to extend a "rights-based approach" into leadership within development, humanitarian, and rights-advocacy NGOs.

Fearless treading once led me into an uncomfortable dialogue with colleagues in my field of public administration. Following a spate of media accounts in 2001 about hundreds of "lost children" in the state of Florida (actually about the inability of that state's Department of Children and Families to track information as to the whereabouts of children supposedly in its foster-care system), I presented a conference paper that assessed whether this bureaucratic predicament amounted to "administrative evil" as characterized by two colleagues and friends, Guy Adams and Dan Balfour, in their provocative book *Unmasking Administrative Evil* (1998). Although my conclusions were notably equivocal, others took me to task, arguing that the lost children conundrum merely reflected an unfortunate but nonetheless predictable outcome of democratic governance—Florida's citizen-taxpayers were unable or unwilling to pay the freight for an ideal mechanism capable of monitoring the progress of all of its foster-care children all of the time, providing the appropriate level of case work for each child, and attending to the psychological care of these traumatized kids. The scolding that came my way was clearly on target; I had to relearn the basic "facts of life" of democratic process in front of a roomful of attendees. Managers in the public sector after all strive either to accomplish their mandated tasks in a competent manner or to "increase public value" on behalf of their collective customers. But for me, the experiences of these invisible children spoke forcefully in calling for rights-focused leadership *outside of government* (if it cannot function within the public sphere), *even in* an affluent society blessed with a responsive government under the rule of law. Years later, I still wonder whether these children had *any less a moral claim* to human dignity and humanitarian care because they "fell through the cracks" of decent governance.

Management rhetoric that alludes to "creating value," "adding value," or "increasing value" offers those with specific concerns for widespread suffering and human degradation intriguing conversation starters. On an implicit level, Peter Uvin deals with the enterprise of "creating value" in his powerful commentaries in *Aiding Violence* (1998) and *Human Rights and Development* (2004) that question the roles of development NGOs in Rwanda during the run-up to the 1994 genocide for their inability to anticipate the impending catastrophe. Apparently, those organizations were so diligently engaged in "creating value" (and creating niches for themselves within state-dependent development [1998, 177]) that they missed the humanitarian dimension, perhaps an example of goal-displacement in tragic proportion. Thus it appears there are "values" and then there are *values*. So in large part, the double entendre that surfaces in juxtaposing the public manager's efforts to create value to save a buck for the indignant taxpayer and an NGO leader's attempt to create (or sustain) values that uphold human dignity is indicative of some challenges encountered in drafting the chapters herein.

The transition from a teaching and research background in public administration to gaining insight that can inform rights-focused leadership involves a significant shift in institutional perspective. In terms of pedagogy, my key objective here has been to "make knowledge plain" (a theme that is underscored in reference to organization learning and knowledge management in chapter 6) for readers (presumably, many of them students) while also characterizing the institutional frameworks in which NGOs function—which are not so easily "made plain." In succinct terms, institutional perspectives look beneath and beyond the technical issues of management to probe the political, social, and cultural explanations of organization behavior. Clearly within NGOs that promote humanitarian or rights-based missions, leadership must first and foremost attend to the imperatives of these institutional environments. In other words, NGO leadership encompasses far more than a bundle of technical skills. In terms of scholarship, various lines of institutional thought offer powerful explanations for how organizations behave in their environments. Nonetheless, I deem it important to maintain a balance between efforts to elucidate pertinent scholarly ideas about institutions and the pedagogical priority "to make knowledge plain" for the reader. Regarding pertinent scholarship, I draw often from Richard Scott's (1995) "three pillars of institutions" that differentiate among regulative, normative, and cognitive elements and processes within organizations. As I point out in chapter 1, NGOs that advance human rights may in fact be normative in character, but those norms *cannot speak for themselves.* Rather, NGO professionals often rely on their cognitive skills to *demonstrate and articulate meaning* that will hopefully be accepted and taken for granted by other relevant actors and societies. In large part, the various chapters in this book focus on how NGO professionals function in, cope with, and relate to particular environments—thus, they deal with leadership issues that are inherently institutional in nature. Yet in this delicate balance between the scholarly treatment of institutions and pedagogical presentation, the latter appears to me the more equal.

In drafting these chapters, I have been able to draw on numerous commentaries wherein authors so ably characterize issues of practical management and leadership with a strong appreciation of institutional parameters and constraints. A quick glance at the bibliography reveals that I have depended heavily on the journal *Development in Practice* that (according to its masthead) "offers practice-relevant analysis and research relating to development and humanitarianism." In that the journal seeks culturally diverse views from practitioners and scholars around the globe, the ease by which contributors integrate practical concerns with robust theoretical explanation strikes me as both remarkable and refreshing. It seems ironic that the editor feels the need to *defend* this body of commentary as "grey literature" that apparently does not satisfy the scholarly tastes of some audiences. From my vantage point, such "grey literature" is in regrettably short supply. Hopefully, my references to this literature can serve as markers for a rich vein of scholarship and experience beyond the horizons of many public administration researchers, students, and practitioners in the United States.

To reiterate, I am lucky to work with those who are partial more to inter-disciplinary wandering (and wondering about the human condition) than to guarding turf. In this regard, permit me to acknowledge my colleagues both in the Department of Political Science and in the wider cluster who sustain our undergraduate Human Rights Studies Program for their keen interest in my work. I am much indebted to Paul Benson, dean of the College of Arts and Sciences at the University of Dayton, and to Jason Pierce, my colleague and department chair, for their support in facilitating my progress in this undertaking. At Kumarian Press, Jim Lance's steadfast enthusiasm for this project and Alexandra Hartnett's sensitive production guidance made burdens light and all the more worth pursuing. Superb editing on the parts of Jessica Begonia and Alisa Bartel—graduate students in the Master of Public Administration Program at the University of Dayton—provided the organization I very much needed to maintain momentum in this work; I am humbly grateful to both for their assistance and optimism. Alisa is an effective human-rights leader as cofounder of "The New Abolitionist Movement," a student organization that lobbied successfully for the 2011 enactment of anti-human-trafficking legislation in the state of Ohio. Lisa Ellison (my spouse) also provided editorial help in proofing earlier chapter drafts, but more important, she demonstrates what it is to *do* humanitarian work day-by-day (rather than write about it). In a *not-so-roundabout* way, she reminds me that we are all "works in progress" and, by extension, that the fruits of our labor (such as this book) represent directions rather than finished products. So I dedicate this book to Lisa.

Introduction
NGOs, Human Rights, and Leadership

The acronyms CAI and CIA can be easily confused. The latter of course is widely recognized as a US government agency pursuing intelligence matters, but the former may be familiar only to readers of a book about building schools in Afghanistan. Appearing on the *New York Times* Paperback Nonfiction bestselling list for 74 weeks, Greg Mortenson's *Three Cups of Tea* (2007) chronicles the author's work through the Central Asia Institute (CAI), the nongovernmental organization (NGO) he founded. In his July 13, 2008, *New York Times* op-ed column, Nicholas Kristof—who writes extensively on humanitarian issues—bestowed high praise on Mortenson: "So a lone Montanan staying at the cheapest guest houses has done more to advance U.S. interests in the region than the entire military and foreign policy apparatus of the Bush administration" (p. A14).

With the passage of time, Mortenson's image as a humble, self-sacrificing humanitarian tarnished amid accusations that he had misstated, exaggerated, or lied about accounts of his experiences in *Three Cups of Tea* and had diverted CAI funds for personal use. In his April 20, 2011, column titled " 'Three Cups of Tea,' Spilled," Kristof speculates that Mortenson's problems may be more attributable to inept organizational leadership than to bad character:

> My inclination is to reserve judgment until we know more, for disorganization may explain more faults than dishonesty. I am deeply troubled that only 41 percent of the money raised in 2009 went to build schools, and Greg, by nature, is more of a founding visionary than the disciplined C.E.O. necessary to run a $20 million-a-year charity. On the other hand, I'm willing to give some benefit of the

doubt to a man who has risked his life on behalf of some of the world's most voiceless people. (Kristof 2011, A27)

Kristof's intuition that associates *disorganization* with a *founding vision-ary* finds corroboration in some existing commentary on NGO leadership. Founders may excel at motivating followers and inspiring social innovation, but they sometimes fail as facilitators who can build an organization's future and *institutionalize* its missions (Uphoff et al. 1998; Smillie and Hailey 2002, 135–37). As noted by Marcuello Servos and Marcuello, time forces vision-ary founders to confront certain realities: "The charismatic founders of NGOs [need to] experience what it means to consolidate an organisation. Idealists' initial dreams [must] give way to the daily routine and the institutionalisation of certain ways of doing things, which usually gain legitimacy as time passes. The pursuit of utopia eventually employs organisational structures" (2007, 395). *In large part, this book intends to equip those called toward leadership in humanitarian work to nurture strong organizations capable of sustaining rights-based missions.*

The introductory chapter of a book titled *NGO Leadership and Human Rights* needs to offer readers working explanations for the three terminological constructs packed into that title. The three sections to follow are intended to provide some preliminary understanding of what the term *NGO* means, ex-plain how "human rights" affect NGO missions, and focus on the meaning of "leadership" in NGOs in comparison to private sector and government agency leadership. A fourth section encourages readers with vocational aspirations in human rights work to think strategically in preparing for their professional futures.

NGOs

Defining NGOs, according to one analyst, "is not an exercise for the intel-lectually squeamish" (Simmons 1998, 85). First used by the United Nations in 1949, the term *nongovernmental organization* resists tight definition as it has been applied to a broad spectrum of organizations including "'voluntary associations,' 'nonprofit associations,' 'international nongovernmental organi-zations,' 'nongovernmental development organizations,' 'new social movement organizations,' 'people's organizations,' 'membership organizations,' 'grassroots support organizations,' and 'membership support organizations,' to name but a few" (Fernando and Heston 1997, 10). Keck and Sikkink's minimalist defini-tion serves as a common denominator among these diverse groupings: "NGOs are organizations that are independent of any government. Typically, NGOs are made up of activists devoted to working on particular issues according to a set of principled ideas or values" (Keck and Sikkink 1998, quoted in Breen 2003, 455).

Beyond the common denominator of "independence from government" (even though some NGOs in fact contract with governments to provide services), there is debate as to whether NGOs are in essence "nonprofit" or "private" organizations. Regarding the former, a 1994 UN document describes an NGO as a

> non-profit entity whose members are citizens or associations of citizens of one or more countries and whose activities are determined by the collective will of its members in response to the needs of the members of one or more communities with which the NGO cooperates. (Simmons 1998, 83)

In addition, many NGOs rely on volunteer assistance to augment the work of paid, professional staff persons. Others understand NGO societal functions and institutional structures more closely aligned to private organizations than to third sector nonprofit entities that interface the boundary between the private sector and government. For example, rural-development specialist Norman Uphoff argues that although "people's associations and membership organizations" (often called "grassroots organizations") link the private and public sectors, NGOs should be regarded as a subsector of the private sector, a private voluntary organization, accountable *not* to a large membership but to a small governing core. He explains, "Service organizations, the category I think most NGOs belong in, deal with clients or beneficiaries. . . . Clients or beneficiaries of NGOs are in a 'take it or leave it' relationship, quite similar to that of customers and employees in a private firm" (1996, 24–25). Others cite the NGO imperative for achieving self-sufficiency as a close parallel to the profit motive in private firms (e.g., Fernando and Heston 1997, 11). Perhaps it is the case that many NGOs do in fact exhibit characteristics common to private firms (e.g., behavioral norms, forms of sanction, and decision-making processes) but find it advantageous to acquire nonprofit legal status as an inducement for contributors.

Given the absence of a universally acceptable definition, an official at the Carnegie Endowment for International Peace offers a taxonomic approach that classifies NGOs according to such criteria as ultimate goal, function, and funding source—for example:

- *Ultimate goal:* Does the NGO change societal norms, improve understanding, influence agendas, implement policies, solve problems in the absence of an adequate governmental response?
- *Function:* Does the NGO facilitate advocacy, information gathering and analysis, information dissemination, generation of ideas and recommendations, a monitoring and watchdog role, service delivery, mediation and facilitation, financing, and grant making?
- *Funding sources:* Does the NGO depend on dues/assessments, donations, foundations, governments (grants or contracts), intergovernmental organizations (IGOs)? (Simmons 1998, 85)

Significant criteria such as goals, functions, and funding sources need to be understood in the context of NGO interactions with other organizations either in particular locales or on the global stage. Two of these contextual relationships stand out as especially important: (1) the funding relationship between donor institutions and indigenous NGOs engaged in development and/or humanitarian efforts and (2) connector relations with other organizations that can advance NGO missions. The first context, also known as "the aid chain" (Wallace 2007), is often characterized as a contentious relationship between *North* and *South*, terminology that has more to do with international power and wealth than geographic location (as a case in point, AusAID—the international development agency in Australian government—is a "Northern" donor whereas most of the 3,000-plus NGOs in Haiti qualify as "Southern" organizations regardless of locations above or below the equator). Thus, the North consists of *multilateral* organizations (with multinational memberships such as the Asian Development Bank), *bilateral* organizations (government agencies such as AusAID that fund NGOs), and large, international NGOs (such as CARE International or Oxfam UK) headquartered in affluent societies.

By contrast, the South consists of poor nations or settings (such as Uganda or even impoverished populations in affluent societies) wherein particular "southern NGOs work to affect change" (Gaventa 2002; Wallace 2007, 12). In regard to the "connector" context, Edwards and Fowler distinguish NGOs from other change-directed organizations in society but emphasize the unique NGO role to serve as "a critical part of the 'connective tissue' of a vigorous civil society [such that] making and sustaining the right connections lies at the heart of NGO management" (2002, 9). The point here is that NGOs' accomplishments in affecting positive social change or advancing rights lie in

NGOs' abilities to "act as bridges, facilitators, brokers, and translators, linking together the institutions, interventions, capacities and levels of action that are required to lever broader structural changes from discrete or small-scale actions" (p. 9). Thus, NGOs are usually more apt to make progress by leveraging their connections than by confronting power actors such as state regimes and development institutions head-on.

Lacking consensus on a precise definition, some analysts evaluate *particular types* of organizations, such as development NGOs, humanitarian (or relief) NGOs, rights-advocacy NGOs, and so forth. This book focuses on NGO capabilities to serve as "connective tissue" in leveraging action on behalf of human rights in conjunction with goal commitments related to development (as it may be characterized), humanitarian relief, and human rights advocacy per se. Each of these mission orientations (including rights advocacy itself) poses certain leveraging constraints. First, the "development community" has tended to distance itself from human rights advocates (and vice versa), prompting appeals for interactive cooperation on the basis that "development" is inherently relational, people centered, and a fundamental right (e.g., Slim 1995; Russell 1998; Sen 1999; Uvin 2004, 2007). Second, organizations involved in relief efforts are inclined to elevate the imperative for political neutrality in the face of abusive power above responsibilities to speak out against rights deprivations and violations (see Slim 1997, 2000). Third, human rights advocates gravitate toward rights talk, "principled" confrontation, and adjudicative processes (in essence, "lawyering") in response to highly visible crises rather than toward low-profile "politicking" (that is, collaboration and negotiation) with adversaries and allies on a continual basis (see Wiseberg 1991; Uvin 2004, 122–29). Given these various obstacles inhibiting human rights connections, it appears useful to pose a few fundamental questions that can ground how readers relate to the chapters to follow, the first of which deals with forces in NGO environments: *How do NGO environments affect organizational capabilities to leverage actions on behalf of human rights?*

Human Rights, Dignity, and NGOs

How can one distinguish a "rights-based NGO" (a designation appearing throughout this book) from other organizations that generally "do good work" for people in various global settings? Any viable response to this question is bound to provoke critical questions, as is the case with the distinction proposed here: A *rights-based* organization enables the rearrangement of power relationships in ways that support the dignity of people *for no other reason* than their humanness and advocate for rights "one should hold by virtue of being a person" (Donnelly 1982, 305). This interpretation calls attention to (1) the controversial nature of "human rights" particularly as related to various philosophical and culture-based understandings of rights, (2) the linkages (or logical incompatibilities) between alternative conceptions of "human dignity" and human rights, (3) the requisite human capabilities necessary to realize dignity, and (4) the nature of human rights' transformative power.

First, make no mistake about it; human rights talk raises controversies concerning the substantive content of particular rights, the legitimacy of the "human rights" ideal in the context of Western philosophical traditions and varying cultural settings, and the inclusion of certain economic entitlements as a human right. Lamenting the lack of agreement on (an "official theory" of) rights content leading up to the adoption of the Universal Declaration of Human Rights in 1948, Charles Beitz speculates that "the framers evidently believed that people in various cultures could find reasons within their own ethical traditions to support the Declaration's practical requirements" (2003, 36). For Beitz, the absence of an agreed-upon theory, or conception, of human dignity is "embarrassing," given its prominence in the US Declaration of Independence and French Declaration of the Rights of Man. With regard to Western traditions, some classical liberal philosophers dismiss notions of human rights and social justice as sentimentalist aspirations in favor of their minimalist position that moral rights entail only the "property rights" (defined in various ways; e.g., see Becker 1977; Cohen 2008; Arneson 2010)—although some *do* acknowledge the plights of "moral patients" who for various reasons are deprived of their property rights (e.g., see McPherson 1984). On the other hand, the "cultural critique" charges that the human rights ideal is a Western liberalist construct that lacks universal applicability. In particular reference to "Asian values" that supposedly justify authoritarian regimes, Amartya Sen argues that the pluralism of political ideas in Asian societies diffuses claims that Asian values are incompatible with human rights (1999, 227–40). Moreover, some find seeds of human rights and dignity within Eastern religions (see, e.g., May 2006). Finally, the inclusion of certain economic entitlements, such as the *basic right* of "at least subsistence" (Shue 1980, 22–29), finds controversy particularly where libertarian ideologies prevail.

Second, notwithstanding Sen's insights on the diversity of political thought *within* cultures, the argument that the human rights ideal reflects Western liberalism holds some merit. In their essay explaining the linkage between a particular (liberalist) conception of human dignity and human rights, Howard and Donnelly (1986) follow the lead of Ronald Dworkin who associates "the heart of liberalism" with the right of equal concern and respect. In Dworkin's words,

> Government must not only treat people with concern and respect, but with equal concern and respect. It must not distribute goods or opportunities unequally on the ground that some citizens are entitled to more because they are worthy of more concern. It must not constrain liberty on the ground that one citizen's conception of the good life . . . is nobler or superior to another's. (Dworkin 1977, 273, quoted in Howard and Donnelly 1986, 802–3)

From this, Howard and Donnelly understand that "conceptions of human dignity" vary among political regimes but stress that only the liberalist conception (of equal concern and respect) supports human rights derived from "merely by being a person" as an autonomous individual. Following this logic, alternative conceptions of "human dignity" (or people's "places" in society) either trade off equality for individual freedom (consistent with the preferences of political libertarians who advocate for the minimalist state) or circumscribe "human dignity" around expected behaviors that support a particular regime. In the latter case, there is no "place" for the individual *outside* of her defined role in (a traditionalist) community, of a homogenous proletariat (in communist societies), of an all-encompassing moral order (in a corporatist, perhaps fascist, society), or of compliance for the future benefits of development (in a development dictatorship; Howard and Donnelly 1986, 808–13). Consistent with a liberalist conception of human dignity, a rights-based perspective celebrates individual autonomy and people's individual and collective agency to control the circumstances that affect their lives. Absent people's *agency*, an authentic rights culture cannot exist *even if* regimes follow through in delivering the substance of a "right" (i.e., adequate housing or health care).

Third, regimes that entertain a liberalist perspective on human dignity (in terms of "equal respect and concern") are obliged to promote conditions that make "a life worth living"—that is, provide basic *capabilities* that empower people as agents to exert control over their lives. Martha Nussbaum explains the connection between agency and capabilities as follows:

> The notion of dignity is closely related to the idea of active striving. It is thus a close relative of the notion of basic capability, something inherent in the person that exerts a claim that it should be developed. . . . In general, the Capabilities Approach, in my

version, focuses on the protection of areas of freedom so central that their removal makes life not worthy of human dignity. (Nussbaum 2011, 31)

Freedom as people's potential to empower themselves can be confused with the market libertarian's "freedom" to make individual choices without interference. As Séverine Deneulin points out, "From this [libertarian] perspective, it is possible to be free while starving to death at the same time. [In other words] the freedom that matters is not the freedom from interference of others, but the freedom one has to lead a good and worthwhile life" (2009, 51). So, what *capabilities* are needed for one to realize such freedom? Nussbaum is explicit in articulating 10 central capabilities that a "decent political order must secure to all its citizens at least at a threshold level": (1) life; (2) bodily health; (3) bodily integrity; (4) senses, imagination, and thought; (5) emotion; (6) practical reason; (7) affiliation; (8) other species; (9) play; and (10) control over one's environment (2011, 33–34). Generally concurring with Nussbaum's capability approach, Sen (1999) prefers *not* to categorize capabilities in deference to others that may be acknowledged in the future. Presumably, rights-based organizations should appeal to "decent" governmental and corporate regimes (even some holding nonliberalist conceptions of dignity) to provide for the development of basic capabilities needed for worthwhile living.

Fourth, rights-oriented NGOs seek to bring about transformative change in the behaviors and actions of states, corporate entities, and individual actors in ways that promote human dignity and empowerment. As Charles Beitz explains, "[Human rights politics] seeks to propagate ideas and motivate political change. Human rights stand for a certain ambition about how the world might be" (2003, 40). That said, the change dynamics at work in advancing rights causes—whether related to authentic "moral discernment" or alternatively to a Machiavellian realization of materialistic interests (or a bit of both) on the parts of states, corporations, or individual and factional motives within either—are *anything but clear* (see Landolt 2004). Is it the case that the transformative potential of NGOs and similar organizations lies in their morally persuasive capabilities as "norms entrepreneurs" to embed new rights norms into the global culture (see Finnemore and Sikkink 1998), or rather that the norms they promote afford new opportunities for those wielding power to pursue their material interests? Or, from a utilitarian perspective, *does it matter?* The following passage reflects this utilitarian stance that Risse, Ropp, and Sikkink assume in *The Power of Human Rights* (even though these authors value NGOs' roles as norms entrepreneurs in the diffusion of human rights):

"Prescriptive status" means that the actors involved regularly refer to the human rights norm to describe and comment on their own behavior and that of others; the validity of claims of the norm are no longer controversial. We argue that the process by which principled ideas gain "prescriptive status" should be decisive for their sustained impact on political and social change. . . . We are not that interested in the "true beliefs" of actors, as long as they are consistent in their verbal utterances and their words and deeds ultimately match. (Risse, Ropp, and Sikkink 1999, 29)

Risse, Ropp, and Sikkink then categorize consistent deeds as (1) ratifying human rights conventions (including optional protocols), (2) institutionalizing norms into constitutions and laws, (3) institutionalizing complaint and redress mechanisms, and (4) incorporating norms into the normal discourse and practice of government. Specifically, these authors situate "prescriptive status" as an achievable milestone within a particular phase of norms adoption. However, *at minimum* the transformative power of rights NGOs lies in its agenda-setting potential to confer "prescriptive status" on issues that affect human dignity. In this regard, Chapter 2 elaborates on the political nature of rights discourse, and Chapter 3 connects institutional visions of transformative change with alternative economic and political ideologies. But for now, it is important to reflect on the *leadership implications* of the controversial issues raised here: *What obstacles can NGOs expect to encounter in adopting a rights-based perspective, and how can those obstacles be surmounted?*

NGO Leadership: Making Hope "Real"

Sometimes the simple questions prove to be the most difficult to answer. Implicitly, the focus of this book is predicated on a fairly simple question that can be stated in everyday language: *What's it like to lead an NGO, particularly one that has adopted a rights-based perspective?* Such a question invites comparisons, for example—*Is an NGO leader like a chief operating officer (CEO) in a corporation such as General Electric (in the United States or elsewhere)? A government executive (like a director of a state environmental protection agency)? A head of a large not-for-profit (like the United Way)?* In terms of similarity, each is an *institutional leader* rather than simply a technocratic manager concerned only with control and authority issues or specific managerial functions (e.g., staffing, reporting, and coordinating; Clay 1994, 239). In other words, corporate executive officers, government administrators, and NGO officials *alike* attend to the longer term, more fundamental issues of conserving institutional *legitimacy* (or general credibility in meeting various societal expectations) and maintaining *stability*—or in the case of NGOs, institutional *sustainability* (see Terry 1995; Lewis 2003).

Put another way, organizations in each of these three sectors must be understood not (merely) as "technical production machines" but as *institutions* that, according to organization theorist W. Richard Scott,

> consist of cognitive, normative, and regulative structures and ac-
> tivities that provide stability and meaning to social behavior. In-
> stitutions are transported by various carriers—cultures, structures,
> and routines—and they operate on multiple levels of jurisdiction.
> (Scott 1995, 3)

As Scott implies, the leader's institutional vision extends outward to lo-cal, national, and global environments wherein the expectations of specific stakeholders and broad publics affect the organization's legitimacy for better or for worse. For example, executives of US corporations must address com-pliance issues related to the 2002 Sarbanes-Oxley Act that oversees corporate governance, accounting, and reporting procedures to protect investors at the national level and with "corporate social responsibility" related to all levels. Government officials in democratic societies need to be as attentive to the norms of fairness, equality, and other ethical concerns (in abiding to the spirits of "due process" and "equal protection" of/under law, of impartiality, of trans-parency, and so forth), as well as to the attainment of more instrumental policy objectives. Finally, NGO leaders must demonstrate that their organizations' development, humanitarian, and rights-advocacy initiatives are not only "cred-ible" but also *necessary* in the pursuit of human dignity.

From an institutional perspective, what is taken as "knowledge" evolves from, and in turn revises, *shared systems of meaning* within both the organiza-tion and its environments (see D'Andrade 1984, 89–96). In this regard, ex-ecutives in all three sectors cultivate "meaning systems" as founts of knowl-edge that support legitimacy at various societal levels. If Scott is correct in his assertion that "institutions consist of cognitive, normative, and regulative structures and activities," it can be said that leaders in business, government, and NGOs similarly avail themselves—*to greater or lesser extents*—to each of these "pillars" of (or elements of) institutions in exacting compliance, convey-ing appropriate logic, and grounding legitimacy (1995, 34–45). Although it might typically rely on corporate (regulative) rules and performance standards, a business firm could engage in cognitive activities by interpreting (or framing) what "corporate social responsibility" actually means (see Shamir 2005) or clarifying what its "expertise" means to its customers (Alvesson 1993, 1000–4). And although government organizations typically derive knowledge from authoritative (regulative) laws and established patterns of routines to "make sense" of complex and ambiguous public environments, public administrators also may engage in "the management of meaning"—for example, by defining what "agency transparency" means by developing procedures for releasing sensitive documents or what "cyber-government" means by designing interactive modes of citizen participation.

If institutional leadership *is similar* among the sectors in relying on regulative, normative, and cognitive activities to validate knowledge, the *differences* may lie in the extent of reliance on each. In an effort to call attention to institutional leadership as a unifying theme in this book, I cautiously advance the proposition that *NGO leadership is distinguishable by its prevalent reliance on cognitive processes to transform altruistic aspirations into operational realities "on the ground."* To borrow from a title of an article examining NGO development partnerships in Africa, I contend that NGO professionals bear the institutional responsibility of "making it [hope] real and making it intentional" (Postma 1994). The purpose of this book is not to compare leadership among the three sectors; therefore, its efforts will not empirically support (or refute) this proposition. Nonetheless, we can envision various situations that would oblige NGO leaders to manage meanings—in response to circumstances calling leaders to

- interpret what NGO accountability (and, for that matter, donor responsibility) means among various stakeholders in the organization's work (see Anderson 2009),
- convey a coherent sense of the NGO's mission within a culturally diverse workforce (see Lewis 2003),
- promote moral learning in terms of what it means for corporations to take responsibility in attending to human rights concerns (see Spitzeck 2009),
- articulate an appropriate meaning of "development" that resonates with how program participants (or beneficiaries) "see their world" (see Easton, Monkman, and Miles 2003), and
- establish a common denominator of "meaning" that can be shared among organizations in an NGO network or coalition (see Postma 1994).

Each of these scenarios directs attention to the importance of cognition and perception as related to a leader's ability to promote change. In this regard, sociologist Neil Fligstein argues that principal actors in an organization can initiate change by offering a particular construct of a "problem," as well as an appropriate "solution," and that "solution" could be expected to enhance the power of the organization (1991, 315). Thus, leaders exercise power through the persuasive reasoning they put forward in (re)interpreting the meaning of ambiguous situations.

For Powell and DiMaggio, *cognition* "refers to reason and the unconscious grounds of reason: classifications representations, scripts, schemas" and so forth (1991, 35, n. 10). In other words, leaders can introduce seemingly commonsensical logics of understanding in response to ambiguity to promote *their* interpretation of reality—in essence, "making it real." For example, given the difficulties of determining an NGO's success in advocating for human rights, a leader might design *categories* indicative of success—such as prestige, self-satisfaction, goals, ability, hard work, and competition (D'Andrade 1984, 95)—that promote the agency's image in annual reports and project proposals. In his "structuralization theory," Anthony Giddens speaks of *rules of signification* (1984, 29) that "restrict and enable agents to make sense of the context they act in and to communicate this meaning and their views of ongoing practices to others" (Sydow and Windeler 1998, 271, quoted in Yang 2011, 270). Thus, the categories and schemas leaders devise to promote sense-making *in* the organization project cognitive interpretations that also influence stakeholders in *external environments*. The strong focus here on the cognitive dimension does not discount the value of the other two institutional processes (the regulative and the normative) in NGO leadership. In emergency relief contexts wherein chaos is rampant (e.g., in a makeshift refugee camp), a leader's ability to impose rules to instill order provides desperate people a humane sense of stability (see Mintzberg 2001). And clearly, "development," "humanitarian," and "human rights" communities all coalesce around inherently normative imperatives. Nonetheless, the "nongovernmental" character of these entities implies that leaders cannot rely on authoritative law to promote legitimacy or sustainability. Furthermore, it follows that adroit and nimble leadership—on behalf of humane *norms*—should take care to avoid doctrinal "traps" that limit essential dialogues with donors, beneficiaries, partners, and adversaries (Smillie and Hailey 2002, 134).

Operating within the cultures of development, humanitarianism, and human rights, NGO professionals confront the institutional challenge of (re) articulating and (re)interpreting meanings in ways that "make hope real and make it intentional." But in terms of professional development, how does one *prepare* for effective institutional leadership in the nongovernmental sector? Such a question seeks out both a wide range of professional skills required of staff professionals and specific competencies that support strong leadership. Along these lines, a recent book on public service management elaborates on a wide array of professional competencies, several of which relate to effective institutional leadership. Specifically, Bowman, West, and Beck group these competencies as follows:

- technical competencies (specialized knowledge, legal knowledge, program management, and resource management),
- ethical competencies (values management, moral reasoning, individual morality, public morality, and organizational ethics), and
- leadership competencies (assessment and goal setting, hard [technical] and soft ["people"] management skills, management styles, political and negotiation skills, and evaluation) (Bowman, West, and Beck 2010).

The authors discuss each of these skills in the context of a new, continuously changing public service that in many ways parallels the complex and fluid settings in which many NGOs function.

Not surprisingly, Bowman, West, and Beck focus on the regulative element (of public institutions) in pointing out the unique roles that public leaders play "as part of an administrative structure that includes career employees and political appointees [and the importance of] networking relationships that characterize the 'new public service' cross-sectoral boundaries" (2010, 99–100). Nonetheless, they are attentive as well to a number of competencies that, when adapted to particular situations, address the cognitive institutional dimension. For instance, these authors refer to adaptive changes in leadership style as "occur[ring] when a leader switches from negotiation to confrontation to attain a goal" (p. 107). Beyond this, Bowman, West, and Beck have much to say about "the use of political and negotiation skills" that rely on cognitive learning techniques such as asking "why?" "why not?" "what if?" "what makes that fair?" and so on. With a few interpretive liberties here and there, all of Bowman, West, and Beck's competencies serve well as standards for NGO professionals in general and leaders in particular. Thus, readers are advised to stay attuned to appropriate leadership skills and competencies in relation to the variety of institutional settings encountered in the following chapters. Specifically, the pertinent question here could be posed as, *What particular competencies do NGO leaders need to understand the distinctive nature of their institutional environments and respond to them effectively?*

Career Development Issues

As previously mentioned, Peter Uvin (2004) specifies some essential elements of a rights-based perspective that could guide organizational development toward a collective consciousness that affirms human empowerment. The chapters that follow in this book examine leadership responsibilities as they relate to institutional concerns such as accountability, organization learning, human resources management, and others. But from a pedagogical perspective, questions arise as to whether *individuals*—and, specifically, prospective leaders in humanitarian endeavors—can benefit from any measure of career development guidance. Since a coherent literature on "career development for rights-conscious leaders" has yet to emerge, the strategy here is to compare the career profiles of two exemplary leaders of large, rights-affirming NGOs (one headquartered in Bangladesh and the other in the United States) to discern patterns that might help others chart their career trajectories toward rights work in the NGO setting.

The first career profile focuses on Fazle Hasan (or F. H.) Abed, who founded the Bangladesh Rehabilitation Assistance Committee (BRAC) in 1972. Abed's career path to NGO leadership led through private sector management in the oil multinational Shell. An accountant by training, Abed spent his early years with Shell in personnel management, a job assignment that afforded him experiences in handling bureaucracy and working collaboratively with employees. Later, Abed directed the finance division there. He reflected on his personnel work as follows: "I learned to put faith in people and appreciate it when they put faith in me. Sometimes, it may happen that people take advantage of you, but you have to accept it, you have to learn to handle the situation and build your own team" (Smillie and Hailey 2002, 152). Abed's commitment to (what could be described as) a rights-based perspective came about abruptly as a cathartic discovery, which he describes as follows:

> Communities are in conflict. . . . There are the rich and the poor, and their interests are in conflict. Ultimately, the benefits of community development accrued to the very rich and the well to do. So we began what we called a target group orientation and focused our attention to the poor. Obviously, this change in emphasis meant

that our staff had to work with the poorest, and this made the rural elites unhappy. They were suspicious of our motives and our staff had to cope with lots of opposition. (Smillie and Hailey 2002, 98)

This discovery marked a significant turning point in the BRAC organization.

Throughout *Managing for Change* (2002), Smillie and Hailey trace the various leadership behaviors of six leaders of NGOs in South Asia, including F. H. Abed of BRAC. Their observations of Abed's approach to NGO leadership reveal the following capabilities and preferences:

- *Ability to learn by doing:* Smillie and Hailey relate that Abed understood learning as a two-way process whereby he acts both as a teacher to his staff and also as just one participant in collaboration with the staff in undertaking analyses of strategies and problems. Referring to the latter, he commented, "This is how we learned. . . . In fact, BRAC started learning by doing, and the excitement was that everybody was learning too" (2002, 75). With regard to problem analysis, Abed was an ardent proponent of "embracing error" (see Korten 1980) through learning, as evident in this quote:

  > You go to a woman's house and find that the [microcredit] loan you have given her has been taken away by her husband. Or a child comes to your school and suddenly has to drop out because the parents have moved away, and the child doesn't learn anymore. These are all failures. . . . You must accept that they are part of the learning process. (Smillie and Hailey 2002, 76)

- *A preference for incremental strategies:* Through his (and BRAC's) catharsis to focus development efforts on the poor rather than entire communities, Abed stressed the value of a targeted, incremental approach to mission and strategy. For example, he explained BRAC's health strategy as having evolved incrementally; after trying a number of efforts (placing doctors in the field, training paramedics in villages, raising public health consciousness, etc.), "So gradually you evolve certain kinds of work that seem effective in getting your objective of better health. . . . So in a way, it is learning by doing and isolating the non-essential aspects and discarding them" (Smillie and Hailey 2002, 95).

- *Ability to instill confidence through communication:* Abed describes his own capabilities to infuse confidence in his staff by engaging them and then "getting out of their way" in assuming a low profile in the organization. He commented that it was not for him to assume a charismatic and highly visible role: "The answers came from them—the staff—more than I gave to them. Even at the beginning, I wanted to do the best thing in the most sensitive way possible, so people should be treated as people, as human beings" (Smillie and Hailey 2002, 142). That said, Abed is less than enamored by the "flat organization," preferring instead to maintain a formal hierarchy within the agency as a means of communication in a large and geographically dispersed NGO (pp. 125–26).

According to his biographical statement,[1] Abed was raised in an area of British India that is now part of Bangladesh. After graduating from Dhaka College in that area, he studied naval architecture at the University of Glasgow. Since shipbuilding work was difficult to find in Bangladesh, Abed joined the Chartered Institute of Management Accountants in London where he completed his studies in 1962. Thereafter, he returned to Bangladesh to work for Shell Oil. In 1970 (and while Abed was employed at Shell), a cyclone struck the coastal regions of Bangladesh, killing over 300,000 people. That catastrophe moved Abed to create HELP, an organization that provided relief and recovery to the worst affected areas. During this time, the struggle for Bangladeshi independence forced him back to London where he established Action Bangladesh, an organization to lobby European governments on behalf of the independence movement. After independence was won in 1972, Abed returned to Bangladesh to find this new nation in ruins with 10 million refugees. Amid this crisis, he founded BRAC to improve the living conditions of Bangladesh's rural poor.

A second career profile—that of Dr. Helene D. Gayle, president and CEO of CARE USA—reveals how an enduring commitment to improving the lives of the world's underserved populations has energized rights-based leadership in both previous government service and current NGO administration. As a physician, Dr. Gayle entered public service as an epidemiologist working within the US Centers for Disease Control and Prevention (CDC) in the Epidemiology Intelligence Service. From that technical role, she advanced to successive leadership positions in programs related to HIV/AIDS prevention and policy coordination in that federal agency. Through these responsibilities,

Dr. Gayle gained international experiences undertaking AIDS-related research in the former Zaire, Jamaica, South Africa, the Ivory Coast, and Thailand and working with (or detailed to) the US Agency for International Development as the agency AIDS coordinator.

An analytical biographer summarizes the skills Dr. Gayle demonstrated in public sector leadership in terms of the following strengths (Riccucci 2005, 91–98):

- *Ability to reframe issues:* In particular, Dr. Gayle effectively re-framed widespread perceptions of AIDS as a "gay man's disease in the White community" to an affliction of acute risk to the African American and Latino communities. In addition, she successfully developed specific preventative strategies for populations that had ignored previous public health messages.

- *Ability to create partnerships:* Dr. Gayle understood that effective leadership depends on building a variety of collaborative networks at community, state, national, and international levels that include the underserved themselves, as well as private sector organizations. In this regard, she comments that "many of the issues around AIDS have led to a good deal of mistrust between communities at risk, as well as communities at large, and I have tried to facilitate bringing a broad cross-section of people more into the process and create more open communications among them" (p. 92).

- *Ability to navigate the politics of public health:* Here, Dr. Gayle's keen political instincts combined with her interpersonal skills to support what could be characterized as diplomatic finesse to move HIV preventative programs forward. She indicated, "As I help to shape the direction of research efforts for HIV prevention programs, I try to provide justification for policy options based upon what we know and what we think will have the greatest positive benefit. While this seems obvious, it often isn't because of the political considerations which underlie diseases such as HIV/AIDS" (p. 94). One of her associates described Dr. Gayle's persistence in tough political environments as follows: "She is unflappable. Helene can take a two-by-four between the eyes and keep going. She, more than a lot of people I have ever met, is able to let a lot of things roll off her back and keep focused on what it is she is seeking to do within the limitations she faces."

- *Ability to set goals and target strategies:* Dr. Gayle is described by her biographer as one who can craft long-term goals collaboratively to support a shared vision and to "foster a pragmatic incrementalism" of short-term actionable steps to reach broad goals. She comments, "Measuring how well we do a particular sub-goal, or short-term actionable goal, isn't going to tell us whether we have reduced the spread of a particular disease, but these short-term actionable goals are necessary steps in order to meet our long-term or end goal" (p. 95).
- *Ability to build trust and confidence:* An agency colleague relates Dr. Gayle's credibility to a resoluteness not to "point a finger" or assign blame in the midst of difficult circumstances. A former US surgeon general spoke to her ability to engender confidence in this way: "I would say that she is probably the most trusted American among the African countries. . . . She has developed a lot of credibility because of her *knowledge* and insight into public health as it relates to AIDS and also because she really cares about the issues, and people see this" (p. 96; italics his).

Particularly evident in Dr. Gayle's career preparation prior to work at the Centers for Disease Control and Prevention and CARE USA is her strident dedication to the ideal of human empowerment as a unifying force that guided her formal education. From a background of family involvement in the US civil rights movement, she successfully pursued undergraduate studies in psychology at Bernard College and subsequently earned a medical degree at the University of Pennsylvania. Norma Riccucci (2005, 87) relates that while in medical school, Dr. Gayle attended a lecture on global efforts to eradicate smallpox, an event that redirected her career trajectory toward more graduate work in public health at Johns Hopkins University. Her continued commitment to humanitarian service first at technical levels (as an epidemiologist and public health researcher) and then at executive levels in a respected government agency and a large NGO distinguishes Dr. Gayle as a fitting exemplar of rights-based leadership.

Clearly, the profiles of F. H. Abed's and Helene Gayle's career journeys that eventually led to leadership in the NGO setting diverge significantly with regard to geographic setting, educational background, professional orientation, and previous administrative experience. Nonetheless, these profiles in fact reveal a few points of similarity that might inform those inclined to follow careers in human-rights-related work. First, the technical competencies of these individuals (personnel and accountancy work for Abed and epidemiological research for Gayle) led to a broader array of institutional leadership responsibilities. Second, a triggering event or experience encountered along the career journey reinforced a calling toward humanitarianism as a career mission; with Abed it was the cyclone that devastated part of Bangladesh in 1970, and with Gayle it was the occasion of attending a lecture on global efforts to eradicate smallpox. Third, each had the inner strength to place faith in other individuals within and outside of their organizations. Fourth, both profiles illustrate combinations of career intentionality and unexpected circumstances that arose as their organizational careers progressed. This last similarity might lead those intending to pursue careers in human rights work and/or humanitarian concerns to grapple with a pair of fundamental questions: *Can one realistically prepare for a career in NGO leadership? If so, how?*

References to "career preparation" by no means imply that one must commit to a particular course of academic study or benefit from a specific sequence of work experiences—is it not our own unique set of experiences and attributes that keeps life interesting? Nonetheless, career preparation for professional work in humanitarian concerns (as in most vocational pursuits) appears a worthwhile undertaking; if NGO leadership depends on one's strategic capabilities, there is cause to think strategically about a professional future dedicated to advancing human rights.

Conclusion

Although difficult to define singularly, the terms *NGO, human rights,* and *leadership* take on salience within a common context of human dignity. Independent from government authority, many NGOs can leverage influence on behalf of human rights causes, and in so doing they can be likened to "connective tissue" that facilitates the collective efforts of allied rights-focused organizations. This book is primarily focused on NGOs that, by the nature of their (development, relief, and/or rights-advocacy) missions, could adopt a rights framework approaching the perspective Peter Uvin prescribes in *Human Rights and Development* (2004). Thus, specific management questions center on both the leadership responsibilities needed to embed a rights orientation into the NGO culture and to act within that orientation and the particular management skills needed to meet those responsibilities. From a pedagogical standpoint, these leadership issues illustrate the career dimensions of NGO leadership, likely of interest to students or other individuals who sense a pull toward human rights work.

This introductory chapter discusses some of the terminology encountered in studying NGOs, human rights, and institutional leadership. This focus on language extends into the next chapter, which examines the strategically crafted nature of rhetoric (or, in Noah Webster's words, "the art of speaking with propriety") related to issues of development, humanitarianism, and human rights. The next six chapters probe a variety of concerns pertinent to NGO management environments in general and human-rights-focused leadership in particular, specifically: transformative change (chapter 3), organization and management (chapter 4), performance and accountability (chapter 5), organization learning and knowledge management (chapter 6), gender (chapter 7), and human resources management (chapter 8). The concluding chapter responds to four fundamental questions:

- *How do NGO environments affect organizational capabilities to leverage actions on behalf of human rights?*
- *What obstacles can NGOs expect to encounter in adopting a rights-based perspective, and how can those obstacles be surmounted?*
- *What particular competencies do NGO leaders need to understand the distinctive nature of their institutional environments and respond to them effectively?*
- *Can one realistically prepare for a career in NGO leadership? If so, how?*

For now, these questions can serve as points of reference to help readers integrate ideas from the discussions that follow.

Discussion Issues

1. One commentator refers to NGO "aid chains" as "ties that bind." Do "ties that bind" constitute blessings or burdens for NGO leaders? Explain.
2. Some human rights NGOs "name and shame"—that is, publically embarrass governments, corporations, or other powerful actors by calling attention to how they violate human rights. How does this practice affect the NGO's "connective tissue," or the ability to connect with other organizations to facilitate change?
3. Are the terms *institutional leadership* and *organization management* synonymous, or do they convey different meanings in the context of the organization? Explain.

4. "Individual morality" and "organizational ethics" are both classified as ethical competencies. Suggest how a leader who is highly
competent in regard to the former but deficient in terms of the
latter could compromise agencies' goals to advance human rights.

5. On a 1-to-5 scale, rate yourself as a strategist in planning your
professional future. What measures could you take to improve
your strategic capabilities?

Note

1. F. H. Abed released his biographical statement on December 31, 2009, in advance of
his appointment as Knight Commander of the Most Distinguished Order of St. Michael and
St. George by Queen Elizabeth II of Great Britain; see http://fazleabed.com/, accessed October 8,
2010.

2

Slippery Terminology

Strategically Crafted Rhetoric in Development and Human Rights

Webster's Online Dictionary[1] defines the *US Civil War* as "a civil war in the United States between the North and the South [between] 1861–1865." Such a bare-bones description, denotative or "in accordance with fact or the primary meaning of a term," is easy to memorize in cramming for a test but offers little if any knowledge of the relevant context or even alternative interpretations of contextual meaning. In this regard, it is significant that online dictionary formats allow space for background and explanation, the connotative meaning (or competing explanations) that "have the power of implying or suggesting something in addition to what is explicit" (*Webster's Online Dictionary*). In reference to the US Civil War, *Webster's Online Dictionary* explains that southerners understand this conflict as "the War between the States" and also includes that southerners have conflicting interpretations of why states seceded, the relevance of slavery in intensifying division, and the course of the war than those in the North have. In other words, battles of interpretation endure long after the cessation of actual fighting. To *understand* the US Civil War is not only to grasp its origins and historical outcomes but also to explain how it has shaped the current political landscape.

That same dictionary provides one (among several) denotative description of *development* as "a state in which things are improving," leading to an arguably humorous multiple-choice question such as the following:

> Dictionary definitions of *development* and the *US Civil War* are analogous since
>   a. neither tell us much

    b. both involve states

    c. both are subject to competing Northern and Southern inter-
       pretations

    d. both a and c

The "d" response is probably best because "a" is fairly obvious and "c" has validity given that Northern political actors and institutions exercise power in formulating "explanations" of and "remedies" for "development" that Southern societies on the receiving end often find difficult to swallow. However, the critical point here is that the terminology surrounding the studies of NGOs, development, and human rights consists of politically loaded, contentious words and phrases—such as "poverty reduction," "participation," "empowerment," "civil society organizations," and "sustainability" among others—that may sound definitive and authoritative but nonetheless invite ongoing controversy. In fact, Wolfgang Sachs's *Development Dictionary: A Guide to Knowledge and Power* (1992) is no dictionary at all but instead a collection of 19 scathing essays, each devoted to driving a stake through the heart of "development" as embodied by the power interests of the North. By contrast, David Robertson's *A Dictionary of Human Rights* (2004) is indeed a dictionary that compiles hundreds of entries related to general terms, governmental laws, legal principles, governmental and multilateral institutions, and rights-related problems in alphabetical order.

This chapter focuses on the nature of terminology related to NGO work directed toward development and human rights objectives *not* as a glossary of easy-to-remember descriptions but instead as a discussion about why significant words and phrases must be scrutinized with caution. Thus, the effort here elaborates on but a few "buzzwords" (see Cornwall and Brock 2005; Cornwall 2007) frequently invoked in development and human rights conversations to show how terminology can be obfuscated, morphed, co-opted, overhauled, and retrofitted, not only to describe but also to "do things" that advance political goals by legitimizing, justifying, building consensus, excluding or including, and/or making promises, all in the name of "making things better." Hopefully, readers will be able to apply these ideas about the political dynamics at work in "word-making that leads to world-making" (Cornwall and Brock 2005) as they scrutinize other terms not covered here. So in a nutshell, this chapter serves as a flashing warning sign along the highway to understanding development- and rights-related conversations: "SLIPPERY WHEN POLITICAL" (which is pretty much all of the time). First, it explains why the ambiguity surrounding often-used words and phrases provides political opportunities to (re)shape meanings and advocate new or different ideas. Second, it focuses on strategic word-crafting in reference to a few specific development and rights-related terms. Third, it elaborates on how controversial policy initiatives to link relief assistance with the interests of interventionist states (e.g., the United States in Afghanistan and Iraq) account for changing discourses and value orientations in the humanitarian community. Fourth, this chapter considers how the metaphorical "slippery when political" warning can inform leadership initiatives in rights-oriented NGOs. Finally, it traces the relevance of this politically strategic terminology to other topics treated in subsequent chapters.

Terminology and Political Opportunity

Words, terms, and discourses (i.e., "ensembles of ideas, concepts, and categories through which meaning is given to phenomena"; Hajer 1993, 45) matter strategically in framing (or shaping) policy solutions, whether by multinational aid institutions or by legislators in government. As Cornwall and Brock maintain, words and terms that convey policy ideas like "empowerment" and "poverty reduction" are seldom if ever neutral but instead implicitly advocate particular understandings and courses of action. In essence, these words "succeed" when they achieve a "taken-for-granted" status or consensus among disparate interests. As an official of the United Nations Development Programme (UNDP) suggests, the "taken-for-grantedness" of terminology and meaning constitutes political accomplishment as "ideas changing minds" as important as aid "money changing hands" (Vandemoortele 2009, 356). In her analysis of development discourse, Cornwall refers to terms having achieved such status as *buzzwords* that "get their buzz" from being in vogue that serve as passwords to funding and influence (2007, 471–72). Because they are typically vague and euphemistic, buzzwords are especially useful in negotiating the ambiguity (or "fuzz") surrounding diverse interpretations of issues and problems, as Cornwall explains:

> Policies depend on a measure of ambiguity to secure the endorsement of diverse potential actors and audiences. Buzzwords aid this process, by providing concepts that can float free of concrete referents, to be filled with meaning by their users. In the struggles for interpretive power that characterise the negotiation of the language of policy, buzzwords shelter multiple agendas, providing room for manoeuvre and space for contestation. (2007, 474)

Thus, some buzzwords also serve as *fuzzwords* that provide room for policymakers to maneuver in ambiguous situations, or in Cornwall's words, "It is, after all, in the very ambiguity of development buzzwords that scope exists for enlarging their application to encompass more transformative agendas" (2007, 481).

Ambiguity abounds in policy environments at most any (global, national, local) level, and consensual meanings of buzzwords constitute workable boundaries around diverse interpretations and opinions (Scoones 2007, 591–92). (For example, as I draft this chapter, many US citizens demand "comprehensive integration reform" even though opinions clash over what that buzzword actually means; nonetheless, it places some sense of boundary around that contested territory.) Policy analyst Deborah Stone asserts that for the skillful political actor, "politics is more like art than a science in that ambiguity is central . . . [because it] enables the transformation of individual intentions and actions into collective results and purposes" (2002, 157). In this regard, Steve Denning, a World Bank official whose ideas prompted the bank to undertake "knowledge management" as an institutional mission (as discussed in chapter 6), is as much a political artist, or policy entrepreneur, as a politically astute legislator or big city mayor. Political scientist Frank Baumgartner offers an apt metaphor characterizing policy entrepreneurs in his analysis of French educational policy:

> Policymakers behave like the navigators of a hot air balloon. . . . They must maneuver their vehicles to the altitude at which the wind happens to be blowing in the direction they wish to go. Though they cannot change the direction of the wind, they can change the altitude until they find the wind that suits them. Similarly, policymakers attempt to maneuver their policies to those arenas in the political and administrative system where they expect the prevailing winds to be most favorable. (Baumgartner 1989, 3–4)

But in comparison to government officials typically hemmed in by statutory constraints and partisan competition, global development actors find it much easier to steer the balloon in formulating development policy because, if for no other reason, they control the flow of aid money. So in large part, these powerful policy entrepreneurs *can in fact* "control the direction of the wind" in their ability to define what words like *development, poverty reduction, empowerment,* and *rights* mean and then deftly use their influence to legitimize those buzzwords. From a general acceptance of those meanings it is possible to build consensus about the nature of the "problem" and interventions they deem appropriate as "remedies."

To the extent that consensus reached about meanings, "problems," and "remedies" sets forth recommended standards of behavior, political actors involve themselves in the dynamics of *norms development*. For example, if a multilateral funding agency frames "empowerment" as poor individuals "pulling themselves up by their own economic bootstraps," that institution (or the officials within it) becomes the vehicle by which new conceptions of norms emerge or, in Finnemore and Sikkink's words, "norm entrepreneurs." In their words, "norm entrepreneurs are critical for norm emergence because they call attention to issues or even 'create' issues by using language that names, interprets, and dramatizes them" (1998, 897). In some cases, global development institutions or multilateral organizations can dramatize issues by sponsoring international conferences, and/or forge a consensus on new goals, that (re)define those issues. In other cases, individuals such as public officials or human rights advocates assume this role. In his presidential inauguration address, Harry Truman was somewhat of a norms entrepreneur in calling attention to the term *development*. Gustavo Esteva's critical essay on "development" in the *Dictionary of Development* shows how that word can provoke antagonism:

> Underdevelopment began, then, on January 20, 1949. On that day, two billion people became underdeveloped. In a real sense, from that time on, they ceased being what they were, in all their diversity, and were transmogrified into others' reality. (Esteva 1993, 7)

By contrast, development expert Robert Chambers savors the realities of rural inhabitants in championing the norm of authentic participation symbolized by drawing planning "diagrams in the dirt" as a means of visual sharing (1997, 151–52). According to Finnemore and Sikkink, whether such newly conceived norms persist in mainstream opinion depends on the power actor's capability to "create a tipping point after which agreement becomes widespread in many empirical cases, and we provide some suggestions about common features of 'critical mass'" (pp. 892–93).

For critics of "the development industry" (and Northern aid institutions in particular), language crafted to dramatize "new ideas or norms" may amount to little more than simply "rhetorical repackaging" (to use Peter Uvin's phrase; 2004, 168–69). Cleary, the critical analyses of Cornwall and Brock on development buzzwords, along with that of others (including Uvin) in a

2007 symposium on *Development in Practice* devoted to parsing development terminology, reflect a level of sophisticated thinking that can discern the human rights implications (the hopeful and discouraging alike) in development language. In other words, the ability to trace the political motives at work in crafting development terminology helps us advocate for human rights. But can the same be said for the human rights cause in itself? In his preface to *A Dictionary of Human Rights*, David Robertson comments,

> This is not a creative or original work, and I have not sought to establish a substantive position of my own in my choice of terms. There are inevitable choices, that have to be made in a book such as this, and the choices cannot be entirely neutral. The bias, if that is the right word, I am most aware of is my own preference for taking rights to mean political and constitutional entitlements and freedoms, rather than economic- and social-need satisfactions. (2004, 3)

Robertson's intentions make sense in compiling a library reference source for preparing term papers and PowerPoint presentations on topics related to human rights (at least as characterized in the West). But Robertson takes a sterile, "after-the-fact" perspective that overlooks rights *claiming* as enduring political struggle (see Stone 2002, 324–53). Analyses that parse "rights talk," corresponding to the work mentioned previously examining "development talk," could help immeasurably in understanding claims-making. For example, in reference to demands for gender rights in Brazil, Pitanguy comments,

> I propose that we analyze gender violence and human rights, taking the concept of citizenship as a starting point, to follow the fragmentation of this citizenship concept. This exercise would result in a map of those who are more or less citizens, more or less excluded in a given country at a given time. Just as geopolitical maps change as a result of wars, disputes, and alliances, this symbolic map of citizenship rights also changes. (1997, 30)

In essence, she calls for the parsing of "citizenship" to understand the marginality of women and to do something about it. But projected onto a larger canvas, awareness that language matters in human rights rhetoric leads to a wide array of extralegal tactics worth pursuing.

What Five Strategically Crafted Buzzwords Can Do

As books on watercolor techniques include a few paintings as illustrations, this section offers five examples of political word-crafting related to terms frequently used in development and human-rights conversations: "poverty reduction," "participation," "empowerment," "civil society organizations," and "sustainability." Hopefully, this sampler will give readers cause to examine the political contours of other terminological meanings encountered either in learning about or working within NGO environments. Three of the terms— *poverty reduction, participation,* and *empowerment*—are those that Andrea Cornwall and Karen Brock (2005, 9) identify as buzzwords that "speak to an agenda for transformation that combines no-nonsense pragmatism with almost unimpeachable moral authority" in a program paper for the United Nations Research Institute for Social Development. Table 2.1 summarizes how each of these terms can advance (i.e., legitimize and justify) particular political agendas, build consensus around them, include or exclude certain interests and stakeholders in or from the dialogue, and promise outcomes that improve human conditions.

Poverty Reduction

From a human rights standpoint, "poverty" as destitution robs people of their capabilities and freedom just as a tyrannical regime would in denying civil and political liberties (see Sen 1999, 87–110). But few other words reflect greater ambiguity in the context of development because "there may be as many poor and as many perceptions of 'poverty' as there are human beings" (Rahnema 1993b, 158). In this regard, a development consultant in Uganda states,

> Poverty does not have a single face, easily recognized and labeled. It has many faces—far too many faces for development agencies from the centre or local government levels to lump them together as a single mass for targeted poverty alleviation interventions, and far too diverse to work with each individual household. The closer we look at poor individuals or poor households, the more differences we see. Therefore, the harder development agencies try to target the poor as a homogeneous group, the less clear it is who they are targeting. (Johnson 2002, 127)

As Cornwall and Brock (2005) see it, *poverty* and *poverty reduction* qualify as fuzzwords as well as buzzwords.

Table 2.1
Five Selected Buzzwords and What They Can Do

	Legitimizes or Justifies	Builds Consensus	Excludes or Includes	Promises
"Poverty reduction"	• It justifies the Poverty Reduction Strategy Papers' consensus—poverty reduction accomplished only through country-driven, results-oriented, long-term strategies associated with strong free markets.	• It links "problem" with "solution" and provides a universal model of development as a basis of consensus.	• It may overlook those impoverished by nuanced contextual circumstances.	• It promises to make the "underdeveloped" "developed."
"Participation"	• It co-opts the virtuosity of radical ideal and puts a "human face" on this neoliberal program.	• It is depoliticized from radical roots to accommodate development status quo. • It is ambiguous about *who participates? why?* and *at what level?* and makes the term attractive to diverse interests.	• It is likely to include urbanites with access to commerce but exclude rural poor.	• It promises reciprocity in dialogue and persuasion and power sharing (from a bottom-up perspective).
"Empowerment"	• It was reinvented to support an individualist "do-it-yourself" ethos that justifies neoliberal development initiatives.	• It co-opts Freire's radical connotation to build consensus for "tweaked" but still conventional development policies.	• It includes involvement of private sector entities as empowerment partners.	• The market offers the road to human improvement.
"Civil society organizations"	• It finds legitimacy in Western political thought; this rhetoric justifies funding civic associations to challenge state authority and traditional political institutions.	• Connotations of more democratic societies and "political neutrality" have wide appeal.	• It excludes (weakens) the state and traditional political institutions (such as political parties, labor unions, the church) as interest brokers.	• It promises solidarity and good will through democratization and "good governance."
"Sustainability"	• Although the term can be used to support any number of stances, its co-optation of ecological meaning has been especially influential in justifying Northern economic self-sufficiency agendas.	• As a fuzzy "boundary term," it provides adversaries maneuvering room for negotiation.	• Although generally inclusive as a "fuzzword," the term can also be used to exclude participant involvement.	• "Prudent" development can be made permanent.

Nonetheless, *development* invites sweeping comparisons of deficiencies related to lacking material "things" or depressed measures of well-being (e.g., annual income) usually from vantage points other than from subjects themselves. As do other commentators, Gilbert Rist recognizes the meaning of poverty largely enveloped in a market-oriented conception of "development" as commodification:

> The essence of "development" is the general transformation and destruction of the natural environment and of social relations in order to increase the production of commodities (goods and services) geared, by means of market exchange, to effective demand. . . . A country is the more "developed" the more limited the number of free things that are available: to spend an afternoon on the beach, to go fishing, or enjoy cross-country skiing is nowadays impossible unless one is prepared to pay for it. (Rist 2007, 488)

Johnson and Rist's observations imply that development agencies approach poverty in terms of straightforward economic criteria that overlook important nuances such as nonmaterial assets (and access to them), risks, and vulnerabilities (Johnson 2002, 128–30).

If one word such as *poverty* reflects ambiguity, it would appear that adding a second (e.g., *reduction*) would obfuscate meaning even further. But Cornwall and Brock suggest that linking buzzwords together forms a chain of equivalence or "words that work together to invoke a particular set of meanings" (2005, 4). The rubric "poverty reduction," which also incorporates "participation" and "empowerment" to the poverty reduction effort, provides the World Bank and International Monetary Fund (IMF) an alternative policy framework that replaced the widely assailed structural adjustment approach (discussed in chapter 3). "Poverty reduction" connotes the "goodness and rightness that these agencies need[ed] to assert in order to assume the legitimacy to intervene in the lives of others" to be embedded in mainstream development (2005, 4). Specifically, that euphemism finds "official" status in conjunction with the Poverty Reduction Strategy Papers (PRSP) prepared by various stakeholders in individual countries as new (1999) conditions for aid funding. The PRSP framework involves "participation" in that individual nations take responsibilities of diagnosing poverty, prioritizing their own policies addressing poverty, setting targets, establishing indicators, and so forth. Similarly the United Nations' actions to adopt Millennium Development Goals evolving from the previous year's Millennium Summit offer additional support for "poverty reduction" associated with the eight goals adopted by member states:

1. Eradicate extreme poverty and hunger
2. Achieve universal primary education
3. Promote gender equality and empower women
4. Reduce child mortality rate
5. Improve maternal health
6. Combat HIV/AIDS, malaria, and other diseases
7. Ensure environmental sustainability
8. Develop a global partnership for development

So in reference to table 2.1, it appears that the World Bank and IMF, along with the UNDP, have relied on poverty reduction discourse as a means of justifying a new iteration of market-oriented development policies that are country-driven and results-focused lending protocols. Notwithstanding critics who argue that poverty must be understood within a wide array of contextual circumstances, "poverty reduction" strategies build consensus in mainstream development as it links the "problem" with "solutions." Although the universality of the poverty reduction framework appears all-inclusive, it may prove irrelevant to significant numbers of the world's poor whose plights result from complex circumstances, perhaps even the ramifications of a global economy. Finally, the promise of "poverty reduction" rhetoric embedded in institutional policy is self-defining, to make people's lives better . . . and who could argue with that?

Participation

Once upon a time, the word *participation* threatened the status quo in the West as a radical idea arising from the Marxist teaching of Paulo Freire, who championed Participatory Action Research (PAR), dedicated to the transformation of political and economic structures. Freire maintained that "development can only be achieved when humans are 'beings for themselves,' when they possess their own decision-making powers, free of oppressive and dehumanising circumstances; it is the 'struggle to be more fully human.'" In other words, social transformation can and should produce development, while institutional development has not historically led to social transformation (Leal 2007, 540–41, quoting Freire 1970, 29). Participation through this radical lens meant that Northern perspectives in conventional development approaches should give way to "different knowledge systems, representing poor people's own cultural heritage, in particular the locally produced [know-how]" (Rahnema 1993a, 121). But, as Rahnema suggests, the authenticity of this radical "participation" in Freire's thinking and subsequently in Chambers's rural participatory approaches (discussed in chapter 3) lends virtue to the term (p. 116). These positive connotations of self-determination make "participation" attractive to political actors as diverse as repressive heads of state and "good governance" organizations that would choose to use it rhetorically.

Critics of conventional development claim that the failure of aid policies during the 1980s led Northern development institutions such as the World Bank to co-opt (or lay claim to) the propriety of participation discourse to justify institutional missions (associated with free-market economics) amid riots protesting development policies in Tunis (1981), Caracas (1989), and elsewhere. In his essay on the ascendancy of *participation* as a buzzword, Leal refers to Majid Rahnema, a former UNDP official:

> In participation, official development found what Majid Rahnema has called "a redeeming saint" (Rahnema 1990, 199). Development's failures were now to be explained by its top-down, blueprint mechanics, which were to be replaced by more people-friendly, bottom-up approaches that would "put the last first," as Robert Chambers (1983) coined in his well known book *Rural Development: Putting the Last First*. (Leal 2007, 542)

Leal goes on to explain that "it would become imperative for the global power elites to seek some kind of palliative solution, to put a 'human face' on inhumane policies" but at the same time denounce governments as the key obstacle to development.

> By having identified the nasty state as the culprit, the World Bank was not advocating a popular government, but rather creating a populist justification for the removal of the state from the economy and its substitution by the market. . . . Thus liberation or empowerment of poor people in this rationale is not linked with political or state power. Rather, the implication is that empowerment is derived from liberation from an interventionist state, and that participation in free-market economics and their further enlistment into development projects will enable them to "take fuller charge of their lives." (Leal 2007, 542)

The point here is not so much to critique policies but rather to illustrate how terminology can be framed and reframed consistent with political agendas.

In this regard, table 2.1 shows that "participation," a term once associated with Marxist liberation ideology, has been commandeered to justify policy alterations in the hopes of building a new consensus around revised development narratives (or stories about "problems" and "remedies"). In this regard, Leal (2007, 543) suggests that the World Bank built consensus around the new meaning of "participation" by depoliticizing it from its radical roots and incorporating it within the development status quo. Consensus here typically incorporates a diversity of interests, each understanding the term differently. Institutional aid agencies, for example, could approach "participation" from a top-down perspective as a means for establishing legitimacy and justifying efficiency (achieved by people taking self-responsibility). But from a bottom-up perspective, it could promise the capability to leverage power (White 1996, 7). Although the refurbished message may have broad appeal, it may resonate more with urbanites with closer access to commerce while excluding those in rural areas where poverty is especially severe (see Patrón 2000). The promise of participation, often put forth by advocates of a "people-centered" development subscribing to Robert Chambers's concept of "new professionalism," implies that participation can create spaces for the marginalized to establish solidarity that promotes reciprocity in dialogue with powerful actors (White 1996; Craig and Porter 1997, 236).

Empowerment

On the basis of her experiences with gender-equity work in India, Srilatha Batliwala laments that "of all the buzzwords that have entered the development lexicon in the past 30 years, empowerment is probably the most widely used and abused" (2007, 557). The title of her critical essay "Taking the Power out of Empowerment" aptly summarizes her central argument that the term was deliberately and deftly co-opted by conservative and reactionary ideologies and the development agencies that embrace them. Specifically, she alleges that these agencies reinvented "empowerment" with the intention of "divesting government of its purported power and control by 'empowering' communities to look after their own affairs" (p. 558). In commandeering it as a buzzword, the Northern aid agencies have mainstreamed empowerment discourse in a diluted form, detached from "its original emphasis on building personal and collective power in the struggle for a more just and equitable world" (Cornwall and Brock 2005, 5). Bluntly stated, the dispute over empowerment interpretations centers on *power* and whether marginal people acquire "the power to" in relation to those who traditionally exercise "power over." In contrast to this transformative connotation of a power-acquiring process, mainstream development conversation dulls the political edge of empowerment by equating it with "helping," "facilitating," "providing access to," and offering "positive support" (see Uvin 2004, 83–120). A gender empowerment trainer explains,

> Empowerment must be about bringing people who are outside the decision-making process into it. This puts a strong emphasis on access to political structures and formal decision-making and, in the economic sphere, on access to markets and incomes that enable people to participate in economic decision-making. It is about individuals being able to maximise the opportunities available to them without or despite constraints of structure and State. . . . It is thus more than simply opening up access to decision-making; it must also include the processes that lead people to perceive themselves as able and entitled to occupy that decision-making space. (Rowlands 1995, 102)

Rowlands's last sentence about "lead[ing] people to perceive themselves as able" raises a question as to whether "empowerment" can occur within the individual as well as in groups mobilizing for political influence. From perspectives of gender equity (e.g., Batliwala 2007) and participatory appraisal (e.g., Chambers 1997), attention usually focuses on the capability of *groups* to mobilize pressure and participate meaningfully in decision making. Nonetheless, issues of *individuals'* perceived competence within that group setting arise, as well as legitimate concerns in rights claiming (Rowlands 1995, 102). In fact, it may be the condition of oppression itself that inhibits one's self-confidence, as a community development program coordinator explains,

> At times, oppression creates a situation in which a population cannot act proactively, is conditioned by its oppression, and is fatalistic in accepting things as they are. In such cases, the role of the external practitioner is more complex: it is noticeable that the more people are oppressed, the more difficult it is for them to participate in their own development and express their own needs. (Schunk 2003, 378)

It is in situations such as this that development professionals walk a fine line between offering needed support and depending on individuals and groups to discover empowerment within themselves (Rowlands 1995, 104; Schunk 2003).

All of that said, it is important to differentiate between the relevance of individual empowerment *within the context of a group* attempting to leverage power and an overhauled meaning of "individual empowerment" as a solitary consumer, perhaps able to purchase designer clothes, or entrepreneur *in the context of free-market development ideologies* (Cornwall 2007, 475). The latter context of individualism offers justification for a "do-it-yourself" narrative of rights empowerment whereby individuals and communities, rather than governments or even international aid programs, are cast as captains of their own fates or as "owners" having stakes in policy outcomes. In particular, this new discourse implies that "ownership" (as applied to individuals or entire nations) can be strengthened through the assistance of "partners," referring to the aid agencies themselves, privatization firms, or development banks (Cornwall and Brock 2005). Microcredit programs intended to provide women small sums of entrepreneurial capital, for example, can be said to empower individual women in an economic sense of the term. Nonetheless, as Mallick suggests in his portrayal of Grameen Bank microlending, economic "empowerment" can in fact disempower women in the family setting. In particular, he alleges that to ensure regular loan repayment, the bank scheduled meetings of "borrowers circles" to enlist gendered coercion as an enforcement mechanism:

> In contrast to [other programs relying on] financial inducements for repayment, the Grameen Bank practices social coercion. The meetings are designed to develop peer pressure to ensure compliance, and women are found to be the most suitable for this. Not only are their neighbors in the borrower circle, but their husbands are there to enforce compliance through corporal punishment. The Bank worker holds up the meeting until everyone has arrived and paid their dues. If this is not done, the meeting continues so the women are late returning home to prepare the meals. This results in physical abuse by the husbands. (Mallick 2002, 154)

Apart from the ethical quandaries raised, Mallick's discussion of how Grameen Bank implements its microlending program offers a vivid contrast of "empowerment" interpretations.

Table 2.1 then shows how deliberate efforts to reinvent empowerment discourse serve to justify, or "put a human face" on, free-market approaches to poverty reduction. Following the lead of the World Bank and other multilateral organizations, development actors in the North achieved success in co-opting this term once tied to Marxist liberation ideology in a manner that builds consensus for conventional development approaches. The rhetorical linkages between "empowerment," "ownership," and "partnership" open the door for corporate sector involvement in privatizing governmental functions as a market-oriented strategy to reduce poverty. This reworked meaning of "empowerment" now promises human fulfillment via the individual's access to well-functioning markets.

Civil Society Organizations

Frequently invoked in conversation about democratization and political rights, the terms *civil society* and *civil society organizations* (CSOs) get their buzz from a rich heritage of liberal political theory dating back to Roman civilization and from the recent decline of socialist regimes in Eastern Europe. Although they generally relate to expected roles of civic associations in strengthening (read democratizing) societies, both appear mired in ambiguity as "hurrah words" lacking definitive meaning (Whaites 1996, 240; Chandhoke 2007, 608). Specifically, Chandhoke summarizes her frustration with the watered-down meanings of these terms in this way:

> If civil society is hailed by almost everyone, from trade unions, social movements, the United Nations, the International Monetary Fund, the World Bank, NGOs, lending agencies, borrowing agencies, and to states as the ideal elixir to counter the ills of the contemporary world, there must be something wrong. . . . The ubiquity of a concept, we can conclude somewhat regretfully, may ultimately prove to be its undoing. For if it comes from everyone's lips, it must have lost both shape and content. (Chandhoke 2007, 609)

Similarly, in her introductory chapter in *Civil Society and the Aid Industry*, Alison Van Rooy (2000) attests to this ambiguity by differentiating among six connotations of "civil society" in contemporary development discourse as

- values and norms,
- a collective noun (representing the entire voluntary sector in a society),
- a "space" for action,
- a historical event (when the prerequisites for its existence fall into place),

- "anti-hegemony," and
- an antidote to the state (1998, 12–27).

Van Rooy's last two meanings, civil society as anti-hegemony and as antidote to the state, correspond to Chandhoke's quip that "civil society as the antonym of authoritarianism is on everyone's lips—government officials, funding agencies [and others] who find inspiration" in the rhetoric (2007, 608). Terminological differences between CSOs and NGOs appear fuzzy at least in part because aid agencies have found it beneficial to promote usage of the former that calls attention to "democratizing" efforts while downplaying their political implications (Van Rooy 1998, 32–33; Uvin 2004, 99). In this regard, Van Rooy relies on quotes from officials in various aid agencies suggesting that "differences" between the meanings of CSOs and NGOs emerged from deliberate intentions to reframe the conversation, for example:

> CIDA[2]: "As new non-NGOs arrive on CIDA's horizon, the term 'civil society' has allowed the agency to encompass the new actors. In Latin America, certainly, we have realized that we have neglected social issues in pursuit of economic ones. In looking for ways to channel support through non-governmental sources to support democracy in Peru, we began to talk about civil society," and
>   UNDP: "We were receiving feedback, especially from our Middle East posts, that the term 'NGO' was seen to mean 'anti-government,' whereas 'civil society' was seen to be more neutral." (Van Rooy 1998, 33–35)

Thus, the CSO discourse appears to offer funding agencies legitimacy in supporting democratizing activities without the appearance of meddling in another society's politics.

However, some coherent meanings emerge in understanding why multinational donors find the "civil society" rhetoric appealing. An official of World Vision UK explains that donors associate *good governance*, as a condition for awarding aid, with the democratizing effects of civil society organizations. Specifically, CSOs are expected to counteract traditional ethnic and political allegiances by coalescing widespread support around various civic issues unencumbered by traditional political (or "primordial") alignments (Whaites 1996, 241–42). In essence, the rise of civic associations, based on this logic, cuts society loose from its traditional politics to pursue democratic "good governance" outcomes. Uvin refers to this strategy of conditionality based on civil society support as "the politics of de-politicization," implying that the "civil society" rhetoric tends to downplay the politics of good-governance-oriented conditionality or to pass it off as "non-political" (2004, 99–102).

The connection between active civic associations as agents of democratization and civil society "as antidote to the State" made sense in the post–Cold War Eastern European setting where "a vibrant and politicized civil society promoted the rebuilding of both political activism and civic virtue" (Chandhoke 2007, 612). But in other contexts, expectations that new modes of civic association would counteract traditional ethnic and political loyalties do not square with reality. In his analysis of civil society and "the politics of democratization" in Kenya, Maina indicates that new civic organizations are looked upon with suspicion as attempting to feed at the troughs of donor aid or as part of state patronage networks. Moreover, CSOs that achieve success there generally do so by networking with established ethnic and political institutions such as the church and farmers associations, *not* by undercutting their influence (Maina 1998, 145–52). In Peru, a nation of deep poverty, donor initiatives have led to a proliferation of CSOs advancing neoliberal agendas, but they are widely distrusted because economic reforms benefit professional elites rather than the impoverished (Patrón 1998, 194–96).

NGOs need to approach the "depoliticizing" and state-weakening agendas entangled in "civil society" rhetoric with caution. It is difficult to reconcile how initiatives designed to weaken already weak states advance human rights interests. First, as Whaites suggests, "the weak state leaves vacuums of power that elites are more than happy to fill" (1998, 345). Second, a weak state that cedes authority to CSOs is under even less pressure to be accountable and responsive to its citizens and local communities. In efforts to "re-conceptualize the overall aims" for rights work, NGOs could be better advised to pursue initiatives that *build capacity within governments* so they can become more competent brokers of diverse political interests whether traditional or emergent (Whaites 1998; Uvin 2004, 134–37, 160–62).

As table 2.1 indicates, Northern funding institutions have used the rhetoric of "civil society" and "civil society organizations" to justify policies seeking to change the dynamics of domestic politics in other societies. These terms build consensus because of their rhetorical connections with a long tradition of Western political thought that advances the virtues of "civil society," the appeal of democratization and good governance, and supposed political neutrality. On the surface, emphases on "democratizing societies" suggests inclusion, but the aid policies behind the rhetoric lessens the influences of traditional political institutions such as the labor union and the church. Lastly, civil society language speaks to promises of solidarity, openness, and general goodwill within the fabric of societies.

Sustainability

Sustainability (the noun) has come a long way since 1712 when Carl von Carlwitz assigned scientific meaning to it in his textbook on long-term forestry management. From there, Scoones traces that word's recent reincarnation as an enabler of "boundary work" that invites negotiation and network building "as a continuingly powerful and influential meeting point of ideas and politics" (2007, 589). Along with *sustainable* (the adjective), this terminology took on new life with the rise of the environmental movement of the 1960s and 1970s and then later as ecological concerns led to contentious political and economic debates. An international commission on the environment and development was influential in focusing on "sustainable development" in its 1987 report *Our Common Future*, also known as "the Bruntlund Report" named after the commission's chair, the former prime minister of Norway. In the late 1980s, technical discussions centered on ecological system capabilities to respond to shocks and stress (Scoones 2007, 590). But at about the same time, economists and business leaders began to approach "sustainability" from the standpoint of capital availability. According to Scoones, these ecological and economic streams of conversation about sustainability converged in 1992 at the UN Conference on Environment and Development in Rio de Janeiro from which the World Business Council for Sustainable Development emerged:

> The Rio conference launched a number of high-level convention processes—on climate change, biodiversity, and desertification—all with the aim of realising sustainable-development ideals on key global environmental issues. Commissions were established, and national action planning processes set in train for a global reporting system against agreed objectives. At the same time, a more local-level, community-led process was conceived . . . which envisaged sustainability being built from the bottom up through local initiatives by local governments, community groups, and citizens. (Scoones 2007, 591, with references to Selman 1998 and Young 1999)

In other words, sustainability's buzz accrues from its potential to reach across the boundaries of adversarial interests (ecology versus business, North versus South, top-down versus bottom-up strategies of development, etc.), and as such it provides entrée to negotiation and alliance building.

Both *sustainability* and *sustainable* can be coupled with other words, just as *poverty* was linked to *reduction*, as discourses that frame the nature of development problems or rights problems, along with the remedies that fit the contours of that "problem" narrative (Cornwall and Brock 2005, 2–3). For example, the adjective *institutional* can be affixed to *sustainability* to imply that since development aid is not perpetual, recipient institutions should "get their acts together" to take over financial responsibility for reforms rather than depend on someone else's money. Such was the UNDP's justification for imposing a cost-sharing model for reforming government operations in Brazil whereby that government's share of costs paid for UNDP consultants to implement reforms and, in doing so, circumventing the bureaucratic institutions in need of capacity-building implementation experiences (Galvani and Morse 2004). In this regard, the term *NGO sustainability* may connote an institutional vulnerability in providing long-term capacity building given donor impatience and changing tastes (Low and Davenport 2002). On a more positive note, Johnson and Wilson (1999) frame "institutional sustainability" in the contexts of consensus building and network formation as learning among stakeholders in the "process of negotiating shared agendas over meaning of sustainability." Their quote from another (Lélé 1991) attests to the inclusiveness of their interpretation:

> In short, [sustainable development] is a "metafix" that will unite everybody from the profit-minded industrialist and risk-minimising subsistence farmer to the equity-seeking social worker, the pollution-concerned or wildlife-loving First Worlder, the growth-maximising policy maker, the goal-oriented bureaucrat, and, therefore, the vote-counting politician. (Johnson and Wilson 1999, 45)

The euphemism "urban sustainability" can justify opposing discourses such as those advanced by neoliberal funding agencies or ideologues as contrasted with others who represent Southern perspectives on development. An example of the former can be found in a housing consultant's structural-adjustment argument that urban sustainability can be achieved by "lowering the ladder" of building regulations that would in turn reduce housing costs (Payne 2001). But advocates of the latter may associate "urban sustainability" with inclusion approaches to involve the poor in urban planning (Mahadevia 2001) and in urban development that displaces the means by which people make a living, such as the local fishing industry (Allen 2001). Using the *un*-adjective, a community development expert refers to urbanization in the Philippines following development paradigms of the North as "*un*sustainable development" that is parasitic in violating the " 'carrying capacity,' or the maximum sustainable load that humankind can impose on the environment before it loses the capacity to support human activity" (Constantino-David 2001, 234).

Put simply, sustainability terminology is difficult to pin down, especially when connected with various modifiers (such as *economic sustainability*, *physical sustainability*, and *social sustainability*) and when it is used *as* a modifier (*sustainable development*, *sustainable growth*, and so forth). As table 2.1 suggests, this terminology commands a sense of legitimacy such that, attached to other buzzwords, it can justify a wide range of policy agendas. Nonetheless, business interests have been particularly successful in co-opting the notion of ecological sustainability to appeal for financial self-sufficiency (among aid beneficiaries) as a vital development goal. Sustainability's various connotations (which at times are "fuzzy" or ambiguous in themselves) add to its consensus-building capability to invite diverse stakeholder interests into dialogue. That said, "sustainability talk" (as the case with discourse generally) can exclude voices advocating "unsustainable" proposals. Although seldom stated, it might be said that sustainability promises that "well-advised" or "prudent" development (in the eyes of beholders) leads to durable accomplishment and lasting benefits.

Slippery Humanitarianism: The Convergence Agenda and "Good Humanitarian Donorship"

Yet another buzzword, *humanitarianism*, takes on diverse meanings within the context of a changing political environment. Emphasizing this diversity of meanings and associated practices, international relations scholar Michael Barnett comments:

> Humanitarianism broadly concerns the desire to relieve the suffering of distant strangers, but there is considerable diversity among agencies regarding which suffering[s] matter and how such suffering should be relieved. Some humanitarian institutions want to relieve all manner of suffering, while others focus only on the suffering of these whose lives are threatened by man-made or natural disasters (emergencies). Some humanitarian institutions subscribe to the view that humanitarian action requires observance of the principles of impartiality, neutrality, and independence, while others are not as concerned with how relief is delivered. (2009, 626–27)

Barnett's characterization of humanitarianism as "in a world of hurt" (in the article's title) relates to relief organizations' collective identity crisis in attempting to preserve core values of impartiality, neutrality, and independence while following a *convergence agenda* that aligns humanitarian aid with political and military interventions by donor states. Barnett's earlier (2005) distinction between two types of humanitarian organizations offers historical context for understanding how and why some humanitarian efforts converged with states' political interests:

> Dunantist organizations [associated with Henry Dunant, the founder of the International Committee of the Red Cross] define humanitarianism as the neutral, independent, and impartial provision of relief to victims of conflict and believe that humanitarianism and politics must be separated. [By contrast, Wilsonian organizations follow] Woodrow Wilson's belief that it was possible and desirable to transform political, economic, and cultural structures so that they liberated individuals and produced peace and progress, desire to attack the root causes that leave populations at risk. (Barnett 2005, 728)

Humanitarian transformation came about, according to Barnett, in the 1990s as many aid agencies adopted a Wilsonian orientation out of the futility of mere aid provision, accepting the possibility that they could help eliminate the root causes that endanger people (p. 724). States on the other hand began to recognize humanitarian endeavor—through alliances with, and in some cases financial support for, relief NGOs—as a viable foreign policy strategy. Contrary to Dunant's principle of humanitarian neutrality, Wilsonian agencies became actors in world politics under the premise that neutral relief provision amounts merely to helping the "well-fed dead" (p. 728). Barnett comments,

> Humanitarian principles were completely shattered in places like Kosovo, Afghanistan, and Iraq, where many agencies were funded by the very governments that were combatants and thus partly responsible for the emergency. . . . Commentators spoke of humanitarianism in "crisis" and warned of the dangers of "supping with the devil," "drinking from the poisoned chalice," and "sleeping with the enemy." (Barnett 2005, 724–25)

Wilsonian organizations in some cases link humanitarian aid and human rights advocacy with political and military interventions intended to bring about peace in conflict-ridden settings. Pointing specifically to US involvement in Afghanistan and Iraq, critics of coherence argue that the political agendas of Western states exploit relief work and human rights concerns as tools to accomplish political and military objectives (see, e.g., de Torrenté 2004; Donini 2004). Moreover, critics maintain that the convergence agenda subverts the humanitarian ethic of immediate relief provision for suffering victims by imposing *conditions on aid* "either as an award or denied as a sanction in the name of a brighter future, which results in many avoidable deaths" (de Torrenté 2004, 3). Put another way, these critics charge that the convergence agenda endangers aid workers in the field by raising suspicions they are partisans working to further the political agendas of intervening states. *To Stay and Deliver*, a recent report on humanitarian work in settings of "protracted conflict and insecurity," explains the situation as follows:

> Providing humanitarian assistance amid conflict has always been a dangerous and difficult endeavor; however, over the last decade aid worker casualties tripled, reaching over 100 deaths per year. From 2005 onwards the largest number of violent attacks on humanitarian personnel ha[s] been concentrated in a small number of countries representing the most difficult and volatile operating environments. Attacks in some of the settings have also grown more lethal and sophisticated and the number of killings has risen dramatically. (UN Office for the Coordination of Humanitarian Affairs 2011b, 1)

For the UN Office for the Coordination of Humanitarian Affairs (OCHA) and 17 Western donor governments, the remedy for humanitarianism's identity crises and security dilemmas involves "strengthening the coordination of emergency humanitarian assistance of the United Nations, with particular attention to humanitarian funding and allocations of assistance and the transition from relief to development" (Marchand 2003). A strengthened coordinative role on the part of this UN agency affects how NGOs acquire finding, allocate resources, and pursue their humanitarian missions. As discussed earlier in this chapter, policymakers (such as OCHA officials in this case) seek to attach their new agenda initiatives to discourses that reframe norms in terms that justify advocated policy change. The policy discourse supporting OCHA's integration agenda culminated in the endorsement of "Principles and Good

Practice of Humanitarian Donorship" by 17 Western states that account for a large share of international aid.

So what does "Good Humanitarian Donorship" (GHD) *mean* in relation to humanitarianism's frenzied condition "in a world of hurt" and the operation of rights-based organizations engaged in relief efforts? Just as a dictionary offers a denotative definition of the US Civil War, an OCHA press release provides "chapter and verse" details concerning each of the 23 principles of GHD adopted by the 17 nations:

- Principles 1–3 reassert objectives and definitions of humanitarian actions,
- Principles 4–10 (re)establish general principles that support the UN's enhanced roles in coordinating humanitarian action, and
- Principles 11–23 articulate "good practices" in donor financing, management, and accountability (OCHA 2011a).

But what is *really* going on here? What is the *connotative* significance of GHD for the donor states, NGOs that deliver relief services, victims of conflicts and disasters, and other stakeholders? Is GHD "a lion or a mouse"? Is it an effort to purify humanitarianism from politics or *more* politicization under the guise of "purification"? Does it signify "progress" in humanitarian pursuit or merely represent an institutional adjustment to a changing political environment (Macrae 2004; Barnett 2009)?

Since our concern here focuses on interpreting the significance of particular policy initiatives (rather than casting ethical judgment on GHD per se), it is fitting to speculate about how the GHD effort relates to the controversy surrounding the convergence agenda. Does the GHD initiative, for example, represent a significant departure whereby donor states commit to "cleaning up their acts" by holding themselves more accountable to the traditional humanitarian principles of impartiality, neutrality, and independence? Or is it actually a Machiavellian ploy to legitimize "convergence" by delegating coordinative authority to an intergovernmental entity, the UN Office for the Coordination of Humanitarian Affairs (reflecting the split personalities of the "good humanitarian UN" and "bad political UN"; see Minear 2004, 55)? Or can GHD be interpreted as an institutional attempt to "make sense" of an inherently complex and dangerous aid environment? Such an interpretation implies that donor nations and NGOs seek to learn from their past mistakes and to pursue proactive measures for managing security risks and protecting their staff.

The conclusions and recommendations of the *To Stay and Deliver* report commissioned by OCHA stress the agency's intent to reinstitute the core values of impartiality, neutrality, and independence and to address the security environment. Specifically, the report emphasizes that "humanitarian principles matter" as essential for underpinning acceptance by parties in conflict. In this regard, the following statement is indicative of OCHA's departure from the convergence agenda:

> While simultaneously calling for respect for humanitarian principles, in the recent past many humanitarian organizations have also willingly compromised a principled approach in their own conduct through close alignment with political and military activities and actors. (OCHA 2011b, 4)

As an institutional response to a changing security environment, the report's executive summary states that "the recommendations address the means by which humanitarian agencies might increase their capability to manage the risks they face in high-risk environments, and to invest in long-term and effective means to maintain access to affected populations" (p. 4). While these statements do not necessarily discredit skeptics who interpret GHD as a (Machiavellian) UN power play, they *do* suggest that institutional forces may in fact pressure organizations to reframe their policy discourses. In such cases, "slippery" terminology can usher in new frameworks of understanding that inform a range of stockholders—in this case, those within the humanitarian community.

OCHA's *To Stay and Deliver* report directs particular recommendations toward humanitarian aid NGOs. In fact, the report offers six recommendations to guide the development of risk management strategies and underscore organizations' "duty of care and responsible partnership." A seventh recommendation for "adherence to humanitarian principles" is supported by noticeably strong statements:

> Ensure organizational policies and operational decision-making on issues such as funding, beneficiaries, modes of operation, liaison with other actors, and security measures are in line with humanitarian principles. Invest in communicating the organization's adherence to humanitarian principles. Review operations in complex security environments on a regular basis to ensure compliance with humanitarian principles. (OCHA 2011b, 49–50)

In essence, this report reaffirms a "back to basics" ethos of humanitarianism whereby organizations can exercise more independence by virtue of their commitments to impartiality and neutrality. For the rights-based organization, independence allows for greater leverage to challenge the objectionable actions of donor governments (see de Torrenté 2004, 4).

Although it lacks punitive sanctions to enforce donor accountability (Charny 2004, 16), GHD reflects a normative shift in the environment of humanitarian assistance. Nonetheless, the institutional reality of resource dependency limits the organization's operational latitude in its relief work. In this regard, Barnett's study of four humanitarian organizations found correlation between resource dependency and a proclivity "to incorporate politics into their activities" (2009, 638). However, he is careful *not* to characterize the resource environment as entirely deterministic in driving adaptive behavior. Instead, Barnett stresses the importance of the organization's *identity* (in relation to unifying values) and its ability "to take its temperature" (or to self-assess) through organization learning. In between the emerging norm of humanitarian independence and the counterbalance of resource dependency, rights-based NGOs need to position themselves to optimize their aid leverage. As Barnett implies, such positioning is better established by spirited debate throughout the organization than by unilateral top-management action (2009, 656–57).

NGO Roles in Analyzing and Affecting Rights-Related Discourse

From the standpoint of practical management, belabored discussions about buzzwords, "fuzzwords," and framing discourse could be likened to proverbial "angels dancing on pins" as irrelevant to day-to-day challenges. But it was an academic who returned from his 1990s rights work in Rwanda asking real life-and-death questions about how genocide could occur in a country so saturated with NGOs and civil society organizations (presumably creating all of that good "civic space") and why none of those organizations could sound the international alarm of impending catastrophe (Uvin 1998). Uvin charges the NGO community there was not merely oblivious but also complicit in "aiding violence" because of its "voluntary blindness to factors [that] allowed it to continue 'business as usual' almost up to the last day [before the genocide began]" (2004, 2–3). Part of the problem may lie in the fact that NGO professionals tend not to realize that they are "being framed" by other power actors (such as donors, host governments, and multilateral institutions) not only by how they must plan, budget, and evaluate (as discussed in chapter 5) but also by what they are obliged to "buy into" regarding favored values and narratives. Rights-focused leaders need to recognize the prevalent and/or imposed taken-for-grantedness in their environments (and organizations). Stated another way, it is important for them to "name the frame" before engaging in "naming and shaming" or other rights efforts (Rein and Schön 1993, 153–54). The balance of this section explores how sensitivity to rhetoric and discourse can inform NGO leadership first by focusing on requisite analysis to know oneself (or organization), allies, and adversaries, as well as knowing the terrain of the discourse, and second by introducing alternative modes for engaging discourse in order to advance human rights.

After sharing 150 specific tactics used by various human rights groups, a workbook published by the Center for Victims of Torture offers guidelines for "developing creative strategies and tactics" based on three recommendations: (1) "Don't believe your own propaganda," (2) nor "your opponent's propaganda," and (3) "know the literal terrain upon which you will meet your opponent" (Cornell, Kelsch, and Palasz 2004, 156). The first two clearly advise rights professionals (and amateurs) to recognize the power of buzzwords and discourse, but so too does the third if the notion of terrain is expanded to include the politics of rhetorical interpretation. As reiterated often in this book, rights work requires competency in analyzing *power* whether it is manifested in explicit government actions or in the nuance of arguments put forward by influential development institutions or the coalitions of consensus they organize. In other words, "knowing the terrain" calls for policy analysis just as intent on probing the rights implications of development discourse as on scrutinizing the actions of governments.

. In their article surveying the rhetorical terrain of development policy, Cornwall and Brock draw on the thought of social philosopher George Sorel, who referred to rhetorical narratives as *myths* that "humanity requires as inspiring images of battle and triumph—for any substantial 'forward movement'":

> Myths are not descriptions of things, but expressions of a determination to act. . . . A myth cannot be refuted since it is identical with the convictions of a group. (Hirschman 1967, 31; Sorel 1941, 33, both quoted by Cornwall and Brock 2007, 15–16)

Based on these criteria, the assertion that *civil society organizations create space for democracy* probably qualifies as myth, important *not* because it is necessarily "false" or "true" but because it conveys the power of its institutional advocates in relation to the poor and disenfranchised.

Much like ecological concerns, development issues and their human rights implications need to be understood as matters of technocratic politics wherein experts and the problem narratives they invoke assume power. Therefore, NGO professionals need the capability to recognize that inherently political "who gets what" issues are often technically framed or dressed in the clothes of "expert," "scientific" explanation (Fischer 1993, 24–27). Furthermore, it is incumbent upon NGO analysts to comprehend how consensus coalesces within a group of diverse interests. Sociologist Maarten Hajer refers to such an alliance as *discourse coalitions* or as "a group of actors who share a social construct," such as "Good Humanitarian Donorship" (discussed previously). He explains, "Social constructs such as acid rain can be seen as a way to give meaning to ambiguous social circumstances (e.g., unexplained dying of forests or lakes)" (1993, 45). By analogy, discourse coalitions in development policy assemble social constructs relating to the ambiguities of poverty within particular settings as explanatory myths supporting the determination to strengthen markets or require governments to deregulate as a condition for receiving aid. NGO leaders might do well to heed Hajer's advice to study the power dynamics of discourse coalitions that are influential in crafting development policy. For him, a focus on these coalitions is especially helpful because

1. it analyzes strategic action in the context of specific discourses and institutional practices and provides the conceptual tools to understand [technical controversies] in a wider political context;
2. it takes the explanation beyond mere reference to interests, analyzing how interests are played out in the context of specific discourses and organizational practices; and
3. it illuminates how different actors and organization practices help [perpetuate or counteract] a given bias. (Hajer 1993, 48)

In general terms, attention to discourse coalitions, the argumentation (or myths) they advance, and the buzzwords they enlist to prop up that argumentation prompt the NGO professional to cut through the elaborate framing of rights-related problems to ask straightforward questions such as the following: Who (i.e., which power actors or coalitions) frames problem narratives and favored remedies? Do those narratives distort political reality, and if so, how? And what roles do powerful development institutions play as "think tanks" in perpetuating discourses on which consensus depends?

Beyond attending to analytical tasks necessary to reveal the power in prevailing discourse, NGO professionals bear the responsibility of argumentation to reframe discourse that neglects or mischaracterizes human rights and how to attain them. In this regard, the approach pursued, or the means rights advocates use, to engage adversaries may be as critical as the substance of the rights argumentation itself. Rights advocates can, for example, opt to follow a confrontational approach that directly challenges how an issue has been framed, but they will likely face a number of formidable obstacles. First, discourse coalitions are seldom "self-reflective" and are therefore not inclined to "second-guess" their standing assumptions and worldviews. Rein and Schön maintain that prevalent policy talk defines "the way things are." But seeing things differently, challengers present a "different world" at the risk of compromising their own legitimacy (1993, 151–53). (As a fledgling member of a local diversity committee, I soon discovered that diversity talk centered on naming city parks after prominent African Americans—and then assigning particular minority groups financial responsibility for maintaining those so-named parks. The possibility that racial intolerance could fester in the local culture was dismissed as inconceivable—they were "raised better than that.") Second, it is difficult to challenge consensus based on ideal abstractions—such as democracy, poverty reduction, or military intervention—to "assure a better future," or even human rights (that *everybody* recognizes as important, or as Uvin quips, "case closed, moral high ground safely established"; 2004, 51). On the other hand, argumentation that can illustrate discrepancies between concrete examples of oppression and the principled abstractions of discourse coalitions could play on "our abhorrence of cognitive dissonance" to reframe the policy debate (Rein and Schön 1993, 159–60; Festinger 1957).

As an alternative to direct confrontation, NGO professionals can seek advisory roles that gradually influence the shape of discourse over time. Bruce Jennings draws on the field of medical ethics to propose a "discourse of counsel and consensus" by which the advocate strives toward "the practical goal of enabling constructive action to move the community from a flawed present to an improved future" (1993, 103). For Jennings, the counsel approach capitalizes on the common ground shared between the advocate and others in the group or community:

> The knowledge possessed by the counselor may be more systematic and reflective, but it is not qualitatively distinct from the repertoire and cultural competency of [others]. Neither counselors or citizens can prescribe a definitive, regulative use of the concepts and categories of public argument, but alternative uses of them—alternative

interpretations of public need, justice, and the common good—can be rationally debated and assessed. (p. 104)

On an individual level, counsel is apparent in the lectures Amartya Sen delivered at the World Bank in 1997 in his attempt to reframe development policy discourse. He explains,

> The World Bank has not invariably been my favorite organization. The power to do good goes almost always with the possibility to do the opposite, and as a professional economist, I have had occasions in the past to wonder whether the Bank could not have done very much better. . . . All this made it particularly welcome to have the opportunity to present at the Bank my own views on development and on the making of public policy. (Sen 1999, xiii)

Sen subsequently drew from these lectures to draft his influential book *Development as Freedom*, with his previous quote included in its preface.

On a collective basis, advocacy organizations can endeavor to assume counselor roles in affecting rhetoric within institutions or discourse groups over time. Policy analyst Deborah Stone points out that in the context of litigation, rights claiming suffers from the power asymmetry between well-funded "repeat players" (in court frequently to fend off claims) over "one-shot" rights lawyers with less familiarity of judges and judicial behavior (2002, 344–45). By analogy, if NGOs can gain legitimacy as participants and advisors in policymaking, they may be able to establish themselves as repeat players able to affect how discourses relating to human rights are framed. NGOs that bring particular benefits to the policy table, for example, information about the realities of implementation, may be especially welcomed as advisors. For example, the NGO Idasa (discussed in chapter 4) is viewed as an authority on children's rights in South Africa by virtue of its monitoring efforts that track budgeted funds for children's welfare (Kgamphe 2004). And in Nigeria, CLEEN supports ongoing dialogue between citizens and police agencies and in so doing establishes trust in the law enforcement community there (Cornell, Kelsch, and Palasz 2004, 128).

Conclusion

Lacking the insight and resolve to cut through buzzwords and discourses that power actors use to characterize "human improvement," NGOs risk having their humanitarian and human rights missions hijacked out from under them. As such, interpretive hijacking occurs when instead of NGOs reforming others on behalf of human rights, the reverse is the case: "it is the aid agency reforming its concept of human right to bring it in line with what it already does" (Duffield 2001, 222–23, as quoted in Uvin 2004, 51)—perhaps as with relief agencies aligning their efforts with national interests (as discussed earlier). This chapter attempts to equip NGO professionals with the interpretive wherewithal to understand how resonant terms in development conversations and rights conversations have been strategically crafted and how powerful actors and institutions can frame that conversation to maintain or advance their political wills. Moreover, it directs NGO leaders toward policy-grounded advice for argumentation that reclaims discourses by authentically characterizing rights claiming in the voices of the poor, disempowered, and victimized.

That said, the following chapters in this book make liberal use of all these (strategically crafted) terms *as if* they conveyed straightforward and inspiring denotations. Short of issuing mea culpas in each instance, suffice it here to conclude with brief comments about political discourses as they relate to the topics addressed in subsequent chapters. In many respects, the discussions about "transformative change" in chapter 3 elaborate on variations among development discourse and rights discourse that *promise* advances in the human condition, each of which is based on alternative development narratives reflecting diverse (and in some cases, opposing) ideologies. Occasions will likely arise when NGO professionals will be ethically compelled to challenge "rights" as interpreted through the prevailing ideological rhetoric (of funding agencies, governments, or other power interests) and champion other, presumably more authentic, conceptions of human rights in their place. With regard to organization and management as depicted in chapter 4, it is essential that NGO leaders mediate the "hard" management rhetoric of structure and control with the softer facilitative leadership discourses that promote organization learning, the wellspring of a range of technical, leadership, and interpersonal competencies. In addition, leaders need self-awareness to discern differences in management discourses appropriate at varying stages of the NGO lifecycle (especially those effective as the organization matures in comparison to the rhetoric and narrative of the founder). A rhetorician could have a field day analyzing the characterizations of NGO "performance," "accountability," and "transparency" included in chapter 5. To paraphrase one commentator (Fox 2007, 663), the operative question could be posed (in elongated form) as *What kind of performance satisfies what kind of accountability based on what kind of expectations of which stakeholder given what degree of transparency?*

The related issues of organization learning (OL) and knowledge management (KM) treated in chapter 6 both focus on intentions to examine and possibly reframe discourses—with OL to encourage reflective scrutiny on taken-for-granted assumptions and practices in the organization and with KM to decipher "what we talk about when we talk about knowledge" (Davenport and Prusak 1998, 1). Chapter 7 endeavors to maintain a sharp analytical bead on socially constructed gender roles as they play out politically in families, workplaces, NGO–client relationships, and elsewhere to keep gender focused on power distribution, as true to its feminist origin. A commitment to analysis is essential for rights advocacy given the complaint that "gender talk is everywhere" (Pearson 2006, 157; Smyth 2007, 583) charging that development actors have co-opted gender discourse and have depoliticized it along the way. In regard to human resources management, it appears that NGOs need to reframe management discourses that consider employees' living and hardship circumstances in efforts to reduce rampant turnover in personnel as explored in chapter 8. Words, meanings, and interpretations matter in each of the substantive areas related to NGO efforts to advance human rights.

Discussion Issues

1. Identify two discourses (or ensembles of ideas) that are taken for granted in your immediate (family, work, university, etc.) environment. Have there been instances when they have been challenged? If so, how and with what level of success?
2. For many, universal declarations and principles provide legitimacy for particular human rights. Nonetheless, some international relations theorists argue that "new" norms emerge over time, sometimes eclipsing existing norms. Do the implications of "norm development" generally strengthen or weaken the case for human rights? Explain.
3. Following the logic in table 2.1, offer alternative interpretations of the term *democracy* and then probe each in terms of capability to (1) advance political interests, (2) build consensus, (3) include or exclude particular interests, and (4) make promises.
4. Probe the dubious propaganda (or self-serving discourse) of an organization or a movement that you hold in high regard.
5. Is a student organization intent on stopping human trafficking in a particular state better advised to pursue a confrontational approach or a counsel role in attempting to (re)frame rights

discourse among legislators and law enforcement officials? Compare the strengths and limitations of both approaches and the ramifications of each for organizational planning.

Notes

1. *Webster's Online Dictionary* can be found at www.websters-online-dictionary.org/.
2. CIDA is the acronym for the Canadian International Development Agency.

3

Rights-Based Leadership and Transformative Change

Envision for a moment that a director of an area (in-country) affiliate of a bilateral NGO provides a range of health-related programs designed to empower the rural poor. Within a six-month interval, her organization confronts the following situations:

1. The "home" bilateral agency (in response to donor complaints) pressures the area organization to become more transparent and therefore conditions future budget support on better and more comprehensive reporting protocols.
2. Turnover among grassroots workers in villages has increased at an alarming rate, allegedly due to low morale and a widespread perception that the area office is indifferent to the day-to-day plight of field-workers.
3. Community leaders in a rural village protest that the NGO's programs fail to address the most pressing health problems and that the workers who implement those programs exhibit demeaning behaviors in their interactions with poor farmers.

Presumably, all of these scenarios would call on the organization to assess the need for "change," but each suggests change of a different sort. The first might elicit a response to an *external* demand, while the second may require actions to alleviate *internal* staffing problems. By contrast, the third—as a programmatic concern—directly focuses on the NGO's potential to empower people, and as such it challenges leadership's capability to sustain a rights-based culture in the NGO.

True, all of these in one way or another affect how well organizations fulfill their rights-oriented missions. Nonetheless, it is helpful to differentiate among various types of change and to treat them in appropriate chapters. Thus, this chapter is devoted to issues concerning transformative change (like scenario 3) that affects program strategies to address particular rights deprivation, strengthen human capabilities, and extend persons' agency over their life circumstances as consistent with Sen's (1999) human capability approach and Uvin's (2004, 122–66) rights-based development. Rights-oriented strategies evolve within a contextual relationship between funding agencies and organizations wherein respective ideological worldviews and priorities are as apt to differ as to converge (Wallace 2007, 19), sometimes pitting Northern donor interests against NGO program logic in the South. From an institutional perspective, the *regulative* effects of donor preferences affect the cognitive—that is, how resource-dependent NGOs (re)interpret their missions. Within the agency, leaders need to "make sense" of glaring differences in program foci (between donors and the NGO), as well as in desired management instruments (particularly in the areas of planning and evaluation) to be utilized (Wallace 2007, 32–34). Leaders in rights-based organizations must often cope with donors' perspectives of "change for the better" as a significant parameter that restricts the NGO's room to maneuver in affecting programmatic change.

"Change" for Advancing Human Rights

Most people, organizations, communities, nations, and so on strive to either "change things for the better" or "leave well enough alone"; few purport to "change things for the worse." Yet disagreements invariably arise over exactly what changes are needed, what is "better" (or "worse"), and who or what can effect those changes. These process issues loom *even if* consensus can be reached on substance, that is, the nature of "the problem" and goals to address it. Within human rights conversation, issues about how to advance human rights (and what that entails) differ among various ideological (political and philosophical) perspectives that are often agenda driven (i.e., intended to justify favored outcomes).

This section presents four different interpretations on "appropriate" change that promotes human rights—as defined by those sharing the interpretation. Three of these four perspectives (discussed in the following section) are introduced as narratives, or stories that characterize the nature of a problem, as well as the remedy—in this case, change remedy—to address it, all of which reinforce the ideological stance taken (see Stone 2002, 138–45). As stories, narratives have heroes, villains, and plots, all leading up to the (change) remedy for "living happily ever after." For example, one (the neoliberal) narrative presented casts *private investors and entrepreneurs* as heroes and *central governments* as villains, with the story lines that *governments have deprived people of rights* and that *people can claim rights through the emergence of free markets*. In another (the participatory narrative), the *people empowering themselves* are heroes, and the entire *development industry* is the villain, with the story line that a *self-serving development industry saps people's rights-claiming, self-empowerment capabilities*. In essence, narratives manipulate symbols and meanings in ways that represent the narrator's subjective interpretation of the policy environment (see Scott 1995, 40). Another interpretation focusing on advocacy (also discussed) appears less ideologically coherent than the first three, so it is presented simply as a perspective rather than a narrative (even though it is tempting to think about human rights advocacy in terms of heroics—see Nelson 2000). Excluded from discussion is a "leave-us-alone" grassroots stridency that categorically rejects development (*We have been developed to death!*) and presumably organized rights advocacy as well (see, e.g., Esteva and Prakash 1998; also see Lofredo 1995 for an example of a cynical antidevelopment narrative).

These four alternative interpretations of change for advancing human rights are intended to represent the predominant thinking in the literature—at the obvious risk of inadvertently omitting other significant ideas. The section to follow explores the opportunities and challenges of rights-based NGO leadership within each of these interpretations.

Technical Narratives of Change

The *technical* narrative regarding change has little to do with the "technical" or scientific nature of a service or benefit provided but rather more to do with presumptions of how changes occur and who the change agents are. Take, for example, agroforestry and aquaculture (fish or shellfish farming)—perhaps *technical* in a scientific and biological sense, but the concern here deals with the logic that drives how NGO leaders and staffs conceptualize desirable change and organize their resources to implement it. NGOs embracing the technical narrative generally presume that experts (either within the organization or available from affiliate organizations) act as the principal agents who can improve forestry practices or expand prawn farming as a viable occupation through formalized, rational processes. (By stark contrast, other NGOs might focus on the rural-poor *participant* as the intended change agent.) Alternatively, NGO personnel, apart from their own personal or professional opinions, might find themselves obliged to follow the will of donors or other influential stakeholders who understand change as a primarily technical undertaking of imparting expertise. The balance of this section assumes a descriptive (rather than critical) tone as it identifies some key development issues as they relate to the technical narrative, or presumptions about how "change" comes about.

Change as a "needs-based" intervention by "expert" outsiders. Those guided by the technical narrative presume that professionalized experts command the skills and wherewithal to intervene by addressing significant needs and deficits that affect people and communities within divergent settings. *Capacity-building* or *empowerment* (to the extent they resonate as issues) are generally limited to training individual recipients, local community organizations, or area-based NGO personnel in acquiring particular skills, for example, reforestation projects (see Anyonge et al. 2001) or use of inorganic fertilizers in prawn ponds (see Kusakabe 2003). In essence, the intervening expert in this mode of development takes on the role of outside consultant—in fact, some authors devote articles to the predicament of flying into a development locale for brief stays (perhaps one or two weeks) in which time they must channel their expertise to meet particular needs, generally through training sessions. Then, off to a different site.

Change as project focused. In common parlance, it may sound quite normal to hear of development efforts as *projects*—for example, an agroforestry project in Kenya. Yet the term *project* places significant time limitations on that effort as it specifies points of a beginning and an end—in contrast to the term *program* that implies a longer term, ongoing relationship between a development organization and a local community. As David Korten (1984) points out, the *project* focus aligns with traditional management assumptions that experts can bring about change by "solving" difficult problems through appropriate planning and programming procedures. The limited time frame implied in the *project* also sits well with Northern donors wishing to leverage (or maximize) their investments by accelerating change—in essence, achieving maximum efficiency for their development dollar rather than committing to an open-ended undertaking. Korten and others explain that donor motivations to accelerate change reflect differing change ideologies and temporal perspective between Northern funding NGOs and Southern grassroots organizations (also see Chambers 1997); both Korten and Chambers attribute the Northern yearning for accelerated change to a cultural impatience on the part of Northern modernity.

Change as an outcome of project planning. Among the change narratives reviewed here, the technical discourse most closely parallels the classical management idea that "appropriate change" can be rationally defined and implemented through sound structures and processes. This orientation emphasizes the need for strong planning and strategic management techniques as important in prescribing desired outcomes and in designing apt implementation procedures. These modern management ideas resonate among donors expecting tangible accountability linkages between their investments and durable development outcomes—in other words, NGOs competing for donor dollars must document the validity of project objectives and the methods and procedures for achieving them. Thus, the presumed capability to "preprogram" "appropriate change" complements the notions of change as expert (outsider) "intervention" and as "project-focused" product (as explained previously).

In development NGOs, the logical framework (or logframe) typically embodies the methodological nexus between programming and planning and subsequently offers the evaluative criteria for monitoring project success. For example, a project to improve children's health in a rural (poor) local village might link various development objectives (e.g., "Children or estate laborers in X district enjoy better health than earlier."), indicators (e.g., "frequency of treatment of relevant diseases, health personnel's statements, mothers' statements"), and indicators for evaluation (e.g., "height, weight/age, frequency of diarrhea") (Dale 2003, 63). Thus, it appears that stakeholders, such as donors, furthest removed from grassroots development work highly value the logframe, while those closest to the change efforts generally discredit (if not despise) it. An author of a published article illustrates the controversial nature of the logframe as a blueprint for the preplanning change in his title: "The Logical Framework: An Easy Escape, a Straitjacket, or a Useful Planning Tool?" (Dale 2003).

Needs-based change as apolitical. Although perhaps not frequently stated as such, the technical narrative elevates the good works of expert intervention above and apart from the political motives of some stakeholders such as governments or bilateral donor organizations. (It is worth noting the parallel between this presumed distance from politics in the technical narrative and the classical thinking in my own field—public management—that the techniques of good administration are or should be separable from the political process.) By this logic it follows that physicians, agronomists, nutritionists, and others depend on technical expertise to support their credibility as change agents—thus, they ought not wander into the "corrupting clutches" of politics. While it might appear that *nongovernmental* organizations serve to "do good" as apolitical humanitarians, such thinking is especially dubious in the pursuit of rights-based NGO leadership.

Neoliberal Narratives of Change

Neoliberal narratives explain "development" as structural and policy changes that enhance economic opportunities and promote civil and political rights consistent with those usually found in Western democracies. (Readers should take care *not* to associate *neoliberal economics* with "liberal politics," as more often those who espouse neoliberal policies engage in conservative politics with preferences toward limited government.) Reflecting classical economists' views of the ideal society, this orientation is also known as "structural adjustment," a term referring to its imperative to restructure power, typically away from central government and toward local organizations and market actors, and to clear the obstacles that governments presumably pose that encumber a market economy. This perspective on change stems from an ideology of globalism (as opposed to the phenomenon of globalization) that devalues nationalism and strong states and elevates the merits of foreign trade and international investment (Malešević 1999).

Guided by its confidence in classical economics as a science for engineering "developed societies" (see Kelly 2008, 329), the neoliberal narrative is advanced by multi- and bilateral institutions that fund international aid, such as the World Trade Organization, the Multilateral Agreement on Investment, the World Bank, the International Monetary Fund, and multinational corporations (see Korten 1995; Fowler 1999). The structural adjustment strategies evoke strong negative reactions, especially from the South, because (among other reasons) of its close philosophical alignment with US foreign policy (Kelly 2008, 329). As will become apparent, neoliberal change narratives can exert profound impacts on the nature of NGOs' goals and organization as they push those agencies to challenge different societal roles and, in so doing, pressure NGO leaders to "bureaucratize and professionalize" (see Feldman 2003). These demands, although perhaps not unreasonable from the standpoint of accountability, may in fact result in compromising or displacing traditional NGO missions.

For purposes of clarity, it is helpful to understand the neoliberal change narrative in terms of both its *ends* (i.e., desired change as particular results) and the *means* for achieving those results. *Ends* relate to three levels of change. First, at the personal level, success involves poverty reduction and/or income growth through individualism, entrepreneurship, and self-reliance on the part of the individual. Consistent with Western democracies, the narrative showcases economic development and national competitiveness in a global economy occurring alongside the development of human and social capital (Rondinelli 2003b; Agosín and Bloom 2003). Second, at the national level, the neoliberal narrative values a minimalist central government (referred to as a "night watch-man" role; see Kelly 2008) as an essential goal. Third and correspondingly, the neoliberal narrative calls for power to be dispersed at local levels among a mul-titude of community and civil society organizations (CSOs), including NGOs. The balance of this section elaborates on principal *means* by which these ends can be realized in the neoliberal change narrative. It should be noted that ad-vocates of neoliberal economic reforms often use the term *good governance* as encompassing the ends that lead to "development" (as discussed previously) and the means to achieve them.

Change as a decentralizing power to autonomous organizations. Consistent with the logic of structural adjustment, funding institutions advance the neo-liberal change agenda through specific programs that call on governments—through either legislation or other means—to devolve policy authority as a condition for development aid. In this regard, Erik Bryld quotes a discussion of decentralization in the World Bank's *World Development Report of 1997* as follows:

> The clearest and most important principle is that public goods and services should be provided by the lowest level of government that can fully capture the costs and benefits . . . decentralisation. . . . In conclusion, the evidence presented in this chapter has shown that improving the capability and effectiveness of the state rests with mechanisms to increase openness and transparency, to strengthen incentives for participation in public affairs, and, where appropri-ate, to bring the state closer to the people and communities it is meant to serve. (World Bank 1997, 129; Bryld 2000, 702)

It is particularly important to note, as Bryld does, that although power rearrangement is usually understood as a political tactic (either changing the sub-stance of policy and/or changing the membership of policy-making bodies—see Stone 2002, 354–75), the neoliberal narrative approaches these power shifts as technocratic, "practical" (and thus, apolitical) improvements. Bryld comments,

> In a technocratic world there is little room for political parties or elitist states. A political issue such as development is addressed, with state involvement, through the use of economic techniques. Sensitive political issues are put in macro-economic boxes, where the highest priority is efficiency. Hence, politics is not seen as a part of the state. (2000, 703)

Since the neoliberal narrative links the prospect of these improved goods and services with proper good governance measures to decentralize power, failures can be readily attributed to "government's ineptness" in implementing decentralization in the first place rather than to other causes—such as fundamental incompatibilities between particular political-cultural contexts and the intent of neoliberal reforms (p. 703).

Change as market deregulation and reregulation. In addition to urging governments to decentralize power, neoliberal funding institutions call on national governments to reform their regulatory policies, usually in the direction of scaling them back. Trade liberalization (in basic terms, the relaxation of tariffs) stands out as especially important among regulatory reforms in the neoliberal change agenda as a means of providing new production opportunities for impoverished workers in the South. Quoting a UN Conference on Trade and Development report, Rondinelli suggests that promoting national (export) competitiveness involves "diversifying the export basket, sustaining higher rates of export growth over time, upgrading the technological and skill content of export activity, and expanding the database of domestic firms to compete internationally" (2003b, 39). Institutions advocating trade liberalization call on governments to enact any number of policies to de- or reregulate markets, such as these recommended by the World Bank's International Finance Corporation to improve the business environment by removing the following:

- expensive and time-consuming regulatory requirements such as licensing and registration,
- the legal framework for commercial transactions and the resolution of disputes that can affect transactions with unknown firms,
- laws governing the protection of business and intellectual property and the use of property as collateral,
- tax structures that distort incentives and discriminate against small firms, and
- labor market rigidities that make hiring and firing workers difficult and expensive and that limit the flexibility and mobility of the labor force (Hallberg 2000, 9–10).

It is difficult, however, to trace direct linkages between trade liberalization, such as the phasing out of the 1974 Multifibre Agreement (a tariff), and improved economic conditions of garment workers among the poor in particular settings, as in Bangladesh. In essence, exactly who benefits from the complex interplay of global market forces and the particularities of national or regional labor markets is hard to predict (see Hale 2002). Yet the neoliberal appeal for regulatory change extends beyond trade liberalization to include various sectors of the economy that affect the lives of the poor. (For example, Geoffrey Payne [2001] explains how scaled-back planning regulations improve housing opportunities for the urban poor.)

Change as the proliferation of CSOs promoting democracy. In the neoliberal change narrative, CSOs—a wide assortment of grassroots groups involved in public service—are viewed as principal vehicles for democratizing societies. More specifically, David Lewis characterizes CSOs as "grassroots organizations, community and neighborhood groups, local development organizations, and NGOs, which have been able to constitute themselves as autonomous social movements challenging the established social order and at the same time have become bridges between marginalized populations and the formal institutions of the society" (1994, 130). Lewis's treatment of CSOs as more trusted alternatives to government bureaucracies reflects neoliberal thinking that the *nongovernmental* status of these service-oriented groups can open up civic space for democratic processes. Rondinelli explains the roles of CSOs in this way:

> As societies become more complex, people also need the help of consumer groups, charitable and philanthropic organizations, and social organizations to bring them together to participate in a wide range of activities. . . . All of these groups, by bringing people together in a common cause, provide them with mechanisms for contributing to the quality of life in their communities and countries. (Rondinelli 2003b, 55)

In their book *NGO Accountability*, Jordan and Van Tuijl explain how since the early 1990s NGOs found legitimacy in the aftermath of the Tiananmen Square massacre through the following syllogistic logic: "*1. Civil society is necessary for democracy; 2. NGOs are civil society;* [therefore] *3. NGOs are good for democratic development*" (2007, 11). Yet if NGOs build credibility through their involvement as public service providers, they risk their autonomy in relation to funding institutions or governments that contract with them for services. Deborah Eade presents the dilemma as follows:

> Many of those civil society organizations . . . find themselves trying to maintain a balance between the difficulties of surviving within a hostile environment and the challenges posed by swimming against

the tide, and seeking alternatives to it. They are caught between accommodating themselves or "selling-out" on the one hand, and being neutralised or cast as outdated radicals on the other. As the ethical and human values that accompany the forces of globalisation are shifting, so it becomes far harder to draw the line between adapting to change and simply abandoning one' s principles. (Eade 2000, 149)

Some critics refer to NGOs' roles as service providers in civil society as "gap filling," suggesting that CSOs "let governments off the hook" by assuming responsibilities for costly and challenging public functions (see, e.g., Whaites 1998, 344). Ironically, an account of an NGO providing services for runaway teenagers in Mexico City shows how EDNICA (Educación de Niños Callejeros) compensates for government's fiscal inability to act—due to that nation's involvement in neoliberal free-trade policies (see Magazine 2003).

Change as private sector involvement in public service provision. The neoliberal change narrative includes an interesting twist given the following assertions: (1) governments should provide fewer services but simply "make sure things get done"—in public management circles, this is known as "steering not rowing" (see Osborne and Gaebler 1993, 25–48)—and (2) government can be strengthened by outsourcing service responsibilities to private sector contractors. In essence, subtraction can be addition. Ridde (2005) offers an account of a World Bank–funded partnership to reconstruct the health system in Afghanistan. Here the Ministry of Public Health relies on private partners' capability to secure private capital (basically, leveraging World Bank aid) in lieu of costs to government that would have been prohibitive for such a large-scale undertaking. Rondinelli explains the incentives for governments to partner with private sector entities:

> By outsourcing or working in partnership with the public sector, governments can benefit from the strong incentives for private firms to keep costs down. Often, private firms can avoid the bureaucratic problems that plague national and municipal governments, and they can experiment with new technology and procedures. PPPs [public–private partnerships] allow government to extend services without increasing the number of public employees and without making large capital investments in facilities and equipment. (Rondinelli 2003a, 221)

Funding institutions have looked to the prevalence of such partnership arrangements in the West (which some public management experts criticize as "hollowing out" state authority; see, e.g., Frederickson and Smith 2003, 207–28) as apt development models (Ridde 2005, 6). Yet there is concern that private contractors circumvent stakeholder participation in project planning (see Estimo 2007 regarding a public–private water and sewer project in the Philippines); such a complaint presumes that, alternatively, government bureaucracy would have honored those mechanisms for stakeholder input.

Participatory Narratives of Change

The term *participation* connotes any number of meanings, forms, and motives within development conversation, sometimes leading to the empowerment of those affected but in other cases merely offering cosmetic "cover" for development professionals to proceed with business as usual (see Pijnenburg and Nhantumbo 2002, 191–93). Yet the participatory narrative outlined here reflects a strident rejection of "development industry" practices whereby outsider professionals exercise power on those to be "helped" who have little, if any, say in project procedures and outcomes. Thus, references to the development industry are typically derogatory in nature, taking aim at the various actors— Northern donors, aid agencies, bilateral NGOs, and so on—involved in perpetuating this large-scale international enterprise viewed as serving itself rather than the poor in particular locales. From this perspective, those subscribing to either the technical or the neoliberal narratives would generally be included as integral parts of the development industry problem.

Although this scathing criticism stemmed from many places, particularly from self-critical development workers themselves, it is Robert Chambers (1997) who is widely credited for advancing a specific framework for participation-directed development: the Participatory Rural Appraisal (PRA) in his book *Whose Reality Counts? Participation* was not unheard of before Chambers's writings—in fact, David Korten notes that in 1973 the US Congress passed foreign assistance legislation known as "The New Directions Mandate" that instructed US Agency for International Development (USAID) to include poor participation in planning and implementation (although those good intentions were seldom realized; Korten 1980, 482–83). Yet Chambers's PRA framework (note that the "R" should not be taken too seriously since the approach is just as applicable in urban as in rural settings; Chambers 1997, xviii) resonates forcefully among practitioners as essentially the embodiment of

Sen's emphases on agency as central in addressing deprivations and on multiple constitutive capabilities. Moreover, in line with Sen's thinking, participation is viewed as an essential *end*—and not simply as just a *means*—that translates to human agency, the person's control as author of one's destiny. But as logical as this may appear, such authorship fundamentally challenges development organizations to reconceptualize how and under what circumstances (somebody else's) change unfolds, as well as rediscover professional responsibilities outside of the traditional, technical change-agent role.

Since participatory-directed change evolves naturally from human agency and therefore rather unpredictably, particular narratives of change through participation seem less evident than with the other two narratives described previously. The following change themes represent but a few of the key issues either emphasized in development literature focused on PRA-modeled participation or attributed directly to Chambers's writings.

Change as only meaningful within "poor people's realities." As explicit in Chambers's book title, the reality of those whose lives are to be affected should "count," rather (or at least more so) than the realities of development professionals, Northern donors, or aid funding institutions (perhaps themselves driven by assumed realities of global politics). Chambers stresses that professionals' realities tend to prevail in development largely because of their exalted power maintained by hubris and lofty status within development organization hierarchies. Standard practices, such as developing logframe planning and evaluation systems and applying best practices (deemed as having "worked" elsewhere), essentially "transfer reality" in ways that impose professional interpretations of "what is" or "what ought to be" on local ways of life (see Chambers 1997, 56–75). To counter such self-deluding inclinations, the participatory narrative conditions development workers to assume roles as catalysts recognizing that persons (often mobilized in collectives) themselves become change agents—presuming of course that they perceive the intended change as desirable and relevant.

As a potential catalyst, development workers need to "get inside" to grasp the indigenous reality in an expeditious manner in order to help others resolve their own problems. Such a learning challenge requires one to start with a "blank slate" (or to discard all presuppositions) with the intention of coaxing out signals and clues helpful in understanding what people view as problems, or obstacles, in their lives *as well as* what they perceive to be their strengths and competencies. For example, an environmental specialist might pursue traditional farming practices that may in themselves control erosion (perhaps to some extent) as entrée for participation and interaction, rather than presume a lack of environmental awareness in need of technical intervention (see Any-onge et al. 2001).

Change as the poor empowering themselves. As Chambers's participatory framework gained stature in the development world, international funding agencies took note—for example, the World Bank adapted some aid programs to incorporate participation by the poor into program planning and implementation (see Pijnenburg and Nhantumbo 2002, 193). Thus, a critical question arises as to whether meaningful participation can be grafted onto existing programs (particularly those reflecting other change logics) without diluting the essence of Chambers's radical imperative of "putting the last first" (referring to the subtitle of his book that clearly references the Beatitudes in the gospels of Matthew and Luke). Although it seems presumptuous to answer this question definitively, a couple of general propositions may be in order. First, Chambers's participation empowers; second, it is even tougher to "put the first last" than to put "the last first" (1997, 210–37). Relating to my own field of public management, public officials frequently enact change (i.e., revising procedures, reallocating staffing, creating citizen participation groups, etc.) to keep things homogenous or maintain stability—this is sometimes called "contingency decision making." In this regard, Gabrielle Appleford elaborates on a joint development venture involving an Australian aid (AusAID) organization and the government of Papua New Guinea that created a number of women's societies (or social-civic groups) as a participatory component of an aid program. Aside from the gendering implications here (to be discussed in chapter 7), Appleford concludes that participation in this case is nominal— certainly not transformative or empowering—and serves merely to legitimize the project (2000, 82–89).

In vivid contrast, Chambers's PRA framework reorients the roles of "uppers" (those with power, particularly development experts) and "lowers" (the poor and powerless)—in doing so, his approach is radical in the sense of getting to "the roots" of power inequity in development and then reversing roles. Specifically, Chambers advocates six particular reversals in professional practice needed to empower the poor: "from closed to open, from individual to group, from verbal to visual, from measuring to comparing, from higher to lower, and from reserve and frustration to rapport and fun" (1997, 147). Although some of these will be examined in some depth in chapter 5 with regard to accountability and performance, the reversal *from verbal to visual* offers keen insight as to how the poor can empower themselves through participation. By reversing the means of knowledge conveyance, the nonliterate poor can plan and evaluate diagrammatically—on the ground. Chambers relates,

Perhaps most important, the ground is an equalizer. The media and materials are often those of insiders—soil, stones, sand, seeds as counters, sticks as measures, vegetation, and so on. . . . Paper often inhibits: it is elitist, valuable, and linked with literacy, and pen marks are permanent. . . . With the ground, more can take part and take part more easily. Passers-by stop and become involved. Paper is private; the ground is public. Paper empowers those who hold the pen; the ground empowers those who are weak, marginalized and illiterate. There is a democracy of the ground. (Chambers 1997, 151–52)

Perhaps this imagery of poor people communicating, possibly planning or evaluating, in the dirt captures the essence of change through self-empowerment at the core of the participatory narrative. It is therefore not surprising that Chambers's framework piques the imagination of self-reflecting practitioners and nudges aid agencies to place greater weight on participation. Regarding the question of whether genuine participation can be an "add-on," it appears safe to respond with a firm "no" regarding Appleford's case of symbolic women's participation in the Papua New Guinea setting. As for other participation add-ons, the test is whether power is fundamentally (or radically) shifted to empower.

Change as "permanently provisional." For some who, like Chambers, value authentic participation as the driver of development, a flowing river stands out as an apt metaphor for understanding change—in fact, one commentator titles his essay about development in the midst of ambiguity and uncertainty as "Stepping Into a River of Change" (Thaw 2002). This imagery of a dynamic confluence also seems to differentiate the participatory narrative from conventional thinking about development goals. Chambers comments,

There are, as it were, two polarized paradigms: one with a structure that is linear, organized, predictable, and converging on equilibrium; and another one which is non-linear, chaotic, unpredictable, divergent, and non-equilibrium. In the latter, everything is provisional and subject to review. (Chambers 1997, 11–12)

Those committed to the first endeavor to counteract ambiguity through attempts to structure and order it, while those holding to the second work with it as containing the seeds of opportunity for people to empower themselves.

In the participatory change narrative, ambiguity can energize democracy in a vibrant but unpredictable and spontaneous manner. From this perspective, democracy is a matter not so much of structures and laws but of community norms either reaffirmed or refined through consensus.

For Chambers, *democracy* is one of the "four Ds" that flow together in the river of change with *decentralization, diversity,* and *dynamism*. As to the relationship between the development worker and the community served, he asserts,

> Decentralization demands trust and permits and encourages diversity: different regions, organizations, and people, when they have the discretion, do different things. Trust has to be two-way in a non-punitive culture: uppers trust lowers, and lowers trust uppers. With distrust, dominance and centralization, truth is distorted . . . and diversity is muted and masked. Trust, in contrast, diminishes misinformation. (Chambers 1997, 199)

Yet at some point, questions arise about uppers' (i.e., the development worker's and organization's) role in the participatory narrative, not as a change *agent* but as catalyst or facilitator—after all, should rights-affirming NGOs *not* have social improvement proposals to recommend? If so, how should those ideas unfold in a nonthreatening manner? An example can perhaps suffice in the absence of a definitive answer. In a fascinating account of one NGO encouraging social change, Easton, Monkman, and Miles (2003) relate how Tostan (a grassroots NGO) offered a women's education program that led participants to reassess traditional practices of female genital cutting (FGC) in Senegal, a Muslim nation. This case-based research characterizes a bottom-up process whereby conscious raising about FGC arises unexpectedly among village women (and a few men) from regular continuing education activity conducted through Tostan. That group found "champions" to curtail the practice of a well-known woman cutter and a respected imam (who at first opposed the reform initiative but subsequently reversed his stance through consultations with women activists and the cutter). Eventually, this community activism led to a village declaration discouraging FGC, which in turn spawned similar movements and actions in other villages (Easton, Monkman, and Miles 2003, 445–57).

Easton et al.'s research reveals democracy as a normative dynamic that flowed from educational program modules on human rights and women's health in an unexpected and unplanned manner. It appears that Tostan stepped into a river of change that, perhaps somewhat due to its prompting, flowed in a direction toward human agency and empowerment.

Advocacy Perspectives on Change

It is fitting at this point to redirect attention toward how NGOs associated with human rights advocacy—as examples, Amnesty International and World Refugee Services—understand change apart from the more development-centered agencies addressed in the previous narratives. The distinction here between "development" and "advocacy" is somewhat arbitrary given that (1) virtually all NGOs (or for that matter, *all* organizations) *advocate* for *something* and (2) both the human rights (or as Uvin calls them, the "PowerPoint-presenter") and development (the "dirty-fingernails") communities recognize the right of development as a human right (see Slim 2000; Uvin 2007; Andreassen and Marks 2006). Nonetheless, the NGO literature documents that traditional advocacy organizations approach both the means and the ends of change from perspectives that are noticeably different from development agencies.

Change as campaigns to alter beliefs, norms, and behaviors. In essence, advocacy boils down to persuasion, and in particular, human rights persuasion needs to change behavior and norms toward a sustainable concern for human dignity. On a theoretical level, some international relations scholars study the nature of "norms dynamics" in order to grasp how alternative norms emerge, sometimes displacing existing norms concerning issues of international importance (see, e.g., Finnemore and Sikkink 1998). In this respect, advocacy NGOs devote considerable effort and resources toward reshaping norms and beliefs among donors and funding institutions, governments, public opinion at various (global, national, local) levels, and recipients of assistance at the grassroots. The literature frequently refers to these norm-changing endeavors as "campaigns"—as examples, the campaign to "advance women's reproductive and sexual health rights" on a global scale (see Merali 2000) or to raise awareness of torture victims (from genocide, famine, or other large-scale injustices) who happen to reside (often relocating) in a particular community (see Cornell, Kelsch, and Palasz 2004).

Advocacy campaigns can be likened to electoral campaigns since both involve the ambiguities of public attention or indifference, the importance of strategies and tactics, unexpected events or circumstances that could work for or against the campaign, and a protracted time period (although usually longer for advocacy than even US presidential campaigns). And, as in the political realm, NGOs need to compete with their counterparts for resources and public attention (see Leipold 2000, 457). Coates and David assert that "advocacy is messy":

> The most common pitfall is to assume that political and institutional change occurs in a linear fashion, as in a recipe that is prepared through the addition of particular ingredients (research, lobbying, public concern, political pressure, etc.) and cooked (campaigned) for a certain period. This is rarely the case. Change often occurs in sudden leaps, in unexpected ways, and in response to the most unlikely circumstances. And campaigns typically evolve through a bewildering range of obstacles, opportunities, and responses. (2002, 534)

Thus, as Chapman and Fisher glean from their observations of a campaign to promote breast-feeding in Ghana (2000, 151–64), NGO leaders need to adapt tactics to a host of variables such as life stage of the campaign, level (international, national, local), and arena (community, national government, multinational corporation, etc.)—and to the nature of the political system (whether pluralistic, elitist, or ideological) encountered (Coates and David 2002, 534). In sum, the analogy between advocacy and electoral campaigning underscores the central theme stressed throughout this book: advocacy work, like other NGO leadership pursuits, is inherently political and tactical, and not simply matters of "naming and shaming" or technical "lawyering" in implementing adopted rights standards.

Change as "fact-making" to empower. As mentioned earlier, Robert Chambers borrowed from the Beatitudes for the subtitle of his book *Whose Reality Counts? Putting the Last First.* These scriptural passages found in two gospels represent "facts" made (or truths determined) about the status of the poor: that not only were they (contrary to prevailing beliefs in that society) on the same footing with others but beyond that they were "blessed." Most would agree that Jesus's fact-making in the Beatitudes was directed toward broad public opinion that rejected the poor as outcasts; yet in addition, the likely message for the poor was that they are indeed "somebody" and that their lives matter (a fundamental assumption supporting Sen's idea of human agency). The latter message can have therapeutic value in the psychological processes through which people find new identities and skills.

Although perhaps an unfamiliar term, *fact-making* occurs repeatedly in social life as those with authoritative (and/or persuasive) voice make pronouncements about what reality is. Obviously the intent can be self-serving and manipulative (*"This used car runs like new."*) or quite legitimate. Regarding the latter, government agencies are typically charged with responsibilities to make findings pertinent to public well-being in areas such as environmental protection (*"Is the water safe to drink?"*), product labeling (*"Does my breakfast cereal really prevent colon cancer?"*), and education (*"Is my child's school effective?"*), among many others (see Stone 2002, 305–23). By now, it should be clear to most readers that the "facts" under discussion here pertain not to things physical or natural (such as load to weight ratios in bridge construction) but instead to social (political, cultural) determinations that affect how we treat each other and what we believe about the social order.

Thus, human rights advocacy must involve fact-making to be effective in redirecting public opinion and in bringing about transformative processes that lead to human agency. For example, most rights-advocacy organizations likely subscribe to the social fact that "poverty is a violation of human rights," even though they might disagree about what poverty means and/or how it should be alleviated. And, as Grahame Russell (1998, 355) points out, it is especially critical that advocacy NGOs make facts that run counter to prevailing public opinion and/or institutional cultures in the developed world (i.e., the North). Organizations asserting that "basic health care is a human right" within a society that recognizes civil and political rights *but not* economic, social, and cultural rights make a fact to empower. Likewise, an NGO that determines that a funding institution's development programs are either ineffective or counterproductive to the advancement of human rights makes facts that challenge prestigious institutions and the governments supporting them. Some criticize human rights as a faddish Western value to be imposed on other cultures. Short of accepting this argument, there is cause to acknowledge the difficulties encountered in "selling" human rights facts to indigenous populations wherein Sen is not yet a "must read."

Advocacy then involves fact-making of a psychological or therapeutic nature as a first step toward human agency that can, in turn, enable persons to either reject or accept whatever someone else advocates in their "best interests." For the question *Where to start?* some suggest going to the roots of religious or cultural beliefs to find supports for fact-making intended to empower. As examples, Wendy Tyndale quotes Hindus that "all human activities are part of a sacred pattern of the universe" (2000, 9), and David Korten (1971) sifts through Ethiopian children's fables to identify those stories' morals as clues to underlying cultural values. Thus, fact-making that is grounded in a faith tradition or cultural heritage can be particularly effective in empowering people. Most NGOs—whether focused on human rights advocacy or on development—must advocate to encourage some sort of cognitive redirection that harnesses self-capability and hope among those served (Courville and Piper 2004; Raab 2008). In some cases, this advocacy of human capability may involve the subtleties of reworking counterproductive program jargon—such as references to "victims" (e.g., HIV-AIDS "victims"; better phrasing is "people *living* with HIV-AIDS")—that project unintended yet fatalistic imagery (see Clarke 2002). In other cases, NGOs may be more direct in facilitating cognitive empowerment by enlisting the abused as workers and participants in advocacy programs. For example, the Black Box Foundation trains victims of human rights abuse in Hungary and Romania to use video technology to expose abuses (Cornell, Kelsch, and Palasz 2004, 138). In this regard, active involvement can be cathartic, and "facts" can be made by enabling fulfilling experiences.

Promoting Rights-Based Change

From Sen's capability approach, it follows that rights-based change expands human freedoms from numerous deprivations and enhances human agency, or autonomy over one's condition. Furthermore, the means by which rights-based change materializes is assumed to be just as important. Despite the NGO's ideology (whether technical/rational, neoliberal, etc.), leaders can nonetheless act strategically to approach initiatives related to change, growth, or scaling up with a more pronounced sensitivity to expanding human capabilities. From a professional standpoint, few of us enjoy the luxury of choosing to work *only* in venues that exemplify our own values—thus, one could be employed in an organization advancing development agendas that are somewhat incompatible with one's political sensibilities (see Wallace 2007, 28–29). Nonetheless, leadership (ideally exercised *throughout* the organization) "leads" in championing movement in valued directions in the midst of divergent ideas and expectations.

In varying degrees, each of the change narratives outlined previously poses particular challenges to leadership efforts committed to rights-based change orientations. The balance of this section revisits the four change narratives to identify particular obstacles that leaders must negotiate to promote rights expansion and to suggest corrective tactics that, while not necessarily counteracting the narrative, can repackage change initiatives in ways that expand freedoms and/or promote human agency.

Working Within Technical Change Narratives

Technical narratives presume that outsiders can ascertain the needs of target populations, design appropriate program interventions, and organize effective implementation to bring about the intended change. Such a presumption runs counter to rights-based leadership in at least two respects. First, *even if* the need addressed significantly enhances a particular human capacity (e.g., instituting forestry practices to prevent erosion), the *means*—that is, the technician's control over goals, plans, and program procedures—excludes intended beneficiaries from determining their own destinies and thereby diminishes agency (or autonomy). Second, the *ends* of changes come into question in probing beneath the rhetoric of needs-based development; whose interests (or to paraphrase Robert Chambers [1997] "whose realities") are actually served in initiating a particular change: those of the NGOs—(1) in competing for funding against other NGOs? (2) in attempting to satisfy the expectations of donors far removed from the specifics of the development context? (3) in currying favor with host governments that may fund and/or certify the organization's activities as legitimate?—or those of the marginalized?

The public management adage that experts should remain "on tap but not on top" holds as well for NGOs that embrace rights-based change. First, it follows that if rights-focused leadership is *inherently political* in nature, technical know-how serves to leverage power or to affect the distribution of power in favor of enhancing human freedom and autonomy. Asking experts to understand their roles in the context of the political obliges them to develop different analytical skills (related to political contexts) and to cope with roles they may find uncomfortable. Regarding the latter, Raymond-McKay and MacLachlan refer to "role shock" that can arise as follows: "It refers to the stresses and frustrations concomitant with discrepancies between expected, ideal, and experienced roles. Role conflict and role ambiguity have received considerable attention from occupational psychologists, and [their] psychosocial and health costs are well documented" (2000, 684). These authors go on to suggest that organization leaders should be aware of the dissonances that individuals can confront in assuming new roles.

Second, experts should be committed to reflective organization learning that places values, structures, procedures, and technologies under a scrutinizing light and be willing to temper their recommendations accordingly. Their expertise should offer a vehicle for affecting power distributions that enhance particular freedoms without detracting from others. Thus, NGO leaders confront the delicate task of placing experts in supporting rather than leading roles, and as Robert Chambers suggests, it is even more difficult to put "the first (that is, the development professional) last" than to put "the last first" (1997, 2). He argues that development professions need to discover and confront their "normal errors" or those that are embedded within their belief systems (p. 15). In this regard, David Korten emphasizes the advantages of "embracing error" as a vehicle of organization learning in development organizations (1980, 498). Although more will be said of organization learning in chapter 6, it bears mentioning here that technical experts—as well as others—in a rights-focused development organization must be able and willing to reassess their professional understandings and opinions as they affect the expansion of freedoms and agency.

Clearly, technical expertise in such areas as health care and agroforestry supports human capabilities to the extent leaders can integrate it into the organization's value system, structure, and procedures (see Padaki 2000). Rights-based leadership can encourage a collective curiosity that subjects the causes (see Stone 2002) of deprivations (that in the first instance call out for change) to scrutiny; for example, does the need to institute better erosion control or establish disaster response plans stem from uncontrollable and unforeseeable natural forces (draught, harsh climate, soil conditions, etc.), from past policy actions or long-standing neglect on the part of governments, or from both? In the United States, the plight of the urban poor in New Orleans during and after Hurricane Katrina in 2005 can be attributed to a long history of discriminatory neglect and to both a catastrophic natural event and a shoddy federal response (see Cooper and Block 2006, 23–44; Cutter and Emrich 2006). Similarly, Amartya Sen argues convincingly that causes of famine are inherently political and can be readily addressed through appropriate relief measures (1999, 160–88). Presumably, change initiatives that offer technical improvements (such as better levee design and construction) *without stressing the perverse politics* that feeds human indignity allow power imbalances to persist and government officials to evade accountability. Rights-based leadership therefore should take care *not* to let government authorities and other power players "off the hook." Instead, NGOs should leverage the assistance offers with a strident advocacy for accountability where policy intentionality or even neglect contributes to needs they address. In other words, rights-focused NGOs need to maintain vigilance against offering technical interventions that serve to perpetuate the political dynamics associated with human indignities and deficits. Thus, rights-based development organizations should be as adamant in "naming and shaming" as (so-called) "human rights" NGOs but use this advocacy as one of many political leveraging tactics at their disposal (see Uvin 2004, 181–82).

Rights-based organizations need to understand that (to paraphrase former US House of Representative speaker Tip O'Neill) all human rights abuses are local—that is, they occur within particular situations and contexts rather than as universal abstractions. This assertion should alert NGO leaders that exhibiting a healthy skepticism toward reliance on best practice technologies (assumed to work effectively here, there, and everywhere) is a strategy for scaling up NGO impact in a variety of settings. As David Korten suggests, scaling up should be built from the bottom up with authentic and meaningful collaboration of those affected by the intervention, *not* as a generalized, top-down diffusion of methods and expertise (1980, 486). This may cause some frustration for leaders under pressure to scale up track records of isolated successes (in a few locations) to achieve wider impact (Edwards and Hulme 2002, 53–54). Nonetheless, leaders should be wary of "blueprints for change" that preprogram desired objectives and outcomes. Since they typically reduce focus to one particular problem rather than to a combination of needs or deficiencies (Chambers 1997; Aune 2000, 689), logframes appear as logically incompatible with Sen's (multiple) capabilities approach. A number of practitioner-authored articles in the development literature recommend various adaptations to the controversial logframe methodology. Those refinements include various strategies to extend participation in planning and evaluations processes to beneficiaries (see, e.g., Korten 1980; Dearden and Kowalski 2003; Willetts and Crawford 2007).

Although the participation narrative of change is treated in depth in the following section, suffice it to suggest here that a project orientation, which compresses development time between rigid initiation and conclusion dates, leaves little space for an ongoing collaboration that sustains relationships between development organizations and local communities. Furthermore, the project orientation can lead to what Marcuello and Marcuello call "projectitis," or a perverse culture that is based on a technical language of exclusion and that leads those affected by development to communicate in sync with what development experts want to hear.

> You see, people see aid coming in from outside and realise that they must organise themselves if they are to get anything. They see that assistance is given not to individuals but only to groups. So they begin to organize . . . so the project culture is generated—I have a need, so I must come up with a project to resolve it. And since neither the State nor the local authorities are doing anything, we have to ask the white foreigners who are the ones with the cash. The

result is "projectitis"—the project culture. (a beneficiary quoted by Marcuello and Marcuello 1999, 155)

Finally, to reiterate the inherently political nature of rights-based development, the illusion of apolitical neutrality (that can surface among technical experts inclined to elevate themselves above politics) invites NGOs to inadvertently serve the interests of the powerful by offering assistance without pressuring for accountability in return. Thus, development agencies expose themselves to the risks of being co-opted by powerful actors in government or in corporate venues. In extreme cases, such co-optation can implicate the organizations as unwittingly complicit in the unfolding of monumental human rights tragedies—such as the Rwandan genocide of the 1990s (see Uvin 1998, 205–23; 2004, 134–39).

Working Within Neoliberal Change Narratives

Can NGO leaders work within programs that embrace a neoliberal vision of improving human opportunity—that is, poverty reduction through income generation and attendant market-investment opportunities—to facilitate rights-based agendas consistent with the breadth of Sen's constitutive capabilities? Opportunities to do so lie within the realities of implementation experiences as they (1) affect NGOs' rights- and development-focused missions, (2) fall considerably short of neoliberal expectations, or (3) offer programmatic justifications for introducing tactics to support human rights. In other words, politically skillful leaders can play the neoliberal cards dealt them so as to enlist rights-facilitating strategies (such as those Uvin [2004, 139–65] identifies— legal machinery, capability building, advocacy, naming and shaming rights violations, organization introspection, the rule of law, problem reconceptualization, and new partners) to refine the development agenda.

First, leaders of NGOs who are inclined to assume public service roles (as CSOs) need to confront the possibility of being co-opted by governments (in their funding roles) and/or losing sight of their missions—in essence, they are at risk of becoming entrenched in someone else's agenda (see Feldman 2003, 9–13). What is the NGO to become—akin to a private sector partner, a community activist, or a quasi-government bureaucracy (Robinson 1999, 80–82)? Yet seeing the glass as half full, the organization could act to reconfigure the service provision to act as a change agent on behalf of human rights. Dorcas Robinson laments that this was *not* the case with NGOs that opted to provide community-based health services in Tanzania. She remarks that this organizational inability to grasp the implications of new civil society roles underscores "a need for a broader understanding of 'public' if reforms are to reflect what is happening in practice, and if they are to allow for more effective involvement by a range of key actors and stakeholders. The notion of *public policy as a process of public action* offers a way of thinking about the public arena which goes beyond a narrow focus on government systems or on policy as a matter of technical expertise" and then quotes Drèze and Sen (1989): "Public action is . . . not just a question of public service delivery and state initiative. It is also . . . a matter of participation by the public in a process of social change" (Robinson 1999, 84). For the rights-focused leader, civil society involvement may be viable so long as service provision offers a vehicle for social and economic transformation (Feldman 2003, 21).

Second, leaders can focus on adverse structural adjustment outcomes as platforms for advocacy that "reeducates" Northern donors and funding institutions. As Sen (1999) in several instances points out, such results can be expected from macroeconomic thinking that views "progress" in terms of aggregate trends (e.g., per capita income over decades). Yet the reality is that human rights violations occur in particular (micro-level) contexts. Magazine (2003), for example, relates how neoliberal fair trade policies serve not only to destabilize families (thereby accounting for a higher incidence of teenage runaways in Mexico City) *but also* to undercut local government's fiscal ability to deal with that social problem. Although not directly part of a structural adjustment aid chain, EDNICA's leaders are nonetheless effective advocates for their program and local fund-raising in the midst of perverse economic forces.

More generally, rights-based organizations can maintain vigilance over the social costs of structural adjustment macropolicies. An observer of the European Union's development and trade policies points out,

> [These policies] have led to rapid liberalization, which has resulted
> in a shift of control over agricultural lands, forests, and fisheries
> from those engaged in subsistence production to property own-
> ers. This has destroyed livelihoods and food security. The shift in
> agricultural production to non-traditional exports has undermined
> the long-term productivity of agricultural lands and domestic food
> security. (Van Reisen 1999, 198)

In this regard, *Washington Post* reporter Jonathan Katz begins his article about Haiti's inability to "feed itself" in the aftermath of its 2010 earthquake as follows:

The earthquake not only smashed markets, collapsed warehouses and left more than 2.5 million people without enough to eat. It may also have shaken up the way the developing world gets food. Decades of inexpensive imports—especially rice from the U.S.—punctuated with abundant aid in various crises have destroyed local agriculture and left impoverished countries such as Haiti unable to feed themselves. (Katz 2010)

As neoliberal funding institutions become increasingly sensitive to the subsequent adversities of their policies such as agricultural trade liberalization, NGOs accrue opportunities to push corrective empowerment initiatives that may now resonate in these neoliberal funding circles.

In particular, NGO leaders would be well advised to scrutinize the actual outcomes of structural adjustments intended to decentralize power and authority within local contexts—in other words, they should determine if neoliberal programs "make good" on program goals to facilitate democratization. Policymakers in central governments may indeed enact formal measures to satisfy aid institutions, yet laws and orders cannot implement themselves as correctives to long-standing power relationships. Although NGOs may have little if any clout exerting pressure on central governments (see Edwards and Hulme 2002, 57), the NGO's capability to flag structural adjustment failures would command respect from donors and aid agencies alike as part and parcel of a collaboration *and* confrontation strategy in dealing with aid agencies. An initial step in monitoring decentralization is to "know the legal (or legislative) machinery" (see Uvin 2004, 129–40) crafted by central governments that ostensibly shifts power in response to conditions imposed for aid. Yet beyond that, NGOs need to amass expertise in what neoliberals discount—the current political dynamics and traditional political cultures of particular local contexts. Such knowledge is essential in assessing whether and/or how structural adjustment measures affect various freedoms or deprivations related to human agency in particular locales.

The irony here is that although "human rights is a political matter" (Uvin 2004, 134), neoliberal narratives cast change making as a rational, *apolitical* enterprise. And notwithstanding this ideology based on a "science" of classical economics that "rises above politics," it appears safe to assume that government leaders themselves command strong grasps of local political histories and therefore must be reckoned with by rights advocates with comparable knowledge bases. Such insight is fundamental for determining whether decentralization measures in response to structural adjustment programs are in reality (1) effective in shifting power to local communities and (2) supportive of human conditions or are instead convenient for governments as pretexts to justify load shedding—that is, "dumping" vital but costly governmental responsibilities on the shoulders of local community leaders.

Third, rights-based NGOs can seek out partners with similar stakes and interests in a particular locale, thereby drawing on neoliberal enthusiasm for partnerships as a means to reconceptualize organization goals in ways that fit human rights commitment into this change narrative. NGO partnerships with private corporations might prove particularly effective, as multinationals' global reputations may foster stronger human rights sensitivities in corporate conglomerates than those found within governments or international aid agencies. For example, a program director of Save the Children in Pakistan and Afghanistan reports on how his area-based NGO assists multinational athletic equipment conglomerates by monitoring the child labor practices of local subcontractors stitching soccer balls (Husselbee 2000). In addition, it would be prudent for NGO leaders to partner (or network) with other NGOs—particularly grassroots, indigenous organizations that are not highly dependent on international aid. Readers with backgrounds in public management might find these "more the merrier" ideas in direct conflict with the thrust of program implementation theory asserting that multiple project participants typically impede effective program management (see, e.g., Pressman and Wildavsky 1973). Nonetheless, partnerships can enable NGOs to leverage (an important neoliberal buzzword) development efforts and dollars to widen their repertoire of rights-advancing tactics.

Working Within Participatory Change Narratives

One might surmise that since Robert Chambers's participatory framework aligns closely with Sen's ideas about freedoms and human rights, NGO leaders working within this narrative would encounter fewer obstacles promoting human rights than those working within the technical or neoliberal narratives. A closer look, however, suggests otherwise—breathing participatory idealism into organizational reality is by no means easy. Addressed here are three particular challenges that arise in elevating PRA-like approaches in NGOs: "preplanning" for the spontaneous and unexpected, identifying who should participate, and motivating self-initiative.

First, in reference to the FGC case (Easton, Monkman, and Miles 2003) introduced previously, Tostan maintains a wide range of programs—among them, continuing education—that support low-key advocacy for human rights. Yet as a practical matter, how does such an organization document its need to maintain a continuing societal presence to satisfy potential donors who relate to shorter term *projects* with tangible outcome measures? What logframe format could be designed to monitor subtle yet nonetheless significant norm shifts attributed directly to programmatic activities? Prudence would dictate that NGO leaders, programming specialists, or others would avoid promises of outcomes as momentous as the curtailment of FGC. Instead, the best course around this predicament probably involves capitalizing on past successes instituted through specific program activities and in turn presenting current or proposed programs in terms of activities and outcomes that can be explained descriptively rather than quantitatively. In short, this narrative appropriately elevates participation as an *end* in achieving human agency and self-determination—nonetheless, making that case on paper for Northern stakeholders is daunting to say the least.

Second, participatory change narratives may ultimately lead NGOs toward close-to-intractable problems rooted in political anthropology—if in fact participation frameworks can counteract the deprivations of the poor in a particular setting, they need to inculcate rights-claiming authority sufficiently bold enough to withstand reactions from dominant groups and community and tribal leaders. In reality, deprivation often occurs amid political heterogeneity and ethnic differences (exploitable by government leaders—see Uvin 1998). Thus, NGOs committed to building rights-claiming capabilities among the excluded should expect to find those they seek to uplift trapped in ethnic prejudices embedded into the political system. As Mompati and Prinsen explain, ethnicity should be understood "as a social phenomenon concerned with negative interaction between cultural-linguistic groups. . . . [It] develops when ethnic groups compete for rights, privileges, and available resources" (2000, 626).

Challenges abound for NGO leaders in the midst of ethnic power imbalances: how to gain initial footholds (overtures to leaders or groups *in power*?) to establish a base of operations, how to include the excluded (in what mode of participation?), and how to deal with in-group intimidation when it surfaces, among others. Mompati and Prinsen describe intimidation witnessed through their observations of participatory representation in an ethnically torn village (Kedia) in Botswana:

> The following example shows how a kgosi [tribal leader] used a police officer to enforce this practice of ethnic exclusionism during the PRA pilot project. In Kedia the authors observed a participatory planning meeting in which one particular woman from a

subordinate ethnic group spoke out loudly against discriminatory practices of the dominant group. Observably, she was helped in breaking gender and ethnic rules by a serious intake of alcohol, but quite a number of other participants were also rather inebriated. The kgosi quickly pointed at a policeman, who [removed her]. . . . Thereafter, the meeting continued as if nothing had happened. (Mompati and Prinsen 2000, 630)

Thus, NGOs that pursue rights-claiming agendas through participation need to both maintain a politically adroit presence that can support marginal groups and fend off subsequent recrimination. Nowhere is Uvin's dictum that "human rights is a political matter" more apt than here: NGOs must master the political landscapes in which they work and from there interact with power in a manner that alternates confrontation with collaboration (2004, 134–37).

Third, the participatory change narrative raises the general problem of motivating people, especially those unaccustomed to assertive behavior, to assume initiative for direction rather than to continually defer to NGO officials; any technique to counteract the dead silence or bewildered looks that arise when people are prompted to take on some leadership responsibility is helpful. David Crawford et al. touch on this problem in their creative account of "A Day in the Life of a Development Manager," which compiled diary entries from several Tanzanian development officials, including one submitted by Michael Mambo visiting a participation group in Usinge:

The chairman opened the meeting in only two sentences: ". . . the meeting is opened and I welcome Mr. Mambo to tell us what he has come with." My first reaction is to think "I don't live in Usinge, so what do I say?" All of a sudden I made up my mind and decided to talk. I said, "This is an opportunity for us all to discuss what has happened to the plans you developed at your CBHC meeting last year. What do you want to talk about?" It was agreed and our discussion went very well. (Crawford et al. 1999, 170–71)

Working Within Advocacy Perspectives

Among advocacy-centered NGOs there are "campaigns" and then there are *campaigns*—the implication here is that this term takes on both figurative and literal meanings. Thus, both opportunities and challenges surface for advocacy leadership. Furthermore, one's interpretation of "campaign" may well depend on where the organization is situated geographically (North or South) and in the funding chain (whether Northern bilateral, Southern grassroots, locally based, etc.). If an advocacy organization engages in a (literal) campaign, it needs to replicate the intricate capabilities of an effective political party able to build constituencies (of "everyday" people and notables alike) and at the same time keep reinventing its tactics. In its workbook *New Tactics for Human Rights*, the Center for Victims of Torture (CVT) in Minneapolis stresses the importance of building constituencies:

> Human rights messages are often directed at the people already familiar with the issues, people who have already expressed interest and support. Reaching out to new people and involving them in human rights work strengthens the potential for more effective action. It brings in fresh energy, fresh ideas, fresh resources, and fresh contacts. The more diverse the group of people acting as advocates on a particular issue, the better able it will be to adapt to changes and the more difficult it becomes for abusers to defend their actions. A diverse and active community creates a far more resilient human rights movement. (Cornell, Kelsch, and Palasz 2004, 118)

This workbook offers several examples of tactics that various NGOs use to build human rights constituencies: (1) using the popular culture to engage young people against fascism and racism—Nigdy Więcej (Never Again) in Poland, (2) passing "international" treaties at the local level to impact public policy and promote human rights standards—WILD for Human Rights in the United States, (3) involving religious leaders in modeling behavior toward stigmatized populations—the Sangha Metta Project in Thailand, and (4) using text messaging to build networks of human rights constituents—Amnesty International in the Netherlands (Cornell, Kelsch, and Palasz 2004, 119–24). To elaborate on the first tactic (using popular culture), the following illustrates the "on the edge" character of these campaigns:

> Nigdy Więcej (Never Again) is using pop culture to build an anti-racist youth network in Poland. At rock concerts and soccer matches the group reaches out to young people and makes them aware of the problem. It then recruits some to join a network of correspondents who monitor and report on the activities of neo-fascist

and racist groups in their hometowns. (Cornell, Kelsch, and Palasz 2004, 119)

These various examples illustrate first that advocacy organizations involved in actual campaigning must think tactically to be effective. *Tactics*, as understood by the former director of the CVT, refer to the "how-to-do-it" issues as differentiated from the "what-to-do" concerns of strategy. Second, even though campaigns seek new tactics, NGO leaders need not mastermind all tactics but rather scan the environment for those movements or groups that find innovative ways to coalesce public attention that, in turn, could benefit from NGO backing. In some cases, these movements appear to arise from thin air as the Abuelas (grandmothers) of the Plaza del Mayo did in Argentina: their initial (1977) efforts to locate disappeared grandchildren ultimately led to the creation of the National Bank for Genetical Data 10 years later (Martínez 1996, 362–63).

The good news for campaigning organizations is that tactics beget more tactics that in turn open up new strategic opportunities (see Leipold 2000, 454; Cornell, Kelsch, and Palasz 2004, 150) *if* the institutional culture is sufficiently flexible in accommodating the dynamic and the diverse. But the more ominous news is in that *if*, that cultures in most organizations are typically embedded in existing values, routines, and professional viewpoints. As can be gleaned from the CVT examples and quotes, effective campaigning that can assimilate "on-the-edge" tactics is likely as well to introduce a diversity of personalities, some of which may be "hard to deal with" and confrontational and others could be iconic superstars, such as U2's Bono and the late Princess Diana of Wales (who was involved in campaigns against landmines), and controversial messages (such as a 2009 televised ad by the German AIDS awareness NGO, Regenbogen, which put the face of Adolph Hitler on the dangers of unprotected sex).

How then does the NGO leader shape an institutional culture that welcomes the spontaneous and unpredictable but simultaneously remains focused on mission and maintains credibility among its stakeholders, particularly funding sources? Should the organization add a campaigning arm, or would such an initiative (to institutionalize spontaneity) essentially sabotage a tactical mind-set? Few easy answers are available for NGO leaders, but perhaps it helps to return to the figurative–literal *campaign dilemma*—if the term is merely used as a euphemism, or in a figurative sense, to emphasize fundraising, media communications, or other activities, then such problems are unlikely to surface. Yet leaders intending to mount aggressive campaigns to build constituencies and seize tactical opportunities need assurances that those associated with the organization (internally and externally) have the will to engage in a potentially opportunistic but nonetheless turbulent and unpredictable environment.

The dynamics of literal campaigning challenges one's managerial inclinations to "rein it in" as an activity to be directed (or controlled) and evaluated just as any other. Yet the conundrum becomes apparent: How tightly should those reins be clutched at the risk of choking off initiatives within the organization and its environment that could contribute to an expanding repertory of tactics? Certainly there are compelling reasons why leaders should monitor a campaign's impact (as a political organization keeps abreast of polling numbers tracking the strength of its candidate; see Nelson 2000), but tough questions arise as to how to track success and on what criterion. In terms of criteria, it appears misguided to expect that a tightly defined, formal planning document (such as the typical logframe) could foretell how opportunities and new tactics will unfold over time. Yet impact monitoring, as Coates and David suggest, ought to integrate open learning into the iterations (if not "twists and turns") of advocacy in general and campaigning, given the ambiguities of rights issues (Nelson 2000). NGO leaders in their own right, these practitioners offer assessment advice in terms of four broad principles:

- ensure that what the NGO values gets measured;
- use methodological approaches that are appropriate to the type of advocacy work being carried out;
- look at the whole, not just the parts; and
- make impact assessment an organizational priority (Coates and David 2002, 536–39).

Among these, the first is especially essential for human-rights-based organizations and for those in the North that advocate for concerns in the South. As a Ugandan economist maintains, the question is whether advocacy campaigns can rightly claim the "authentic voice of the poor," particularly if the NGO is based halfway around the world from that community. In elucidating this point, Warren Nyamugasira refers to a "linguistics" problem in aligning advocacy with grassroots needs:

> Whether from North or South, advocates must obtain people's mandate and regularly return to have it renewed. . . . This is not the monopoly or preserve of people from one hemisphere. An advocate

from the North should not be written off just because of geographical origins. . . . We believe that the poor, in spite of the supposed
proliferation of Southern NGOs, do still lack "linguistics." . . . Ex-
ploiters have never been limited by language barriers so why should
do-gooders be so limited? (Nyamugasira 1998, 303)

Presumably then, prime attention to a central mission could frame a reasonable assessment approach that directs attention to the whole or "big picture."

At times, NGO leaders play supporting (rather than lead) roles in campaigns against systemic deprivations that can be waged only through the allied efforts of many organizations. On some occasions, systemic human rights
abuses—as a result of perverse interactions of economic forces and government motives—call for broad complexes of NGOs and allied organizations to
spearhead movements such as antisweatshop and anti-NAFTA campaigns for
workers' rights or prodemocracy campaigns aimed at repressive regimes. Introducing the term *complex* (of activities) as a "diverse set of organizational alliances," Anner and Evans (2004) characterize the interrelationship between two
complexes, each involving an intricate array of interests. First, a basic human
rights complex, consisting of workers' rights campaigns against Latin American employers, interacted within a broader (Western) hemispheric complex of
labor organizations campaigning against the economic injustices of free trade
as embodied in NAFTA. In addition to achieving victories in their respective
struggles, the two complexes together "bridged a 'double-divide'": the first between workers' interests in the South and those in the North, and the second
between NGO agendas and labor unions.

Anner and Evans's scholarship illustrates the vast scale of organizational
efforts needed for effective campaigns to address human rights problems en-
grained in (often global) economic and political systems. Yet how does involvement in a "coalition of coalitions" affect leadership responsibility within
the NGO? Presumably, leaders should cast impending decisions to participate
in joint campaigns in terms of potential benefits and pitfalls with particular
scrutiny on the latter: Will the alliance "bog us down" in endless, contentious
negotiations? Will it veer us off message from our central mission and jeopardize our credibility with stakeholders? Although interdependent on others,
will we not be held responsible nonetheless for adverse alliance outcomes? On
a lesser scale, NGOs can enter into partnerships with particular economic actors (e.g., labor unions or corporations) to facilitate campaigns against rights
deprivations stemming from market practices. In such cases, NGO professionals need to anticipate what specific leadership tasks will be required in nego-

tiations, as well as afterward, as the partnership evolves, including developing clear policies prior to negotiations, identifying a consistent advocacy role that stakeholders can endorse, building trust both within the NGO and with the partner, maintaining other alliances with outside groups, promoting a continuous stream of public communication, and developing a consistent (abuse) response capability (Husselbee 2000, 384–85).

Although NGOs need to weigh the possibilities of not achieving desired outcomes (as mentioned previously regarding alliance involvement), so too should they, oddly enough, anticipate the conundrums of *winning* campaigns. Gerd Leipold comments on the success of the UK's Jubilee 2000, a coalitional campaign to bring about debt relief for poor nations of the South, as follows:

> Winning the argument, however, is a double-edged sword in campaigning. The new consensus that develops is typically less radical than the original campaign position. By adopting the new consensus, the mainstream also demands the authority to define it. Once finance ministers are in favour of debt relief, they will also assume the authority for defining the level and form it should take. Those who campaigned over the years now find themselves easily sidelined, their arguments portrayed as the predictable response of special-interest groups which are never satisfied. (Leipold 2000, 457)

The problem of winning assumes added meaning within particular political and ideological contexts in which campaigns are framed; Leipold comments, "In the West, the argument about debt was highly politicised. The left was for debt relief, the rest of the political spectrum saw it as ideologically motivated, communist propaganda under a thin veneer of concern for the poor" (2000, 456). As an aside, it is worth noting that some link the proliferation of structural adjustment programs with funding agency reactions to the forgiveness of these debts (see, e.g., Bökkerink and van Hees 1998, 324–26; Keet 2000, 463–64). In academia, organization theorists call attention to the problem of domain substitution exemplified by the March of Dimes's predicament a half century ago when its goal of eradicating polio was realized through the development of effective vaccines—after prolonged floundering, it successfully redirected its focus toward birth defects (see Perrow 1965; Whetten 1987). Although a concern for organizations generally, the goal succession issues acquire particular significance among NGOs, given the highly charged nature of their campaigns and the potential for ideological adversaries to "spin" NGO efforts in myriad ways. As Deborah Stone suggests in *Policy Paradox: The Art of Political Decision Making* (a primer for "down-and-dirty" political tactics that NGO professionals ought to read), sometimes winning is losing (2002, 1–2).

As suggested in the previous section, advocacy for human rights involves making "facts," or pronouncements, about reality that can redirect thinking among the poor or deprived and promote rights-based agendas in the broader public. In other words, fact-making asserts that advocacy organizations can channel persuasion that moves people along in capacity-building processes—in essence, the "fact" conveys the new perception that either nudges people toward empowerment and agency or identifies where that process leads. Essentially, rights advocacy gambles on its own competency to "make good" on this sensitive and intricate causality in human behavior, but such gambles are inherent within leadership generally.

Questions thus surface as to what is required of organization leadership in orchestrating the conversion of its audacious persuasion to a self-realization of agency in others (and the leader's awareness of the cognitive institutional processes introduced in chapter 1). Effective persuasion typically depends on the acceptance of the persuader's authority. Nonetheless, rights advocacy competes (or contends) with governments, local officials, faith leaders, and so on whose authority has affected people's lives. But what type of authority fuels advocacy? Given that advocacy advances *social* (and emotional)—rather than technical, rational, or natural—facts, it follows that authority derived from technical expertise (at least in itself) is unlikely to motivate behavior change in the direction of self-realization. It is just as implausible that leaders can rely on their formal titles in the organization to affect change outside of it. Instead, leaders should base their authority on recognizable *competence* (apart from technical expertise per se) that projects the capacity to actualize the mission, in this case act effectively as a change agent. NGOs that are recognized as competent can be especially persuasive in settings where cynicism toward government or other authority figures prevails.

Competent advocacy, as one NGO program director notes, "foster[s] the propensity to accommodate in people and organizations" (Raab 2008, 433). Raab works from Piaget's learning theory of "accommodation and assimilation," explaining,

> Accommodation makes us act "out of sync," suspend familiar schemata, and engage in activity that is intense but somewhat non-instrumental (we don't know yet whether and how we will obtain any result), even "irrational," sometimes in open contradiction to

existing knowledge. It begins with the realisation that something is missing or wrong in existing mental models, and that we do not yet know what exactly is missing. (Raab 2008, 433)

Sometimes advocacy can draw on core faith or cultural beliefs (e.g., the Jewish ethos "Where there is no bread there is no Torah.") to support accommodation in recognizing that "something is missing or wrong here" (Tyndale 2000, 9). Assimilation then involves adapting one's subsequent actions and behaviors to the newly accommodated point of view. NGOs can reach out to well-known community figures (such as the woman cutter and imam in the Senegalese FGC case mentioned previously; Easton, Monkman, and Miles 2003) who as "champions" can pass along their own cognitive redirection to others. If new "facts" about human rights and empowerment are to be accommodated, this likely occurs through face-to-face experiences with NGO workers. Thus organization competence depends on internal human resources practices aimed at promoting an enabling environment that supports "a propensity for accommodation" through organization learning. Ultimately, an authority based on competence depends on a culture that values learning and self-initiative more than conformity and structure.

Competence relies as well on sustaining legitimacy (or credibility) as the foundation of effective persuasion. In general, leaders need to "be right" in making facts—at times, US presidents have suffered for their dubious facts, such as *trees cause air pollution* and *[Leader X] has weapons of mass destruction*—if missions are to be preserved (see Terry 1995, 101–11). Yet to what extent are facts in the furtherance of human rights merely aspirations or best guesses of what empowerment can promise? Advocacy leadership must delicately balance "making good" as a change agent with the risk of overselling the message. This dilemma heightens when facts actually take the form of predictions; in this vein a director of policy and advocacy for World Vision wonders whether NGOs should extend prophetic voice when disasters appear imminent and in so doing lay their credibility on the line (Whaites 2000, 506–16). In his account of factors leading up to the Rwandan genocide of the 1990s, Peter Uvin makes a convincing case for the affirmative in his scathing indictment of the in-country development community's inability or unwillingness to signal the alarm during the lead-up to that catastrophe (1998, 163–79). Yet what if they had done so but no genocide had occurred or had not been categorized as such? As public management scholars Frederickson and LaPorte (2002) ask (in reference to other leadership contexts), which is the appropriate direction to err, toward a "false positive" (crying wolf and nothing happens) or a "false negative" (negligent inaction)? Although essential in advocacy, fact-making is risky business.

Conclusion

This chapter elaborated on the institutional challenges NGO leaders confront in affecting transformative changes to expand human rights and promote empowerment aligned with their development and/or advocacy missions. In large part, these challenges arise out of relationships between resource-dependent NGOs and the funding agencies that support them. Specifically, NGO leaders need to navigate funding environments wherein aid agencies entertain fundamentally different, ideologically driven notions of appropriate change than do NGOs as recipients of support. Four particular interpretations were presented in the first section of this chapter—three as change narratives (the technical, neoliberal, and participatory), along with a fourth advocacy perspective—that characterize how respective funding environments affect NGO strategies for facilitating transformative change.

The second section explored leadership strategies for advancing human rights within each environment. In each case, it appears that effective rights-based leadership depends on a skill set that combines tactical agility with political adroitness and that the various managerial functions (such as planning, budgeting, evaluating, and others) should support political and tactical leadership rather than predetermine or skew its direction. Among the four change interpretations, it could be said that the neoliberal and advocacy perspectives impose similar challenges on NGO leaders. In both cases, leaders need to advocate for counterintuitive conceptions of human rights (e.g., economic, social, and cultural rights in cultures that value only civil and political rights) in the midst of adversarial political cultures. Beyond this, NGOs in both environments should seize network- and coalition-building opportunities that promise to advance human rights in ways that promote credibility through the eyes of the aid community. The technical narrative directs leaders to concentrate internally in reorienting professionals' (especially technical experts') preconceptions about "how to help people" toward a more robust understanding of human rights as means (to human agency and empowerment) and ends in themselves. Appropriate socialization and organization experiences assume high priorities in rights-based organizations wherein technical cultures might otherwise prevail. Socialization and open learning are important as well in NGOs committed to participatory involvement of the poor and disenfranchised. In these contexts, leaders must shape an organization culture that elevates an intricate knowledge of local political history and current reality as prerequisites for engaging the disenfranchised (especially in ethnic minorities) into participatory experiences. In the absence of this knowledge base, well-meaning participatory efforts are as likely to place those at the margins of the community in harm's way as they are to empower them.

Discussion Issues

1. Propose a socialization strategy that orients newly hired technical experts (such as agronomists and nutritionists) toward effectiveness in rights-based work. What priorities should be stressed? How?

2. Is it possible to convince donors that change is "permanently provisional"? If so, how? How could that argument be worded in relevant agency publications and documents? (Draft a sample paragraph.)

3. What is meant by "best practices"? Why might they inhibit empowerment? Can they nonetheless be useful in organization learning? If so, how?

4. Is it prudent for organizations funded by neoliberal aid agencies to publicize the adverse outcomes of structural adjustment programs (i.e., "bite the hand . . .")? Could Uvin's strategy of "collaboration and confrontation" work in such circumstances? Explain.

5. Physicians follow the ethic of "first, do no harm." How might this apply to NGOs committed to involving the disenfranchised as participants in particular communities? Craft a few agency rules or guidelines that might convey this ethic throughout the organization.

4

Organization and Management in Pursuit of Rights-Based Missions

In Woluf, the language of Senegal's dominant minority group, the word *tostan* means "breakthrough" or "coming out of the egg." As discussed in chapter 3 on transformative change, *Tostan* is the name of an Africa-based NGO that integrates human rights and people-centered development in its mission "to empower African communities to bring about sustainable development and positive social transformation based on respect for human rights" (Tostan 2007). Easton, Monkman, and Miles's (2003) observations of Tostan's successes with participative initiatives that curtailed female genital cutting—along with its commendations from the World Health Organization, UNICEF, and other organizations—attest to its accomplishments.

Fortunately, a record of Tostan's good works, along with those of other successful rights-oriented NGOs, is available to study and emulate. But lamentably, commentaries on how to manage NGOs in pursuit of human rights and empowerment are elusive in the existing development and human rights literatures. What *can* be deciphered about the management realities of these organizations often appears paradoxical, confusing, and somewhat chaotic. On one hand, if—as the term *tostan* implies—rights-based organizations need to be emergent, or transformative and changing forces in themselves, they call for "soft" managerial guidance that unleashes these positive dynamics. On the other hand, if the funding environment of NGOs has become increasingly competitive (as most commentators suggest; see Edwards and Hulme 1996; Eade 1999; Wallace 2007; Jordan and van Tuijl 2007), then NGO managers need to "tighten up" (or leash) their organizations with governance structure, rules, and routines to appeal to donors' expectations for "good governance."

Regarding organization structure, it would appear that NGOs become trapped in an unrelenting dialectic that pits the imperative develop control mechanisms that coordinate by standardizing effort and skills (to gain legitimacy among external stakeholders) the need to work for change through mutual agreement in rather unstructured settings. In the former case, top leaders would focus primarily on regulative institutional functions associated with standardization, but in the latter, they would focus on functions with cognitive activities related to team building and organization learning (Mintzberg 1993, 280–81; Scott 1995, 40–45). The question essentially boils down to which organization structure and related managerial roles best fit a rights-based development agency such as Tostan:

1. A standardized work environment wherein leaders maintain and fine-tune coordinated efforts to maximize efficiency and effectiveness?
2. A team-oriented adhocracy with leaders as active participants?
3. An organization (regardless of structure) with leaders who direct prudent responses to externally imposed threats and opportunities?
4. All the above in varying measures.

Those who are proficient in taking multiple-choice tests will likely intuit the "all the above" response as best. But how can choices 1 and 2 as apparent contradictions both have merit?

In *Images of Organization*, Gareth Morgan (1998) introduces eight metaphors of organization (as machines, organisms, brains, cultures, political systems, psychic prisons, transformation and flux, and instruments of domination) that direct attention to particular dimensions of an organization and its management. Although each can help elucidate particular circumstances in rights-based NGOs, one of these—the transformation and flux metaphor that represents the "unfolding logics of change"—characterizes leaders who confront complex problems as dealing with "attractor forces" that threaten the agility of the organization as a change agent (Morgan 1998, 222–36). For example, donor demands for strong internal controls, accountability compliance, and financial reporting could serve as attractors that pull the NGO away from innovative work with people at the grass roots. In these situations, Morgan relies on complexity theory as a basis for encouraging leaders to understand their organizations in an emerging state:

> Complexity theory invites managers to rethink the nature and order of organization. Instead of seeing these qualities as states that can

be externally imposed on a situation through hierarchical means or through predetermined logic . . . managers are invited to view them as *emergent* properties. New order emerges in *any* complex system that, because of its internal and external fluctuations, is pushed into "edge of chaos" situations. Order is natural! It is emergent and free! But most interesting of all, its precise nature can *never* be planned or predetermined. (Morgan 1998, 116–17; italics his)

Morgan's thinking about the emerging organization that "pushes into the edge of chaos" positions the leader to champion Uvin's strategy to "re-conceptualize the overall aims of development agencies." Uvin comments, "One of the main advantages of a rights-based approach to development is that it can bring people to reframe the nature of the problems they seek to address and the levers for change they can employ" (2004, 160). Within the leadership context, Morgan refers to this reframing as

the art of managing and changing "context" . . . rest[ing] on the idea that *the fundamental role of managers is to shape and create "contexts" in which appropriate forms of self-organization can occur.* Managers have to become skilled in helping shape the "minimum specs" that can define an appropriate context, while allowing the details to unfold within this frame. In this way, they can shape emergent processes of self-organization, while avoiding the trap of imposing too much control. (Morgan 1998, 227–29; italics added)

An institutional leader's competency as an artist who creates and shapes context depends on how she articulates meanings to reinforce the learning culture.

In summarizing the key management insights gleaned from their observations of leaders in South Asian development NGOs, Smillie and Hailey (2002) say very little about the typical "command-and-control" functions of classical management textbooks but instead focus on leadership activities associated with the dynamics of emerging organizations: the influence of context and culture, the implications of time and timing, the balance of formality and informality, and participation and participatory management. This chapter follows Smillie and Hailey's lead in approaching rights-based leadership in terms of these four issues (although in another sequence and with slightly different wordings). To these, a fifth section is added that discusses some management control functions (specifically, budgeting and information technology [IT] applications) from a rights-based perspective.

Reconciling the Formal and Informal

As Smillie and Hailey conclude in *Managing Change* (2002), leaders steer development NGOs through the crosswinds of formality and informality at various organizational life stages. Thus, commentaries sometimes depict leadership as pairs of contradictory roles whereby the first coordinates efforts through formal control, but the second depends on interpersonal agreement, or mutual adjustment, in the informal organization. For example, Mintzberg (2001) describes how leaders of a makeshift Red Cross refugee camp in Tanzania "managed exceptionally" through a push-pull of contradictory, or at least complementary, roles—controlling versus communicating information, leading versus linking people, and doing versus dealing as a basis for action. Similarly, Kaplan characterizes leaders as working within three sets of polarities: confronting versus supporting people, grounding versus focusing in developing structure, and giving meaning versus mobilizing in articulating an organizational identity (2002, 427–31; also see Soal 2002). To reiterate, Gareth Morgan suggests that leaders can negotiate these opposites, or as he calls them, "attractors," by analyzing the underlying forces that lock organizations into these polarities. In other words, NGO professionals should become adept at reconciling priorities to promote the interactive synergies of the informal organization with those to conserve external legitimacy (i.e., to demonstrate outward appropriateness in governance structure, formal reporting procedures, and accountability standards). This section examines leadership responsibilities in balancing governance structures with the informal organization, integrating strategies and tactics in planning processes, and enabling self-organizing capabilities in individuals and teams within the bounds of fundamental organization values.

How NGO leaders balance external pressures for *governance* and accountability structures with the workflow of the informal organization is critical in determining the organization's effectiveness in serving beneficiaries. Following Tandon's definition, governance "requires the creation of structures and processes which enable the NGO to monitor performance and remain accountable to its stakeholders" (2002, 215). Increasing emphases on NGO governance since the 1980s appears somewhat paradoxical. On one hand, Northern neoliberal institutions have looked upon NGOs as "magic bullets," or as *autonomous* agents equipped to democratize societies with not-so-democratic regimes. But on the other hand, it is precisely that autonomy—or at least the variety of NGO operational schemes (run by eccentric founders, families, religious groups, and so forth)—that raises the eyebrows of donor institutions calling for more rigorous governance and accountability controls (see Edwards and Hulme 2002). Clearly, the issue of governance structure is critical within expansive, international organizations that need to arrange interactions among global, regional, and national levels of operation (see, e.g., Moore and Stewart 1998; Young et al. 2002). Nonetheless, discussion here focuses on the more immediate balancing act that juggles governance mechanisms to satisfy external stakeholders, strategies that facilitate the team-focused efforts of the informal organization, and the need to coordinate current and future projects to ensure the organization's continuing viability. In this respect, NGO leaders assume roles as institutional jugglers, much like their counterparts in governmental agencies (see Kaufman 1981, 175–79; Radin 2002).

Appeals for strong governance measures prompt leaders to institute formalized, or at least well-established, accountability mechanisms within NGOs (more detail on accountability awaits in chapter 5). But to what extent should the organization, in the interest of "responsible governance," be formalized or structured for fear of disrupting the interdependencies of team-oriented work? Rights-based NGOs do not (or at least ought not) function as mass-production firms that pride themselves on uniformity and consistency, like Holiday Inns where "the best surprise is no surprise" (Mintzberg 1993, 173–74). To the contrary, they are more akin to television networks that value creative, often divergent, thinking that needs to be protected from the conformity associated with overformalization and bureaucratization. From this logic (developed by Mintzberg 1993), rights-based development and advocacy organizations more often resemble *adhocracies* that innovate and solve problems on behalf of—or better, *with*—their clients or beneficiaries.

Within adhocracies, control and coordination occur through *mutual adjustment* or shared agreements rather than direct supervision or standardization (Mintzberg 1993, 4–5, 256), even though some operational protocols and reporting requirements required by donors might promote standardized outputs. Leaders also need to prevent NGO adhocracies from becoming professionalized where technical experts can (like university professors) maintain their independence and aloofness from team-based work activity. As Soal (2002) relates, the issues of *professionalism* and "professionality" can be misunderstood in development and advocacy settings wherein workers from interdisciplinary backgrounds appropriately view themselves as professionals committed to human development and empowerment. Nonetheless, those workers shy away from notions of professionalism associated with power and prestige that might imply detachment from the concerns of those they serve. Returning to the issue of governance, it may well be possible that the organization's need for accountability mechanisms can serve to reinforce the team ethos in adhocracy, primarily by fostering a multidirectional accountability that addresses the interdependencies involved in both collective strategy formation and decision making within the informal organization (see Padaki 2000, 429).

Elaborating on the balance of formal governance mechanisms with the informal work culture, Smillie and Hailey question whether organizations are managed more effectively through formal systems and controls or left to consensual processes that motivate staff and facilitate collective learning (2002, 166). Comments by an official in a South African community development organization reinforce the latter:

> As a staff we are in a tremendously privileged position . . . free to devise our strategies and approaches and select who we work with. To that end, and because our work is in pursuit of a social vision, we work closely, mutually accountable, with individual practices subject to the scrutiny of the team as a whole. This is not simply good professional practice (although it is that too), but is also about holding the organisation as a whole on course, ensuring that its resources are put to best use. (Soal 2002)

On the basis of their study of particular South Asian NGOs, Smillie and Hailey suggest leaders support informal processes to the extent they buffer the staff from information demands placed on them. Although information is vital for staff learning, demands for excessive documentation, case study reports, and field-worker diary entries can crowd out collaborative efforts that support interactive strategy formation. One leader rejected demands for documentation, claiming, "We are implementers, not researchers—I don't have the funds or time for process documentation." Another NGO founder echoes the sentiments of the first, maintaining, "If we get in the documentation business, it consumes a lot of time, at least 30% of the time we could spend in four or five villages" (2002, 86). Thus, leaders can effectively balance the formal and informal as gatekeepers who minimize the external reporting demands that warrant the attention of staff.

Cross-pressures of formal and strategic planning procedures often collide with informal, emergent strategies that derive from competent, bottom-up work in advocacy and development organizations. On one hand, donors may expect that recipient organizations commit to formal, top-down strategic planning that flows from global mission statements and goal statements crafted in London or New York and then is passed down to in-country offices (e.g., in Botswana). Nonetheless, NGOs invest heavily in training and capacity building *precisely* to enable their professionals to both conceptualize and initiate emergent strategies and tactics in order to address the particular power complexities and change dynamics in local contexts. NGO leaders can balance this tension between essential emergent, bottom-up strategy and externally imposed, formal planning first by promoting ongoing collegial debate as a learning outcome. Uvin maintains that such an environment of understanding and trust

> will not happen overnight. But if agencies manage to do this, they can radically reinvent themselves: people may begin reporting the truth to their superiors, create explicit ethical bases for joint action, develop with senior foreign staff strategies of advocacy and protection of their employees, and learn to think in advance through the likely human rights impact of various scenarios of action. (Uvin 2004, 154)

To the extent possible, leaders can crosswalk or reconcile local courses of action within the broad strokes of formal planning language to buffer, or as Smillie and Hailey put it, "keep outsiders at bay while insiders figure out what to do and how to do it" (2002, 166).

In the best-case scenarios, leaders are themselves skilled tacticians who can encourage others to think tactically or in terms of how to accomplish a rights-affirming outcome. Speaking retrospectively of his own professional development, Douglas Johnson, the former executive director of the Center for Victims of Torture, reflects on his early leadership experience creating the Infant Formula Action Coalition that boycotted the food conglomerate Nestlé:

> I am proud of that campaign and nearly a decade of work. But, like all beginners, we made a few mistakes. . . . As I have more experience in the shaping of the strategy of an organization, it has become clear to me that the more we understand about tactics, the more flexibility we have to set more strategic directions. I am not arguing, then, that tactical thinking or training supersedes strategic thinking, but rather that tactical development enriches strategic thought. (Johnson 2004, 15)

For Johnson, *tactics* imply short-term measures to position the organization to carry out strategic plans. He argues that emphasizing tactical thinking enables individuals within NGOs, allied organizations, or even victims participating in human rights work to improvise in particular situations: "I think of this phenomenon as something similar to a musician learning a new piece of music. . . . As we practice, it gets easier" (Johnson 2004, 18).

In *New Tactics in Human Rights*, the Center for Victims of Torture stresses the importance of tactics for human rights advocacy organizations and thus offers specific examples of tactics various organizations use in preventing and intervening in rights-abuse situations and restoring victims (Cornell, Kelsch, and Palasz 2004). But, as Johnson suggests, a tactical mind-set enables managers to cultivate a dynamic, team-oriented workforce. Thus, a tactics-oriented management approach appears appropriate as well in development and emergency humanitarian settings. With regard to development, Robert Chambers explains, "Development projects can be paralyzed by overload at their centers of control. . . . Projects deal with varied environments and with idiosyncratic people as independent agents" (1997, 200).

Chambers also recommends that managers adopt a leadership strategy of "minimum specs," or limiting themselves to only a few simple rules needed to facilitate what is essentially self-organization in adhocracies (also see Morgan 1998, 105–6). Speaking about leaders intending to promote self-organization, organization scholar Gareth Morgan maintains, "They have to avoid the role of 'grand designer' in favor of one that focuses on . . . creating enabling conditions that allow a system to find its own form" (1998, 106). Morgan's understanding of "minimum specs" in leadership align with Chambers's (1997, 199) "four Ds," or reversals of upper-lower relationships needed to facilitate participatory development—decentralization (power at the periphery rather than at the center), democracy (dispersed equity rather than unitary authority), diversity (differentiation rather than standardization), and dynamism (change rather than stabilization). As outcomes of self-organization, the capabilities of development professionals are substantiated by successes in forging productive alliances and agreements with participants in the field. In her account of an Anglo development organization offering business expertise to a Navajo organization engaged in tourism, Debebe (2002) elaborates on the finely honed skills of the adviser from the Anglo organization to calibrate and suppress his own economic values in reference to those of the Navajo group. This capability enabled him to identify the common ground as a footing for assistance and to overlook those divergent issues that could undermine the cooperative endeavor. Although Debebe says little about management within the Anglo advising organization, it is likely that its representative (identified in her commentary as "Tom") personifies a collective, self-organizing effort endorsed by his organization.

Focusing on emergency humanitarian settings, Daly also stresses the importance of self-organization based on team learning, suggesting, "Teams which are at optimum efficiency in the routine are likely to be the best prepared for emergencies" (1998, 365–66). Teams and organizations that place a premium on continuous learning are likely to make the best crossover between the two. A project officer with the World Food Programme, Daly also discusses the particular skills that supervisors and team leaders should draw on in the midst of emergency situations, when goodwill within teams can unravel under the tensions of the situations, mistakes, and criticism of performance. In these emergency settings, Daly advises supervisors "to know when to back down and when to remain firm," largely on the basis of which response is more likely to facilitate pressure learning (pp. 364–65). In large part, Daly recommends that supervisors become tacticians themselves in steering teams through the turbulence of emergency humanitarian responses.

In summary, leaders must balance efforts to facilitate self-organization that draws on the improvisational capabilities of teams and individuals within appropriate, minimum parameters needed to conserve its values. In reference to learning and self-organization, Morgan characterizes this balancing act as follows:

> One challenge is to help . . . work teams, research groups, or individuals find and operate within a sphere of "bounded" or "responsible autonomy." Another challenge is to avoid the anarchy and the completely free flow that arises when there are no parameters or guidelines, on the one hand, and over-centralization on the other. (Morgan 1998, 106)

A management trainer who advises NGOs arrives at similar conclusions by reasoning that organizations need to align their core values, organization structures, and management systems (Padaki 2000). Padaki suggests that two organizations that describe their respective missions alike—for example, "people-centered, working for social justice," and so on—may involve different value-structure management-system alignments. From Padaki's standpoint, it follows that managers can draw on core values such as trust, team interdependency, and collaboration as parameters for managing professionals capable of self-organization and commitment to organization learning.

Emphasizing Context and Culture

As frequently mentioned in the previous chapter devoted to transformative change, rights-deprivation and human development issues relate to the particular, local context rather than to general abstractions. Rights-focused leaders in advocacy and related development organizations therefore need to (1) integrate management approaches and learning activities around core values in ways that nurture competencies to monitor the political and cultural dynamics at work in particular contexts and (2) direct accountability downward to address the expectations of the poor or the victimized. In the broad strokes of leadership, the executive role centers on conserving the core values of an organization or institution in the midst of countervailing pressures on it. Here "core values" are understood as "objects of desire that are capable of sustaining group identity including any set of goals or standards that can form the basis of shared perspectives and group feelings" (Selznick 1957, 121; Terry 1995, 116).

Stated differently, executive leaders conserve values largely by "running interference" so that those working in operational activities enjoy the liberty of staying focused on the moral commitments that hold the organization together or, in the case of rights-based advocacy and development organizations, the commitment to local participants and beneficiaries. Nonetheless, leaders also need to address the top-down demands and expectations of the powerful in donor organizations or in host-government regimes. With regard to donor organizations, Hailey characterizes the issue as follows:

> It is in the context of this increasing concern about the efficiency and effectiveness of such over-stretched organisations that new management controls, organisational criteria, and indicators of performance are being introduced. While these are perfectly legitimate management tools that are commonly applied in both the public and private sectors, there is also growing unease that, with the advent of this new managerialism, many of the original values that made NGOs distinctive are under threat and will become increasingly marginalised. (Hailey 2000, 403)

Therefore, as Smillie and Hailey argue in their analyses of leadership in five South Asian development NGOs, any concerted effort to keep programmatic operations directed toward the intricacies of context requires a corresponding set of strategies for "running interference" or "'buffering strategies' to keep the worst aspects of donor interference at bay" (2002, 162). It follows then that leaders willing to conserve values and mission, and in so doing "buffering" operations from interfering pressures, cannot shy away from certain political risks and uncertainties. In this regard, a study of relationships between transformative leadership and cultural values (among graduate-level leadership students in Pakistan, Kazakhstan, and Turkey) found negative links between "uncertainty avoidance" and the ability to "inspire a shared vision" and "model the way" or set an example (Ergeneli, Gohar, and Temirbekova 2007, 718). Conserving contextually focused values then requires leaders to take prudent risks. Although much has been written on risk management as a rational exercise in weighing opportunities and potential liabilities in development NGOs (see, e.g., Wilson-Grau 2003), the rights-based leader more often develops sound judgment to evaluate risks intuitively through experience.

The balance of this section subdivides into two related discussions—the first identifies some basic leadership strategies for buffering (contextually directed) NGO operations from the distractions of other external pressures, and the second surveys leadership attributes and skills that support commitments to the particular circumstances affecting people's lives, or as Smillie and Hailey put it, their "concern for the poor, a driving ambition to improve society, and ability to adapt and change, [and] a willingness to learn . . . [that] can be turned into powerful forces for positive change" (2002, 163).

Buffering Strategies

As characterized by Smillie and Hailey, managerial efforts to "buffer" or shield NGO activities from external pressures reflect a tactical response to the broader issue of intensified accountability pressures associated with the New Policy Agenda—the neoliberal movement of the 1980s and 1990s to enlist NGOs as instruments of "democratizing" and structural adjustment agendas. Biggs and Neame address the problem directly in a chapter—aptly titled "Negotiating Room to Maneuver: Reflections Concerning NGO Autonomy and Accountability Within the New Policy Agenda"—in an anthology devoted to NGO accountability (see Edwards and Hulme 1996). To focus on a particular externally imposed distraction, Biggs and Neame elaborate on the Northern donor pressure to "scale up"—or to replicate or "mass produce" program successes in a particular area or community in *other locales*. Clearly, the entrepreneurial pressure to scale up, deriving from market ideologies, could threaten core values of addressing the contextual nuances that affect empowerment efforts. Although buffering actually constitutes a means of "managing accountability" (discussed at length in chapter 5), it is pertinent here as a prerequisite for implementing contextually focused NGO missions.

A consultant serving an NGO clientele proposes four elements of effective organizations that allow NGOs some breathing room or "ensure independence in the new [highly scrutinized] funding environment":

- "A programme that is in response to ongoing need, whether provided by empowerment, enabling, or service provision.
- Perception—how the organisation is perceived, the extent to which it is known—including its reputation, and independent brand and positioning.
- The extent to which it has built a constituency of popular support—the number of people or organisations who support the work *in addition to the beneficiaries.*
- A revenue mix that provides a degree of security through a range of income sources, with no over-dependence on any single source of funding" (Wells 2001, 74).

Rights-based leaders can incorporate these indicators of organizational or programmatic strength into credible and influential positions that justify (or conserve) values directed toward the contextual conditions of human experience.

First, with regard to an ongoing program mission, leaders can articulate rather direct messages for donor consumption that emphasize contradictions between donor expectations and the realities of working in particular locales. Social auditing initiatives to bring donors and local participants face-to-face in joint planning and evaluation activities can offer Northern donors a ground-level perspective on human development (see Zadek and Gatward 1996). Along these lines, any experience that offers neoliberal aid officials a broader and more intricate understanding of chronic poverty, as related to specific conditions, could substantiate NGO missions (see Nevile 2002). Subtler messages could be conveyed by including a host of qualifying assumptions and caveats in the drafting of initial planning documents—most notably the logical framework—to underscore the uncertainties that can affect (and in some circumstances undermine) the "preplanning" of intended outcomes amid the complexities of political and cultural dynamics that may not be well understood (see Dale 2003).

Second, leaders can pursue proactive accountability-directed initiatives that, by "institutionalizing suspicion" in various ways, enhance the legitimacy of the NGO as perceived among aid donors (see Moore and Stewart 1998). Talking specifically about institutionalized suspicion, Moore and Stewart correlate the need to develop a verifiable, legitimate governance structure with the maturing of an NGO beyond its embryonic stage under the purview of founders. Although they recommend that similar NGOs work together to form credible self-regulating associations, they indicate that suspicion can be institutionalized in a variety of ways to effectively provide "strict external auditing; recruitment of personnel by open competition; submission of frequent detailed reports to funders; formal minutes of meetings; and elaborate measurement and reporting of the 'impacts' and 'outcomes'" (1998, 337). Furthermore, enumerating the advantages of self-regulating systems, Moore and Stewart—albeit indirectly—touch on how these arrangements can buffer the organization from intrusive outside scrutiny:

> They provide donors with some kind of quality rating that can be traded off against more expensive, detailed, intrusive individual inspections or output evaluations. If donors know that membership of the . . . association is really "earned" and not a rubber stamp, they will be that much more willing to fund members without attaching tight strings. If membership of reputable NGO Associations becomes the norm, then the reputation (and financial health) of the NGO sector as a whole can only improve. (Moore and Stewart 1998, 340)

Similarly, Golub chronicles the development of the Philippine Council for NGO Certification (PCNC), originally established to determine tax-deductible status but ultimately to serve as a "Good Housekeeping seal of approval" that legitimatizes NGOs in the Philippines. His commentary suggests that PCNC certification can buffer NGOs' operations in some ways but jeopardize them in others. With regard to the former, the certification process involves *other NGOs*, not aid institutions, examining the applicant, often sharing information and advice along the way. But in terms of the latter, the checklist of certification criteria works against the efforts of successful but lesser-established organizations that defy easy quantification:

> Some of the best organizations to which the Asia Foundation provided start-up support might not have been able to present the clearly defined missions, goals, policies, systems, and plans required by the PCNC. Such groups . . . defined their work through their post-funding experiences rather than through pre-funding presentations. (Golub 2007, 104)

Another leadership strategy to protect the organization's commitment to contexts of development involves declaring the NGO's obligation to accountability *in the broadest* sense of the term. In effect, NGO officials become proactive in (re)defining the meaning of *accountability* by drawing on their capabilities to manage the cognitive elements of organization. Scott-Villiers recounts how and why the British NGO ActionAid adopted its Accountability, Learning and Planning System (ALPS), which features "360 degree accountability" as follows:

- 360-degree accountability, emphasizing accountability to the poor and marginalized, women, men, boys, and girls;
- commitment to gender equity;
- application to the whole organization at all levels, not just to the front line;
- relevance of information to both the people who supply and those who receive it;
- feedback to the information provider on reaction to information;
- learning rather than writing long reports;
- linking financial expenditures to quality of actions;
- critical reflection: learning from success and failure (Scott-Villars 2002, 425).

This 360-degree pledge enhances the organization's legitimacy and, in so doing, preempts the expectation that any one stakeholder might establish exclusive domain over NGO operations at the expense of others.

Third, NGO leaders can expand the popular support their programs have generated and convince outside external donors that their missions in particular communities and regions are sustainable over the long term. Specifically, an organization's ability to tap into local funding signals the potential to scale up since recognition of success spreads beyond one locality (see Hailey 2000, 75). Two cases discussed in chapter 3 showcase how successes in local constituency building empowers agencies to expand their contextually focused missions in a prudent manner. Both Magazine's (2003) commentary on the Educación de Niños Callejeros (EDNICA)—supporting street children in Mexico City—and Easton et al.'s discussion of Tostan's educational programs—curtailing female genital cutting practices—demonstrate how constituency building and local funding support offer institutional donors evidence of sustainable development. Magazine explains how EDNICA's leaders leveraged existing bases of support to scale up activities among various areas in Mexico City:

When I first learned of EDNICA, it was getting ready to leave the first street club in the hands of the [neighborhood] community. The local parish had provided land to build the street club beside the church, and the priest was an active participant in the project. The club counted eight employees, half paid by the NGO and half paid by the parish. EDNICA was waiting for the community (the parish or otherwise) to provide enough funding or volunteers to take over the project, after which EDNICA would move its employees on to another club. (Magazine 2003, 246)

As Easton, Monkman, and Miles describe, Tostan expanded its programs by capitalizing on the notoriety of its successes in much the same manner as EDNICA did in Mexico City:

The village improvement projects and income-generating activities that typically followed the education modules were a significant part of the attraction and momentum of the programme. With the aid of a variety of donors, Tostan tried whenever possible to make available small amounts of seed capital and microcredit for communities and groups that took the initiative to organise and propose projects. Initiatives typically included well-baby clinics, improvements to local water supply, small livestock projects, consumer cooperatives, collective farming efforts, and crafts marketing. The follow-up activities added to the successful aura of the programme and helped increase demand for it. (Easton, Monkman, and Miles 2003, 447)

As Tostan is a Southern NGO committed to human rights in the local contest, its donor environment is especially salient and likely representative of that in which similar grassroots organizations function. Given the broad, qualitative character of its human empowerment activities, Tostan would experience considerable difficulty documenting its efforts with quantified output measures required by rational preplanning processes (such as the logframe). Nonetheless, it can present a strong case on behalf of its continuing program momentum based on past success and expanding constituency support. As Easton et al. suggest, subsequent negotiations between Tostan and its institutional donors (its current website indicates several donors) is directed at the margins of how Tostan should expand its activities—rather than at the core of its operation:

Given Tostan's apparent success, more donors were willing to offer support and those already involved were ready to up the ante, but most asked Tostan to trim down its programme and to focus on the four modules directly relevant to FGC: human rights, problem-solving skills, community hygiene, and women's health. Literacy elements were relegated to the continuing-education phase of the programme, and emphasis was placed on immediate and highly focused change. The new strategy was called the Village Empower-ment Programme (VEP). (Easton, Monkman, and Miles 2003, 451)

Drafted several years beyond the time frame of Easton et al.'s study, To-stan's 2006–11 strategic plan articulates "challenges to achieving our visions" that (re)frame the donor environment toward marginal or incremental issues, leaving the core of its participatory- and human-rights-focused operations ba-sically intact and as a given:

Challenges to Achieving Our Visions

This Strategic Plan seeks to address the following challenges:

- Challenge 1: Maintain Tostan's program strengths while ex-panding to multiple new countries;
- Challenge 2: Build upon current successes in FGC abandon-ment while developing other result areas;
- Challenge 3: Develop mechanisms to share Tostan's model while maintaining the integrity of the program;
- Challenge 4: Increase Tostan's operational capacities while maintaining Tostan's unique organizational culture;
- Challenge 5: Minimize risks while proactively pursuing fu-ture growth;
- Challenge 6: Maintain a cost-effective model while expand-ing operations to new countries in Africa (Tostan 2007).

It could be said, then, that by capitalizing on its constituency of popular sup-port, Tostan can buffer, or "more loosely couple," its community-focused op-erations from donor funding scrutiny.

Wells's fourth point, that NGOs can realize independence through find-ing multiple sources of revenue, appears implicit in the broader discussion. At this writing Tostan's website reveals the following external donors in addition to the funding that local communities provide:

Agencia Española de Cooperación Internacional

American Jewish World Service (AJWS)

Anonymous donor

Comunidad de Madrid

Jacob and Hilda Blaustein Foundation

James R. Greenbaum, Jr. Family Foundation

JustWorld International

Nike Foundation

Sigrid Rausing Trust

Swedish International Cooperation Development Agency (SIDA)

UN Foundation

United Nations Population Fund (UNFPA)

UNICEF

US Agency for International Development (USAID)

Embassy of the United States, Dakar, Senegal

Wallace Global Fund

The Wallace Research Foundation

Although exact fund breakdowns are not provided, one could speculate that such an impressive list of institutional donors provides Tostan room to maneuver in its efforts to promote human development in local contexts.

Fifth, leaders in Northern NGOs may find it advantageous to buffer their Southern partners or affiliate organizations from the rational planning conditions that aid agencies place on funding. Such protection allows grassroots organizations flexibility in nurturing participation with beneficiaries in particular locales and leaves planning—for example, developing logical frameworks—to better-resourced organizations. As Wallace relates in explaining how UK NGOs functioned with affiliates in South Africa,

> the project managers wanted to buffer their southern partners from
> the rigid planning and reporting requirements and felt that when

reworking the documents they were becoming aid administrators rather than development workers. Smaller organizations especially tended not to be particularly good at report writing, and UK staff keen to support grassroots NGOs had to augment and tailor their documents for funders. (Wallace 2007, 98)

Thus, the UK NGOs offer maneuvering room for their partners in South Africa to address particular needs in that societal context.

Rights-Based Leaders, Context, and Culture

In his firm belief that the multitudes of development organizations can and should advance human rights in their in-country settings, Peter Uvin challenges leaders to integrate a number of right-based strategies—such as "knowing the legal machinery," "capacity building," "advocacy," and others—as organization priorities (2004, 139–65). To understand Uvin in context, one needs to appreciate his outrage associated with his Rwandan experiences in the run-up to genocide there in the mid-1990s—specifically, that the proliferation of supposedly "democratizing" civil society organizations were either incapable or reluctant to warn the global community of impending atrocities. In his book *Aiding Violence*, Uvin implores the development community to work against "the politics of exclusion" whereby regimes set "boundaries of obligation" that wall out "the expendables" from those worthy of recognition. Uvin writes,

> In his 1994 presidential address to the American Sociological Association, William Gamson discussed the politics of exclusion, in which certain groups of people are not considered part of the moral universe of a society. He added that "in most societies, the boundaries of some of the universe of obligation are often hotly contested and changing. Social movements that challenge cultural codes . . . typically challenge those boundaries of obligation." In Rwanda during the 1990s, the boundaries of obligation changed toward further and deeper exclusion, and, ultimately, genocide. (Uvin 1998, 178)

Juxtapose Uvin's statement here with the remarks of the keynote speaker at the 2005 conference of the International Academy for Intercultural Research held at Kent State University:

The Kent State tragedy was not a chance convergence of forces and people. Rather, it was the opposite—an over-determined encounter between two radically different subcultures that had been years in the making. . . . The cultural differences between those seeking peace and American withdrawal from Vietnam and those attempting to continue the struggle at any cost were as different as night and day. Their templates for reality had no convergence, no overlap, no similarity. How much of this is evident today in a variety of contexts? Such questions provided the foundation for this conference. (Anthony Marsella, as quoted in Cushner 2005, 635–36)

From his summary statement in *Aiding Violence*, Uvin's exhortation to rights-based development, and, for that matter, advocacy, agencies to combat the politics of exclusion in the particular context makes perfect sense, as does his claim that human rights work is inherently political in nature. Thus, the leader's role is to mold a resilient and flexible learning organization collectively capable of scratching beneath a society's veneer, both to ascertain the political-cultural fissures that limit human agency and to craft tactics to work beyond them. In other words, to take action *before taking stock of the political landscape* risks overlooking critical individual attitudes and value orientation that are formative in leading the NGO toward either rights-based missions or elsewhere.

To assert that rights-based leaders should be "interculturally sensitive" is to state the obvious. Nonetheless, this broad notion of sensitivity can be broken down into some discrete components that apply to leadership (within and outside one's native culture) in general and to rights-focused NGOs in particular. A first component, for example, could relate to the "worldview" (or cognitive structure) in which leaders process or evaluate experiences of intercultural differences (Bennett and Hammer 2002). A second might track to the leader's awareness of intercultural differences in work-related values that could apply within (subordinate–superior relationships in) the organization or between the organization's embodiment of the NGO mission (e.g., a non-structured, team-oriented adhocracy) and perceptions of "appropriate organization" held by the host government or participant beneficiaries (see Hofstede 1984). A third could involve the leader's style of mediating intercultural conflict relative to conflict resolution traditions within particular cultures (David-heiser 2005; Hammer 2005; Marsella 2005; Worchel 2005; Cingöz-Ulu and Lalonde 2007).

To momentarily digress, I argue that these three dimensions (and possibly others not mentioned here) are fundamental requisites of several of Uvin's rights-based initiatives, such as alternatively "collaborating and confronting," "looking within the agency," and "reconceptualizing the overall aims of the agency." The NGO leader's responsibility for intercultural astuteness hardly requires graduate training in cultural anthropology; indeed, he or she can absorb the competencies in much the same manner as expatriate managers in multinational corporations. In her qualitative study of 11 expatriate middle- and upper-level managers, Cassiday reaches two general conclusions—first, that international experiences profoundly affect one's worldview—asserting,

> The leaders who were most satisfied with their own performance were able to reflect on the cultural paradigms influencing their perceptions and assumptions. The ability to hold the tension of differing realities in a respectful manner precipitated leaders' ability to work effectively within the opposing cultural paradigms. Many leaders made statements emphasizing the importance of learning from, not just about, the host culture. (Cassiday 2005, 403)

The second conclusion relates to the importance of relational development in the midst of task accomplishment, a principal tenet of participatory approaches to rights-based leadership. On the basis of this, Cassiday proposes a support model for the expatriate leader that incorporates both a personal development and a multicultural team component. Within the first, she recommends befriending a "cultural informant" who can offer assistance in navigating the culture:

> Having someone in the host culture . . . can greatly relieve concerns about the move. Having this support continue in-country adds continuity. Cultural informants in the work setting are important. As one participant commented, after a friend suggested that his actions were offensive: "It was my second assignment in that country, and I thought to myself, what other cultural rules am I missing? What are the nuances of this thing that I am not even aware of?" (Cassiday 2005, 405)

Upon his retirement, a CEO of a US-based multinational corporation in India credits much of his success in "building a business from scratch in a county about which he knew nothing" to friends like Montek Singh Ahluwalia who remains his informal adviser, confidante, and mentor (Bhandari 2007). Perhaps like successful expatriate managers, rights-based leaders could do well to make prudent choices of friends in-country to guide them within complexities of the culture.

Although drawn from an intercultural relations literature heavily oriented toward global business, the three "sensitivity" dimensions mentioned previously are pertinent to training people in various NGO positions and to leadership fitness and development. Referring back to the first, a worldview for processing intercultural differences, Hammer and his associates have built an Intercultural Development Inventory that can distinguish interculturally competent (or ethno-relative) worldviews from deficient ethnocentric orientations.

While the scalar logic of Hammer's inventory is intricate, it suffices here to describe "intercultural competence" as reflecting a "worldview that can comprehend and accommodate complex cultural difference. This can range from *acceptance* (a tendency to recognize patterns of cultural difference in one's own and other cultures) to *adaptation* (tendency to alter perception and behavior according to cultural context)" (Bennett and Hammer 2002, 1). By contrast ethnocentricity is understood as the inability to resolve the complexities of these differences, or a worldview that "simplifies and/or polarizes cultural difference. This orientation ranges from a tendency toward disinterest and avoidance of cultural difference . . . to a tendency to view the world in terms of 'us' and 'them,' where 'us' is superior" or that "*reverses* the 'us' and 'them' polarization, where 'them' is superior. This *reversal* orientation is the mirror image of the *denial/defense* orientation and is similarly considered to be ethnocentric" (p. 1). Starting with leadership and permeating throughout the rights-based organization, competence needs to advance far beyond *acceptance* of differences to cognitive and behavioral *adaptation* that energizes capacity building and tactical improvisation in response to emerging contextual realities.

As stated often throughout this book, rights-based organizations need to rely on collaboration, participation, and team learning as expected modes of action. But as Hofstede (1984) explains, culture indeed has consequences in shaping the mental processes that affect one's orientations toward work in organizations. In *Culture's Consequences*, Hofstede conducts a 40-nation study of intercultural differences influencing work-related values by measuring four dimensions of culture: power distance, uncertainty avoidance, individualism, and masculinity. "Power distance" measures a cultural receptiveness to inequality, perhaps better understood as a pecking order within organization work and especially between subordinates and the boss (1984, 65–73). The cultural roots of a high power-distance country extend from many sources such as parents demanding obedience, a general lack of trust, and the strength of conformity as a social norm. Hofstede shows the Philippines, Mexico, and Venezuela as high power-distance nations; Austria, Israel, and Denmark as low; and the United States almost at the mean (p. 77). But particularly revealing for development organizations committed to Chambers's participatory approach in empowering the poor, Hofstede attributes power distance to societies "in tropical and subtropical climates," "with traditional agriculture and less modern industry," and "less national wealth." Paradoxically, development efforts to empower people work against the inertia of their cultural acceptance of inequality.

Hofstede's "uncertainty avoidance" dimension relates to a cultural intolerance for uncertainty and ambiguity, which has origins in particular religious faiths based in absolutism and certainty, and the games (particularly those of chance and of strategy for "gaming" the system) that people play (1984, 137–38). Controlling for age, Hofstede finds high uncertainty avoidance in Greece, Portugal, and Belgium and low avoidance in Singapore, Denmark, and Sweden (p. 122). In organizations, uncertainty avoidance calls for rules and control-oriented technology intended to reduce uncertainty (pp. 114–18). Generally, a cultural orientation toward uncertainty avoidance limits rights-based leaders and organizations that often work with the ambiguities of unpredictable individual and institutional behaviors and that in turn build capabilities to cope with those and other uncertainties. In addition, these organizations could encounter difficulty in recruiting in-county (in societies with high uncertainty avoidance) talent to assume transformative leadership roles that by nature involve taking risks (see Ergeneli, Gohar, and Temirbekova 2007, 719–20).

The "individualism" dimension relates to cultural tendencies to value self-concept in relation to the collective, as well as an inner directedness; it seeks out "personal time," freedom, and challenge in the workplace (Hofstede 1984, 148–58). Among Hofstede's 40 nations, the United States (highest), Australia, and Great Britain rank high, and Pakistan, Colombia, and Venezuela score especially low (p. 158). The implications of individualist tendencies in rights-based organizations appear murky. On one hand, autonomy and inner-motivated initiative are important in less-structured settings, but in extreme cases they could deflect the team focus of organization work.

The "masculinity" dimension actually taps the tenacity of gender differences embedded within social roles in the culture. Gender role (non)distinctions are perpetuated by family and school socialization processes and in the workplace setting. With regard to the latter, work goals may vary between men (advancement and earnings) and women (cooperation and security; Hofstede 1984, 176–91). Japan, Austria, and Venezuela score high on the masculinity index; the United States places above the mean; and Sweden, Norway, and the Netherlands rank low (p. 189). Rights-based NGOs intent on promoting women's economic empowerment, possibly associated with sustainable democratic improvement, should take heed of Hofstede's masculinity dimension. Again, empowerment efforts pose numerous challenges, not the least of which involves surmounting cultural resistance.

The implications of Hofstede's intercultural differences extend to issues concerning conflict and resolution strategies, matters that can inform rights-based leadership as related both to interpersonal dynamics within the organization—and with its participant beneficiaries—and to programmatic concerns. Within NGOs staffed by individuals from diverse cultural backgrounds (e.g., where in-country field-workers are hired to interact in communities), care should be taken to tailor responses to uncomfortable disputes with cultural sensitivity. Some research finds that those with a collectivist orientation (i.e., from societies scoring low on Hofstede's individualist scale) prefer withdrawal from the rancorous situation, or at least face-saving compromise, rather than candid and direct focus (see Holt and DeVore 2005, 183). In such cases, an accommodative leadership style of emotional restraint rather than confrontation appears helpful (see Hammer 2005, 691). Attention to conflict, conflict resolution, and the injuries and deprivations that emerge from conflict offers programmatic bridges between rights advocacy and development. As advocates against torture, the Center for Victims of Torture provides human development programming in the form of psychologically related services to a number of refugee communities in southeastern Minnesota. Conversely, development agencies can integrate conflict resolution and peace initiatives as means for building rights cultures into their institutional missions. This, however, may become ethically perilous if peacemaking and conflict resolution become Trojan horses or guises for advancing interventionist agendas among conflict-ridden regions in the world (see Uvin 2004, 195–96).

Participation and NGO Leadership

On one level, nearly all development and rights-advocacy NGOs espouse the virtues of "participatory empowerment," along with management techniques designed to facilitate them (Smillie and Hailey 2002, 162). But on another level, the moral absolutism of the participation discourse—that has managers and their organizations as "culprits" obstructing empowerment—discourages candor in grappling with problematic, operational questions like "How exactly should an NGO leader define *participation*?" and "How can it realistically happen in organizations under pressure (by donors) to formalize operations?" Smillie and Hailey note the irony of Robert Chambers's invectives against the "uppers" (presumably NGO managers and professionals) whose reality is, by his account, oblivious to the life situations of the poor—whose reality *ought to count*—given that Chambers had based his advocacy for participation on observations of NGOs already utilizing participatory approaches:

> Technical excellence and adaptive learning were high on the agenda of [the Aga Khan Rural Support Program, India] from the outset, but the process of development was equally important. Robert Chambers paid several visits to the organization in its early years, helping to improve its organizational processes and culture, while at the same time developing his own ideas about rapid and participatory rural appraisal. (Smillie and Hailey 2002, 102)

Another commentator poses irony somewhat differently in her critical examination of the participatory approach:

> Why is so little debate about these tensions [inherent in the participatory approach] seen in the development literature? Is it that development practitioners fear criticizing local practices and being seen as the professionals roundly condemned in Chambers' work? Is there not a danger from swinging from one untenable position ("we know best") to an equally untenable and damaging one ("they know best")? (Cleaver 2002, 233)

Among her other criteria for critiquing participation, Frances Cleaver elaborates on "myths of community" common in the participation discourse that communities are unitary and easily identifiable, units of power solidarity, resourceful, and foundations of social cohesion (2002, 231–33). Regarding the myth of a unitary community, Cleaver asserts, "The very definition of community in development projects involves defining those who are 'included' in rights, activities, benefits and those who are excluded because they do not belong to the defined entity" (p. 231). These realities complicate efforts to implement Chambers's participatory approaches, as shown in Mompati and Prinsen's account of a community planning initiative in Botswana in the mid-1990s:

PRA process involved the selection and training of ten villagers in each village to assist in the proceedings and to lead project implementation when the PRA team was gone. As villagers were "free" to elect their trainees, almost invariably members of the dominant ethnic group were elected. It should be noted that even subordinate ethnic groups generally tended to vote for a candidate of the dominant group. The well-entrenched belief among the ethnic minority groups was "We cannot speak so eloquently and do not understand things." (Mompati and Prinsen 2000, 628)

Should planners implementing such efforts interpret minority group deference to the majority as evidence of "unity and solidarity" in the community or as enduring rights deprivation that denies human agency? In such cases, whose reality does Chambers's PRA (Participatory Rural Appraisal) actually endorse? Should "uppers" external to the community reengineer the community for the sake of real participation? What *can* be said is that purist ideals are tough to implement in an imperfect world.

Concerns about what exactly is meant by *participation* are especially significant because virtually all development actors extol its virtues, at least in the abstract (Smillie and Hailey 2002, 167). Even the neoliberal donor institutions that have traditionally embraced structural adjustment to bring about economic growth have tweaked their missions to welcome participation as a poverty reduction strategy (see Wallace 2007, 19–29). As advocates of women's participation in development can attest, participation can be easily "spun" or exploited "for show" to legitimize governmental or organizational agendas (see Appleford 2000). On the other hand, NGOs authentically committed to participation may encounter a number of practical problems relating to the vagueness of the term, passive behaviors of aid recipients, people's traditional interactions with authority figures, and cultural proclivities for avoiding conflict (see Crawford et al. 1999; Pijnenburg and Nhantumbo 2002, 194–97). In other cases, well-intended participatory approaches simply prove inadequate for dealing with people's most pressing needs. For example, one NGO administrator laments that his PRA approaches did not help farmers deal with El Niño's torrents that drowned crops in Tanzania. Reflecting on his own frustrations, an NGO official quotes a farmer who is unimpressed by the organization's help:

I used to think I was poor. Then they told me I was needy. Then they said it was self-defeating to think I was needy instead I was

deprived. Then they said deprived had a bad image; I was really underprivileged. Then they said underprivileged was overused; I was
disadvantaged. I still don't have a cent, but I have a great vocabulary.
(Crawford et al. 1999, 173)

In reference to agricultural programs in Mozambique, Pijnenburg and
Nhantumbo differentiate among various levels and modes of participation
that essentially fall into one of two categories—they serve either as *means* for
facilitating the organization's purposes or as *ends* of self-empowerment or self-
mobilization for people (2002, 193). Presumably, rights-based leaders would
be inclined to understand participation in terms of the latter. But from an
operations standpoint, how can NGO managers, even if directed toward participatory empowerment, fit such a commitment in the organization's agenda
crowded with Northern stakeholder demands to scale up and formalize operations (Smillie and Hailey 2002, 168)? The good news here is that organizations can be operationally effective to support empowerment through informal, one-on-one interactions wherein NGO officials assist people in clarifying
their own circumstances and possibilities instead of solving their problems for
them. This implies that organization representatives should interact in an advisory capacity that displaces dependency relationships with a resolve to counsel
in problem solving. One development manager tells about meeting with a
group of women at a community extension center discussing entrepreneurial
possibilities:

> They discussed how they can find a market for their groundnuts.
> They agreed to make oil from the nuts, and use some in their daily
> cooking and sell the rest to their fellow villagers. The women asked
> if we can find a refinery machine to help. I told them that in town
> there is someone who sells different machines. I will go there and
> see if there are any and then I will tell them how much it costs so
> they can decide/plan how to buy it. (Crawford et al. 1999, 172)

Here the official assumes the role of "gopher" and in doing so is unlikely to be
heralded by World Bank or Northern institutional donors; while her motivations may appear rather insignificant, she nonetheless demonstrates a willingness to put "the first last," consistent with the ideals of participatory approaches
to empowerment. In this case, willingness to act as a gopher sends a powerful
cognitive message of authentic assistance on behalf of empowering others.

According to Rowlands, the one-on-one interaction promotes two of the three critical dimensions of empowerment from a feminist perspective: the *personal*, "where empowerment is about developing a sense of self and individual confidence and capacity, and undoing the effects of internalised oppression," and the *close relationship*, "where empowerment is about developing the ability to negotiate and influence the nature of the relationship and decisions made within it" (1995, 103). Because outsiders cannot impose empowerment, the tactic of accompaniment or *being there*—that some might dismiss as touchy-feely fluff—becomes instrumental in agency. Rowlands translates *acompañamiento*, a term used often in a Latin American development context as

> an outside agent's sense of solidarity and willingness to share risks with poor and marginalised people, and a willingness to engage with the processes of social change in which they are directly involved. It contrasts with the position of outside agents—whether these are church workers, development NGOs, or funding agencies—which maintain a greater sense of distance. (Rowlands 1995, 106)

Since accompaniment by nature necessitates listening skills, it is not surprising that development practitioners are likened to therapists, as Schunk does:

> A therapist should guide the patient towards a state of well-being. What exactly is that state of well-being? What is to be the benchmark? And who decides? Once again, we need to refer to our own vision of the world in order to find an answer and then to "negotiate with the patient." . . . Such a process sets the preconditions of real self-development: a given population, besides building its own road to self-improvement, addresses itself to the causes of and reasons for its current situation, and not simply to international cooperation as a surrogate of itself or some local state authority. (Schunk 2003, 379)

In terms of operations, it can be said that authentic participation can proceed from low-key and low-tech accompaniment enriched by interpersonal skill competencies. However, the bad news for management is the obvious disconnect between NGO workers essentially doing one-on-one "social work" with poor people—or sitting with villagers under a tree (Smillie and Hailey

2002, 168)—and Northern donor expectations focused on hard results and productivity. As Eade puts it, "The 'old guard' may still talk about Freirean conscientisation processes, or class conflict; but what today's hard-headed NGOs demand are skills in Project Management and Strategic Planning, and fluency in the language of input, throughput, and output. Accountability and appraisal replace 'accompaniment'; counterparts become clients" (1997, 502). The challenge for leaders involves packaging diffuse, interpersonal empowerment work in planning and evaluation formats that resonate with funding institutions.

Timing, Prudence, and Sustainable Accomplishment

In their observations of successful leaders in South Asian development NGOs, Smillie and Hailey underscore the issues of "time and timing" as recurring in various problematic contexts: (1) the early period of organization creation amid turbulent political environments, (2) the time it takes to develop a distinct organization culture that "pays off" in terms of knowledge and wisdom, and (3) the time to determine the type of leadership required (2002, 163–64). Taken together, the issues reflect the temporal dimensions of organization stewardship or even prudent leadership in pursuit of sustainable accomplishment (whether development focused, rights empowering, or both). Writing for a public sector management audience, J. Patrick Dobel maintains that public integrity requires leaders (among other considerations) to use their power and resources in a politically astute manner in order to achieve durable accomplishments that improve the community. Dobel's prudent leader needs to (1) develop capacities for "disciplined reason and openness to experience"; (2) master the modalities of deploying power, timing and momentum, and the proper relation of means and ends; and (3) attend to outcomes that are durable and legitimate in benefiting the community (1999, 76).

Astute timing, as situated in the broader capacity of prudent political leadership, is fundamental in setting agendas to push rights claims forward and/or to undertake empowering development in the midst of adversaries. Regarding the former, Dobel points to how civil rights activist "Thurgood Marshall and the NAACP Legal Defense Fund crafted a twenty-year plan of numerous and difficult court challenges to set legal precedents that cumulatively undermined the legal edifice of segregation in the United States." For the latter, he recounts how "President Harry Truman and Secretary of State George Marshall used the communist threat in Eastern Europe as the opportunity to overcome domestic opposition and isolationism and push the Marshall Plan to reconstruct Europe after World War II" (1999, 203–4). Although Dobel understands political prudence as a combination of virtues essential for effective stewardship in the public sphere, it resonates just as (or perhaps more) forcefully in rights-based leadership that (1) advances "human rights [as an inherently] political matter" (Uvin 2004, 134–37), (2) at times obliges leaders to reframe and reconceptualize problems (pp. 160–62), and (3) demands durable, *sustainable* accomplishment.

As for the first, the wording from a CARE policy paper inspires Uvin's vision of a rights-based approach to development: "A rights-based approach deliberately and explicitly focuses on people achieving the minimum conditions for living in dignity. It does so by exposing the root causes of vulnerability and marginalization . . . [and by] empowering people to claim and exercise their rights and fulfill their responsibilities" (CARE 2001, in Uvin 2004, 135). This affirms that rights-claiming most often involves a political struggle in opposition to prevailing opinions that associate rights with whatever powers allow or currently exist under formal statute (assuming enforcement). Policy analyst Deborah Stone characterizes rights making as a struggle within the broader political mosaic of society:

> In the end, rights are not tools or instruments, operating mechanically and consistently. They are dependent upon and subject to larger politics. Perhaps their most distinctive feature, as policy instruments, is that they provide occasions for dramatic rituals that reaffirm or redefine society's internal rules and its categories of membership. . . . They are a vehicle for telling stories about what society means and what it stands for. (Stone 2002, 351–53)

Thus, rights-based leaders chart deliberate courses of political action with foresight and long-term vision in a manner that capitalizes on a judicious sense of timing that Dobel explains as vital in prudent leadership:

> Political leadership involves the ability to act with care and wait with patience, then move with quickness and surety when the opportunity arises. . . . Prudent leadership does not mean cautious or cramped leadership. Although it is profoundly important to avoid harm and loss, Saint Thomas Aquinas argued that prudence actively seeks to accomplish good. A prudent leader's intelligence looks for opportunities that permit action to be taken consonant with goals and power. As long as one does not expect a utopian

fulfillment of all goals, then every action and attainment will only approximate moral aspiration. (Dobel 1999, 77–78)

Uvin's appeal for this rights-based approach imposes an especially important challenge for those in the development community inclined to characterize assistance they render as "apolitical."

Second, Uvin's connection between a rights focus and the need to "reconceptual[ize] the overall aims of development agencies" (2004, 160–62) underscores the virtue of "disciplined reasoning and openness" and modalities of deploying power in Dobel's model of prudent leadership (1999, 199–203). Uvin characterizes a rights-based commitment as more likely to reframe problems like hunger around imperatives to *respect*, *protect*, and *provide* than more conventional, technical perspectives of development (2004, 161; italics his). Alan Thomas coaxes out more thinking about these leadership virtues in his article titled "What Makes Good Development Management?" (1999). Like others, he approaches this question from a value commitment to "people-centered development" (a term coined by Korten 1980, 1984, and further developed in Chambers 1997) and concludes that the difference in the terms "management of development" and "managing for development" carries substantive weight beyond clever rhetoric. "Managing *for* development" generally abandons command and control as the principal mode of power deployment in preference to the empowering-and-enabling approach wherein others (in the organization or in the beneficiary community) can share in the experience of exercising power (Thomas 1999, 16). That said, Thomas indicates that there may be times when development managers can and should revert to command-and-control authority but does not offer specific examples. However, Henry Mintzberg (2001) makes a strong case for "conventional management in unconventional settings"—such as in the operation of refugee camps or other large-scale relief efforts—suggesting that if top-down control can instill a measure of stability in the lives of people experiencing chaos and tragedy, it facilitates the lengthy processes of restoration and empowerment.

On the other hand, Mintzberg argues an equally convincing case for "empowering and enabling" or, in his words, "engaging management" in an article relating to his visit to Ghana where he was called on to recommend strategies for developing indigenous leadership:

> I think of true leaders as "engaging": they engage others with their thoughtfulness and humility because they engage themselves in what they are doing and not for personal gain. Such leaders bring

out the energy that exists naturally within people. If there is a heroic dimension to their behaviour, it is not by acting heroically so much as by enabling other people to act heroically. (Mintzberg 2006, 5)

From the outset of his visit, Mintzberg resisted the temptation to endorse best practices for teaching leadership from the developed world. Instead, he asked his host (who directs a leadership center), "So how do you teach leadership here?" The host responded, "We show it" (2006, 5). Thus, NGOs with affiliate offices in regional and local settings should avoid prejudgments about "good leadership" and "appropriate training" that overlook the strengths of indigenous leadership in promoting rights-based missions.

Third, sustainable accomplishment from a rights-based perspective requires leaders to guard against reversals whereby previously gained ground for empowerment may be (inadvertently or otherwise) sacrificed in pursuit of other rights-related goals. Development NGOs, for example, face pressures from donor institutions to scale up their local successes—indeed, many in the North associate the ability to diffuse accomplishment (analogous to selling a new product in several geographical markets) with sustainability. In his 1980 essay on community development, David Korten maintains that program expansion (or scaling up) constitutes a third organization learning stage—subsequent to "learning to be effective" and then "learning to be efficient"—that evolves over protracted time and countless learning iterations (1980, 499–501). Matthew Clarke's (2002) account of World Vision's efforts to address HIV/AIDS in Thailand reveals that learning to be effective—that is, to develop appropriate program strategies for changing behaviors of those affected—evolved slowly over a ten-year period. Regarding prudent leadership, pressures for sustainability can trap NGOs in a time bind that pits the immediacies of funding demands against the gradual pace of organization learning that promotes Dobel's virtue of "disciplined reasoning and openness." The prudent leader would do well, as Johnson and Wilson (1999, 47) advise, to look beyond the sustainability catchword to focus on sustainable development *not only* as an end *but also* as a means to support the "security of livelihoods and resource use for future generations."

Returning to Smillie and Hailey's study of strong NGO leaders in South Asia, it follows that Dobel's model of prudent leadership clarifies the three key timing issues they raise. First, in regard to organization creation during times of political adversity, founding leaders should expect longer time horizons for reaching organizational maturity than would be the case within placid or supportive environments (2002, 163). In *The Nursing Father: Moses as a Political Leader*, the late (and great) policy analyst Aaron Wildavsky discusses how Moses's "career" began as a "passive leader of a passive people" amid the Egyptian regime of slavery:

> With a passivity bordering on aggression (Why me! Poor me! Woe is me!), Moses bargains [with the Almighty] for greater resources, commensurate with his task. The complaints of modern administrators about insufficient authority to fulfill their responsibilities receive a supporting echo. But it can never be. Authority has got to be less than responsibility or the task would be completed before it was begun. Closing that gap is what leadership is all about. (Wildavsky 1984, 60)

Moses had to learn institutional leadership on the job amid government's (Pharaoh's) suspicions, just as the founding leaders of the Bangladesh Rehabilitation Assistance Committee and PROSHIKA maneuvered around the governmental hostility to NGOs in Bangladesh (Smillie and Hailey 2002, 163). Prudent leadership through these adversities demands "foresight [over] the long term" (Dobel 1999, 199–201) to weigh accommodative, survival strategies to ease tensions in the short term against the risks of compromising rights-advancement opportunities in the future. Regarding the latter, Vanessa Pupavac (2006) draws on her experiences working for the UN Criminal Tribunal for the former Yugoslavia to urge leaders of relief organizations to grasp "the politics of emergency" that could inadvertently perpetuate rights abuses in weak states. Riak comments on similar concerns in reference to World Vision's relief efforts linked with peacekeeping in Sudan and warns NGOs not to succumb to the "tyranny of the urgent" (2000, 503; also see Anderson 1999). Focusing on the long run, Wildavsky illustrates how Moses made several stylistic "U-turns" in his leadership as political cultures shifted from slavery to anarchy (among his followers), to equity, and ultimately to hierarchy (1984, 25). More contemporarily, Jordan and van Tuijl point out how changing legitimacy logics imposed by governments and global institutions affect the external stakeholder expectations placed on NGOs (2007, 3–20).

Second, prudent leaders need to anticipate that the internal work of developing "a distinct organization culture" and of aligning core values with management systems and structures (see Padaki 2002)—often evolving from earlier periods of strong (founder) leadership direction—takes considerable time and effort. Hailey argues that instituting viable organization learning, in the absence of the miracles Moses had working for him, constitutes no small undertaking. He maintains that NGOs are no more "naturally good learners" than business firms or government agencies and that the success of learning cultures depends on "the attitude of the leadership towards learning: at the heart of a learning organisation is a 'learning leader'" (Hailey and James 2002, 398).

Third, and related to the other two points, Smillie and Hailey focus on "the role of time in determining the type of leadership required" (2002, 164). But as the organization assesses this need, those in leadership positions need time to develop or refine their skill capacities related to persuasive appeal, risk taking, and the concept of leadership apart from management functions.

Management Control Functions in a Rights-Based Context

Although the thrust of this chapter directs attention to the nuances of leading dynamic or emergent organizations, some attention to the more conventional management control functions (related to planning and evaluation, human resources management, budgeting, and information technologies) is warranted to the extent that they impede or enable rights-based advocacy in NGOs. Since the managerial implications of planning and evaluation protocols arise often in chapters 3 and 5, and chapter 8 is devoted entirely to human resources management, this section will focus on budgeting and IT related to rights-based leadership. Although budgeting generally enjoys prominence as a core management theme, comprehensive treatments of NGO budget strategies, processes, and document preparation are conspicuously "missing and unaccounted for" in the development and human-rights-advocacy literatures. The paucity of articles on IT applications in NGOs appears more understandable given the recent evolution of these technological tools. Each of the following discussions is premised on the assertion that these management control issues are relevant *not simply as* constraints imposed on NGOs but as learning opportunities for building internal capacity and for monitoring how other powerful entities honor or violate people's rights and human agency.

Budgeting Dilemmas and Opportunities

Commentaries on budgeting and budget processes in the NGO literature are in short supply. In business and government, hierarchal budget authority enables managers (in varying measures) to plan strategically, manage the acquisition and utilization of funds, and control how funded activities are carried out (Schick

1966/1992, 261). But in the NGO context, the specter of centralized budget authority runs counter to core development values that "put the poor, disenfranchised, or rights-deprived *first*" in planning and allocating recourses for themselves. Three community development professionals begin their article on "bottom-up learning" with the following illustration subtitled "What's Wrong With This Picture?"

> In 1995, a leading international NGO (INGO) fielded two community organisers in Harare, Zimbabwe, to live and work with residents of two different urban poor areas. In the ensuing months, the organisers unhurriedly tried to encourage "bottom-up" development: building on the local people's material resources, creativity, knowledge, and views. . . . Hoping their bosses would come to understand the communities' perspectives and adjust their expectations, they resisted pressure from headquarters to spend money. . . . In the end, . . . the organisers finally relented. The funding tap was turned on, and the INGO reported to donors in 1997 that the projects were reaching their targeted benchmarks. (Power, Maury, and Maury 2002, 272)

These authors identify the "problem in the picture" as the INGO using operational control over the budget as a convenient opportunity to show donors results of funds put to good use, "especially in an environment where funds are becoming difficult to obtain, and bilateral donors are demanding tighter controls" (Cammack 1997, 79). In essence, budget authority was directed backward as an accountability contortion to keep the money flowing. Power et al. refer to this problem as the "alien-hand syndrome," a symptom of

> an organisational learning disorder "which involves a disconnection between organisation intentions and actions. . . . Organisations may have clear goals and well-defined routines, yet lack adequate incentives to ensure that actions are consistent with intentions" (Snyder and Cummings 1998). An alien-hand syndrome afflicting INGOs has its origins in a model of organisation and learning borrowed from the for-profit world that is inappropriate to the goals and outcomes of development initiatives, but that is nonetheless beneficial to the INGOs' survivability. (Power, Maury, and Maury 2002, 274)

By contrast to Power, Maury, and Maury's Harare example where spending characterizes "good budgeting," financial accountability in the government sector typically coordinates strategic planning, management control, and operational control in ways that promote frugality. In terms of strategic planning in NGOs, some characterize budgeting as the costing out of goal-directed activities identified in logical frameworks as project proposals (e.g., see Patra 2007)—note that this budget behavior defers to the authority of donor agencies rather than enhances NGO capability. With regard to operational control (i.e., "the process of assuring that specific tasks are carried out efficiently and effectively"; Schick 1966/1992, 261), Ahmad suggests that NGO managers can use budget controls as means to exact performance improvement from those working in the field (2002, 183–84). Presumably, rights-based leaders would think long and hard before passing along donor-imposed pressures for results to the most vulnerable and least compensated among the NGO workforce.

Although the literature on NGO budgeting is sparse, development and advocacy agencies need nonetheless to develop budgeting strategies not so much to amass control as to complement organization capacity building and competence. Conceivably, somewhere in-between cost budgeting in logframe preparation and worrying about performance in the context of *separate projects*, NGO leaders must attend to meeting payrolls and other operating expenses on a month-to-month basis with an eye toward NGO mission. Undoubtedly, managers should craft a semblance of an operating document from disparate revenue sources—perhaps from multiple projects and funders—as a basis for covering expenses. One solution to the management control question is simply to adopt business management routines as some state-of-the-art system, as packaged by management consultants—just waiting to be adopted by NGOs. Two management consultants attest to the success of the Cambodia Trust, an NGO that produces prosthetic limbs for mobility-impaired people, in adopting the ISO 9000, a business management system (Walsh and Lenihan 2006). (It is worth noting that the Cambodia Trust was the only manufacturing, or "widget-making," NGO encountered in writing this book.) But another management expert strikes a hopeful chord in his article titled "Finance: Friend or Foe?" that casts budgeting and accounting skills as a means to strengthen NGO capacity (Cammack 1997). In this regard, Cammack proposes that NGO staffs collectively undertake learning initiatives to become competent in using accounting tools, interpreting financial statements, and understanding internal control systems so as to embed these capabilities throughout the organization (1997, 80).

If NGO professionals can rise above their money-phobic tendencies, they could marshal a shared understanding of financial management principles to monitor how governments live up to their human rights commitments. In a report published by the Center for Victims of Torture, Kgamphe argues that since "the budget is the key policy instrument used by a government to ensure that things happen," NGOs can "follow the money" using government budgets as a monitoring tool for assessing rights implementation (Cornell, Kelsch, and Palasz 2004, 6–7). Kgamphe illustrates how knowing the mechanics of budget processes leads to effective rights monitoring in her analysis of the South African government's efforts in enforcing political, socioeconomic, and environmental rights as constitutionally mandated. Specifically, she outlines the five steps the Children's Budget Unit (CBU), a research arm of the NGO Idasa, followed in tracing governmental responses in upholding these rights:

1. Determine the nature of the government's legal obligations.
2. Measure the extent of child poverty.
3. Review program conceptualization and design.
4. Analyze budget allocations and expenditures.
5. Make recommendations.

Consequently, this NGO's ongoing budget analysis on behalf of child rights yields prestige and respect not only among its network of advocate collaborators but within the government as well:

> The CBU continues to use this tactic. New information is constantly being generated and used widely by policy makers, advocacy groups, and the general public. We have also formed closer partnerships with other organizations. Because we had the right information at a time when the government needed it, we have developed a good working relationship with the National Treasury, which has led to our participation in government task forces, increasing our influence in promoting our policy recommendations. (Kgamphe 2004, 15)

Thus, Idasa has institutionalized its analytical competency of government budgeting to leverage its advocacy capability. In *Human Rights and Development*, Peter Uvin recommends "knowing the human rights law machinery" (2004, 139–40) as a rights-based strategy. That, in turn, can only be strengthened by a research capability to "follow the money" in budget (in)actions involving implementation.

In summary, rights-based leadership calls for a proactive stance in integrating finance and budget expertise into operating procedures and into organization learning throughout the organization. A widely shared knowledge of budget principles and processes provide a realistic political perspective for program development and a platform from which to monitor government actions in fulfilling its rights commitments.

Information Technology and Rights-Based Organizations: Dilemmas, Responsibilities, and Opportunities

IT encompasses a wide range of computer-aided communication processes (from simple word processing to large-scale interorganization coordination systems) that frequently pose dilemmas for those using them or those affected by their implementation. Jane Fountain captures the significance of such dilemmas in the first paragraph of her influential book *Building the Virtual State*:

> In governments around the globe, from Indianapolis to India, from San Francisco to Singapore, policymakers view the Internet either as a force to increase the responsiveness of government to its citizens or as a means to further empower the state. In developing nations, new wireless information and communication technologies signal an unprecedented opportunity to hasten the pace of development and connection to the developed world. . . . In authoritarian regimes, the Internet threatens domination by the state over information and communication but at the same time, paradoxically, serves as an instrument of consummate state surveillance and control over society. (Fountain 2001, 3)

At a symbolic level, the chasm between IT as a tool of Northern institutions and the realities of poor societies in the South is blatant. In fact, Chambers argues that the rapidly changing character of the technology magnifies these opposing realities (1997, 4).

Chambers also extends this imagery of IT as a Northern weapon in his description of the World Bank as a "frightening" institution: "It comprises the greatest single mass of development professionals in the world. It is an extraordinary concentration of clever people connected with each other through computer networking, and through e-mail, fax, and telephone" (1997, 97). In this regard, the centrality of IT in neoliberal development ideology is evident in program justifications in World Bank project documents. For example, a report on the Thailand-Rural Information Empowerment Project states,

> Information technology is increasingly recognized as an effective tool in rural, social, and economic development, in that it can improve the efficiency of governance, the targeting of social services, the building of communities, the cost-effective access of local producers to markets and to market information. The World Bank has considerable experience in innovation funds as well as in designing programs for IT access. More importantly, it has been able to draw together different constituencies working towards a common purpose. These include government, civil society, the IT hardware and software communities, and the rural business community. (World Bank 2001)

Although IT should not necessarily stand guilty by its association with neoliberal agendas, NGOs contemplating its benefits may do well to acknowledge how IT has been championed by the World Bank and other Northern institutions.

With varying degrees of success, government bureaucracies have drawn on IT to institutionalize e-government (Internet communication with citizens or businesses), agency internal networks (coordinating actions within a bureaucracy), and cross-agency integration among several bureaucracies (Fountain 2001, 98–100). Although some IT systems merely facilitate information sharing, others in government are designed as management control systems intended to govern work output—and, in so doing, minimize human discretion (see, e.g., Fountain 2001, 167–92; Currie and Proctor 2002; Boonstra, Boddy, and Fischbacher 2004).

By contrast, rights-based NGOs are considerably less likely to impose information management systems as management control strategies, if for no other reason than because the thrust of aggressive management control so blatantly counteracts the core values of team-directed work and organization learning that many organizations espouse (see Padaki 2002). Nonetheless, development and rights-advocacy NGOs need low-end computer systems to sustain ongoing research efforts and to retrieve and disseminate vital advocacy information. For example, an NGO focusing on public health improvement in Nepal relies on microcomputers to publish monthly reports concerning tuberculosis patients in the region (Wells 1993, 36–37). NGOs can also use computerized information sharing as a basis for creating and mobilizing "virtual networks," or, as Brinkerhoff (2005) calls them, "digital diasporas," for combining development and advocacy efforts. For example, one such virtual network, the Communication Initiative, describes its function as

> an online space for sharing the experiences of, and building bridges between, the people and organisations engaged in or supporting communication as a fundamental strategy for economic and social development and change. It does this through a process of initiating dialogue and debate and giving the network a stronger, more representative and informed voice with which to advance the use and improve the impact of communication for development. (Heimann 2006, 603)

Heimann elaborates on five specific areas of the Communication Initiative's activity: knowledge websites, electronic newsletters, network communications, virtual interactive processes, and strategic review and critique initiatives (2006, 605–7). The relationships between IT networks and knowledge management will be explored in the following chapter on organization learning.

Nonetheless, field-based agencies that utilize computer systems typically cope with a variety of technical frustrations related to the acquisition of appropriate hardware and software, the availability of needed system support, and the training needs of nontechnical staff members. In regard to acquisition, NGOs must either budget for computer-related costs in their donor funding proposals or accept donated equipment and software that may or may not match their needs and capabilities. Technical support (to install the system, protect it from viruses, and repair and maintain it) may not be readily available in isolated locales (Wells 1993). Thus, NGO managers must grapple with a number of "small" technical problems in order to enable their staffs to utilize technology in support of development and advocacy work.

NGOs' interests in IT should range beyond simply how computer systems can be utilized in-house to analyzing how and why powerful institutions affecting development and human rights—most notably, donors and government bureaucracies—implement sophisticated IT systems. The rationale for this argument is twofold. First, on occasion, locally based NGOs are called on as "grassroots intermediaries" to facilitate the large-scale adoption of IT innovations (e.g., "government-to-people" e-gov systems) within a particular community (see Cecchini and Scott 2003). Presumably, prudence would demand that a rights-based organization diligently grasp both the system's logic and the cultural, social, and political implications of that logic—especially those with

the potential to promote or compromise human freedoms—before it endorses
the innovation.

Second, just as budgeting provides a window for observing government's
actual resolve in taking (or avoiding) rights-enabling action, the design and
implementation of IT in government offers a lens for ascertaining how bureaucracies work. Furthermore, since IT arrangements are by nature *sociotechni-
cal systems*—that is, the interaction of people (a social system) with tools and
techniques (see Trist 1981)—people working within the agency affect how the
IT innovation is actually implemented. Thus, Fountain refers to *enacted technology* (in contrast to *objective technology*, as designed) as the way technology
may be altered or enhanced by those at the operating levels in bureaucracy that
put the system to use (2001, 10–4). Since it sheds light on the internal politics
surrounding system implementation, this enactment perspective alerts analysts to the possibilities of conflict, resistance, and dissent inside government
bureaucracies—or, for that matter, key global aid institutions. As mentioned
previously, Peter Uvin claims that *human rights is a political matter* (2004, 134)
and that rights work depends on astute political analysis of power centers. That
said, attention to IT utilization in powerful institutions can simultaneously
uncover potentially divergent official government goals (related to IT use),
managerial priorities within relevant bureaucracies, and who the players are in
the intra-agency politics of enacting IT.

Some examples help in clarifying both rationales for analyzing how IT
implementation processes and outcomes may affect human rights. With regard
to NGOs assuming the roles as "grassroots intermediaries" in governmental IT
projects, the World Bank–assisted Gyandoot program to institute an e-government system in rural India is illustrative. Established in 2000, the Gyandoot
is an intranet system intended to connect citizens with the Dhar district government through computer kiosks. In this structural adjustment venture, the
Dhar government collaborates with the Gyandoot Samiti, an NGO that manages the project. As one analyst relates, governmental purposes in providing for
the Gyandoot are twofold:

> First, to increase the international economic position of the nation
> by building on the success of the Indian software export industry;
> second, by developing programs of "IT for the Masses" (in the words
> of a recent Government of India report) that would play a critical
> role in solving the as yet unsolved problems of development that
> beset large sectors of the Indian population. (Keniston 2002, n.p.)

The Gyandoot's successes are connected with its capability to leverage social capital, or human goodwill, in attempting to reach citizens with little or no experience using computers (Batchelor et al. 2003).

Nonetheless, the weaknesses of the Gyandoot system are readily identifiable as (1) technical failures (in particular, irregularity in the electric power supply), (2) generally low usage, (3) insufficient revenue for sustainability, (4) few services actually used, and (5) nonparticipation of the poor. Specifically, a World Bank–Centre for Electronic Governance (CEG) study reports that the poor are typically unaware that the Gyandoot exists or that it was intended for "common people" (CEG 2002, 25). Furthermore, the study discloses that the perception of the traditional caste barrier discourages system use by the rural poor (p. 25). On the other hand, educated farmers are attracted to the Gyandoot as a source of reliable commodity data that are necessary for maintaining their positions in the marketplace. Although the efforts of the NGO Gyandoot Samiti are probably commendable, there is little evidence here of rights empowerment on behalf of the poor. Instead, it appears that the NGO assisted the Dhar government (and the World Bank) by offering conveniences for farmers who had *already achieved prosperity*.

Examples of IT endeavors revealing bureaucratic behaviors that enable human rights can be found in some of China's municipal governments. Under pressures related to China's entry into the World Trade Organization and criticisms of its response to the SARS outbreak, the central government encourages municipal efforts to promote government transparency through creation of e-government systems. But the dilemma (and *opportunity*) for bureaucrats centered on how to enact the principles of "rule of law" into system design and utilization in a society lacking rule-of-law protections in its central government. Referring to the general issue of administrative reform for democratizing Chinese society, Kenneth Foster explains,

The challenge lies in increasing transparency, accountability, and responsiveness while political leaders, as cadres of the Chinese Communist Party, remain in crucial ways both above the law and not beholden to public opinion. What local-level democratizing reforms can do in China, at the present time, is to make officials more accountable and responsive to the public even while they retain final and unquestioned authority over political decisions. The question is, what does it take to make this happen? (Foster 2005, 97)

In its 2006 symposium on open government in China's municipalities, the journal *Government Information Quarterly* published a number of articles in which municipal committees (i.e., government agencies) describe their work in crafting administrative rules (called "provisions") and institutional norms for operating e-gov systems in their respective cities of Shanghai and Guangzhou (Guangzhou Municipal Government Legal Affairs Office 2006a, 11–17; Guangzhou Municipal Government Legal Affairs Office 2006b, 18–27; Qiao 2006, 28–35; Shanghai Municipal People's Government 2006, 36–47). In formulating administrative rules, these committees—as do government bureaucracies in most societies—define and clarify relevant terminology (what precisely is meant by "open," "information," "disclosure," etc.), identify the sensitive and contradictory areas of "open-government" implementation (e.g., how to handle classified or proprietary government information), develop guidelines for how the contradictory issues should be handled (exempted information must be the *exception*; disclosure must be the rule), and establish evaluative standards for assessing e-gov effectiveness. With regard to norms, the nature and tone of these administrative rules create a culture of openness in centers of dense urban populations. Uvin argues that a rights perspective should focus on monitoring how (or whether) governments implement the rule of law. These accounts of e-gov in China's municipalities offer rights advocates glimpses of rule of law "in the making" within a society that severely limits political and civil rights. Although central government interference in municipal e-gov is theoretically possible, the democratic enactment by IT bureaucrats coaxes "the genie out of the bottle" for the world, and the World Trade Organization, to see.

Leaders in rights-based organizations are more likely attentive to acquiring appropriate low-end IT for professional staff use than to impose management control systems that structure work. NGOs that facilitate IT innovations on behalf of funding institutions or governments bear responsibilities of ascertaining whether their efforts actually enhance rights or freedoms. In addition, it is suggested here that NGOs can benefit by scrutinizing how rights-pertinent IT systems are institutionalized and implemented in government.

Conclusion

A footnote appearing in an influential book on leadership in government agencies reads as follows: "According to the *Compact Oxford English Dictionary*, Janus is the 'name of an ancient Italian deity, regarded as the doorkeeper of heaven and the guardian of doors and gates, and as presiding over the entrance upon or beginning of things, represented with a face in the front and another on the back of the head.' The term *Janus-faced* often means duplicitous or two-faced" (Terry 1995, 183). Larry Terry uses this Janus figure to convey two faces of institutional leadership, one directed at virtuous public service but the other in an opposite direction toward morally questionable tactics (p. 173). In a more general sense, the Janus imagery meaningfully summarizes the nature of management in rights-oriented NGOs, although in a less melodramatic fashion for bureaucratic executives. In regard to development, two faces of leadership could be expected of NGO managers who must straddle the North–South chasm between donor expectations for governance structures with top-down accountability and value commitments within the organizations that put beneficiaries first. Here, the two faces of leadership do not appear so much duplicitous or ethically compromising as prudent in reconciling the formal and informal natures of the organization.

Furthermore, an NGO leader's intentions to buffer the informal organization from powerful, external demands can be understood as principled managerial practice of adapting core rights-grounded values that mimic the normative power of human rights cultures. In effect, it is incumbent on leaders to run interference against tight funding standards in ways that allow professional staffs ample room to maneuver in addressing particular needs. The potential for creating maneuvering room for the informal organization to work effectively within context is especially promising in NGOs that can tap into local financial support or diversify their funding sources. Those who manage in-country or in-field offices need to recognize the intercultural differences in internationally diverse workforces relating to such issues as hierarchal power, risk assumption, conflict resolution, and gender roles.

The moral stridency in calls for participatory approaches in development serves on one hand to energize, but on the other hand to disarm, NGO leaders in attending to empowerment. On the positive side, leaders can capitalize on the appeal of the participation message, so influential as to penetrate global funding institutions—for example, as part and parcel of World Bank projects to raise living standards in particular regions. Thus, the resonance of the participation ideal offers NGOs cover for interpersonal work in communities not typically associated with impressive benefit-cost ratios. Yet on the other hand, the best of intentions directed toward participatory empowerment inevitably raises questions of representation, or precisely who should represent the concerns, needs, and outlook of the community involved. Connected with this

representation conundrum is encountering poor people's passivity and deference in articulating their circumstance and goals. As Janus figures, NGO leaders confront institutional dilemmas that pit time-consuming, one-on-one skill
building against pressure to scale up those empowerment efforts on a cost-
effective basis.

If human rights work is indeed political by nature, then managers in
rights-focused NGOs must take on roles as political leaders capable of prudently orchestrating resources and tactics for sustainable accomplishment—
the claiming of human agency over the long term. Leadership that is dedicated
to political accomplishment calls on managers to acquire an acute sense of timing that can exploit opportunities and circumvent obstacles as they arise. In essence, the Janus face of the shrewd tactician converges with that of the virtuous
enabler through competent judgments of timing, foresight, and trust building.

For the most part, the thrust of commentary on NGO management has
stressed the "softer," more intricate, skill areas—such as positioning the informal organization, working with cultures, enabling participation, and timing
an accomplishment—more so than the application of conventional control
functions (e.g., budgeting) in NGO settings. Nonetheless, NGOs stand to
benefit from organization learning that diffuses competencies related to budgeting and IT throughout the organization.

Discussion Issues

1. A commitment to "minimum specs"—or a deliberate effort to
   rely on *only* a few simple rules—facilitates collaborative efforts
   within the informal organization. Identify and articulate *three*
   basic rules that could serve a rights-focused NGO well as "minimum specs."
2. How would you encourage an NGO employee raised in a risk-
   aversive culture to assume responsibilities that involve uncertainty and risk taking?
3. Discuss the risks that NGO managers assume by encouraging
   professionals to pursue empowerment through one-on-one interactions.
4. In regard to timing, would it be more advantageous for an
   empowerment-oriented NGO (such as Tostan) to seek funding
   from a large global or bilateral aid agency later in the organization's life cycle than in its first few years of existence? Why or
   why not?

5. Identify a US president (or historical leader in any national set-
   ting) whose "impeccable sense of timing" could be emulated by
   NGO leaders directed toward accomplishment in human rights.
   Explain your reasoning.

5

Performance and Accountability in Rights-Focused NGOs

As advocates of particular ideals, aid institutions such as US Agency for Development (USAID) and UK Department for International Development (DFID) expect the NGOs they fund to transform program intentions ideals into reality. Imagine for a moment that you lead an NGO working in Zimbabwe that strives to empower local citizen involvement in the midst of a repressive political regime. Your principal donor, USAID, requests that you validate how effectively the NGO has worked to strengthen democratic governance in its work with citizens as a basis for future funding decisions. Clearly, the ongoing solvency of the project hangs in the balance.

Since the aid agency expects your organization to persuade government to adopt policies that permit more local autonomy, it asks you to assess the NGO's efforts along a number of criteria, such as whether your NGO

- systematically consults the public about the government policy in question,
- formulates a viable alternative to the government's existing policy, and
- builds coalitions and networks to mobilize support for the policy alternative.

Specifically, you are asked to respond to each of these (and others) along a 1-to-5 rating scale from "very little capacity/a lot of room for improvement" to "capacity is very strong/almost no room for improvement" (this example is adapted from Hirschmann 2002, 23–24).

At first, it might appear that your NGO is clearly on the defensive, as it may in fact be, but Hirschmann explains that in this particular case, USAID worked face-to-face with its partner organizations in Zimbabwe to adapt these advocacy criteria to NGO realities "on the ground." Furthermore, NGO representatives participated with USAID officials to construct the criteria in this instrument and approved certain "principles of evaluation" that specify how this advocacy study will be used by the aid agency (2002, 23–29).

On one hand, the example shows the obvious—that nearly all organizations stand accountable to those who exercise authority over them, especially funding authority. But other issues surface as well: (1) accountability demands oblige organizations to meet specified performance objectives, and in turn those organizations can demonstrate accountability by providing evidence of performance; (2) organizations may enjoy some latitude in managing the terms by which they are held accountable if they are offered the chance to explain circumstances affecting what can be done; and (3) advocacy organizations (e.g., Hirschmann's grassroots organizations in Zimbabwe) attempt to hold *others accountable* (government officials), while answering to the expectations of the aid institution (USAID) supporting them. However, this example is not so clear with regard to the issue of *impact*. Does it necessarily follow that NGOs rating low on the advocacy criteria have little or no impact in civic life in Zimbabwe or that others scoring high will leave lasting beneficial impacts? Measures of performance can serve as predictors of impact but fall short of demonstrating sustainable accomplishment, which can only be realized over time.

The USAID–Zimbabwe example suggests that issues of performance, accountability, and the relationship between them tend to be more problematic and open to interpretation than commonly presumed. This chapter coaxes out multiple meanings of both and shows how these alternative understandings relate to various NGO contexts. First, four interpretations of performance—as production protocols, competence, results, and (rate of) productivity—are considered in reference to NGO work. Second, four contexts of NGO accountability—answering to stakeholders, managing expectations, holding others accountable, and managing others' expectations—emerge in integrating two alternative understandings of accountability, (answerability and managed expectations) with respective obligations to stand accountable and to demand rights accountability of other actors. The final section repositions the performance and accountability issues within the broader scope of impact assessment. Related to rights-based organizations, the contours of performance, accountability, and impact run along two dissonant counterpoints. The first—the commonsensical and matter-of-fact—conveys that NGOs must answer to those who support them. The second—the realistic and problematic—follows the contextual nuances and ambiguities encountered in missions to influence behaviors and power relationships in efforts to promote human rights.

Performance and Accountability: Critical Challenges for Rights-Based Leadership

What is it about performance and accountability that confounds leadership in most organizations in general and rights-focused NGOs in particular? Among many plausible explanations, four appear especially pertinent to NGO settings. First, those who demand accountability and evidence of performance are often detached from those directly affected by the agency's efforts.[1] Second, it is difficult to agree on specific definitions for performance and accountability in a particular agency setting; some suggest that it is more reasonable to approach both as conversations or debates (about the actual meanings of either) than as narrow and precise definitions.[2] Third, reforms to strengthen accountability and performance generally call for standards to be applied across the board as universal criteria for performance measurement, but human rights concerns typically relate to particular contexts.[3] Fourth, methods to strengthen accountability and performance essentially simplify what is in reality quite complex.[4]

Organization theorists differentiate between closed-systems and open-systems perspectives on organizations: the former focuses only on issues interacting within the defined boundaries of the system, while the latter scans a broad array of external influences and probes deeper, more intricate subsystem components. In development work, accountability- and performance-based systems (e.g., the logframe) simplify NGO efforts within a closed-systems perspective of issues important to stakeholders with funding authority, even though development is by nature complex. Fowler explains,

> The further one moves from tangible NGO outputs—wells built, credit provided, trees planted, people trained, buildings constructed and so on—to impacts on people's lives, the more significant become less tangible factors such as socio-economic divisions, power relationships, human motivation, individual and collective behaviour, cultural values, and local organisational capacity. In other words, where it matters most, at the end of the aid chain, human development results from a complex mix of non-linear processes which are largely determined by non-project factors. This means that the actual change in people's lives is contingent: it is an open system. (Fowler 1996, 59)

Moreover, performance measurement closes the system by positioning the user (or evaluator) *outside* of that under scrutiny. This makes sense in traditional rigors of scientific inquiry where *objectivity* depends on impartiality in measurement. Yet it is often the case that the roles and behaviors of users affect how the organization functions; in other words, they are part of the open-systems picture.

Performance issues related to rights advancement clearly stand out as critical leadership questions. Later in this chapter, concerns about performance measurement are woven into a broader discussion of impact assessment that broadens the performance focus in relation to the wide range of various stakeholder interests. The next two sections examine multiple meanings of performance and accountability in support of a third discussion of impact assessment as a tool for "making sense" of what rights-based NGOs accomplish.

Performance in the Rights-Based Organization

"Results, of course!" is what donors expect of rights-based organizations. Yet those donors could find it difficult to clarify what they mean: what kinds of results, based on whose definitions of (human rights) goals, how significant those results are and on what scale, and so on. Indeed, "results" constitute the critical element in the logical framework—a published guideline for crafting the logframe maintains that "outputs describe WHAT you want the project to deliver. . . . If you provide the necessary resources, you can hold the project team directly accountable for achieving these results" (Centre for International Development and Training n.d., 7; uppercase in original). In terms of leadership, these issues center on the basic question "What is performance?" in both the general sense and as related to human rights advocacy and human development work in particular.

Performance and accountability, as mentioned previously, assume a multiplicity of meanings, as administrative theorist Melvin Dubnick comments:[5]

> Outside of any specific context, performance can be associated with a range of actions from the simple and mundane act of opening a car door, to the staging of an elaborate reenactment of the Broadway musical *Chicago*. In all these forms, performance stands in distinction from mere behavior in implying some degree of intent. A performance in these senses is a behavior motivated or guided by some intent or purpose—whether it is to exit a vehicle or to entertain a paying audience. (Dubnick 2005, 391)

Dubnick tries to extract some analytic sense out of this "looseness of meaning" by differentiating among specific types of performance (see table 5.1) based on two criteria: the quality of action performed and the quality of what has been achieved as a result of the action.

Although each of Dubnick's four types of performance shown in the table relates to human rights work, each varies according to its perceived importance among stakeholders and the burdens it places on organization leaders. Consider each of these types in regard to rights-based work and leadership.

Production. This, according to Dubnick, is performance "in the broadest and narrowest senses of that term. For example, we speak of theatrical productions as the staging of performances. We also speak to manufacturing forms of production that are associated with the design and operation of machinery and foster a machine view of work. In the first case we think about the performance/role as a scripted and ritualistic endeavor that allows for interpretation by the performing agent" (2005, 392). Most organizations have established systems, protocols, and procedures that guide how work is performed. In this regard, critics of "the development industry" (mentioned in chapter 3) may consider the mechanics of logframe planning as a ritualistic endeavor that may or may not be effective in empowering people.

Competence. This second mode of performance directs attention to the knowledge bases and analytical skills of NGO personnel responsible for carrying out critical work. Dubnick explains,

Table 5.1
Varying Modes of Performance

		The quality of action performed	
		Low	**High**
	Low	Production	Competence
The quality of what has been achieved as a result of the action	**High**	Results	Productivity

Source. See Dubnick, Melvin J. "Accountability and the Promise of Performance: In Search of the Mechanisms." *Public Performance and Management Review* 28, no. 3 (2005): 376–417.

Anyone can read a recipe and think of themselves a halfway decent cook, but a professional chef is a cook with a level of knowledge, experience, and skill that allows us to define cooking performance at a different level than merely producing a meal. Under the assumption that a highly competent performer will be more likely to generate more and better quality output from an activity most of the time, performance becomes associated with the competence of the performer. (Dubnick 2005, 392)

Competence—or "distinctive competence" (Korten 1980, 495)—and personnel capacity building are especially critical in rights-based NGOs that need to command formidable knowledge bases of the social, political, and legal contexts in which they function. Yet the fact remains that *competence*, as vital as it is to human rights work, does not in itself constitute accomplishment in the form of tangible *results* or *productivity*. Thus, the NGO leader faces the dilemma of, on the one hand, investing scarce resources into necessary competence-building activities but, on the other, of convincing external stakeholders that the organization's capacity to perform is tantamount to actual performance. In other words, leaders must argue that competence-development initiatives are legitimate proxies (or substitute indicators) for accomplishment. In terms of institutional leadership, it becomes incumbent on NGO officials to advance discourses that outline a cognitive connection between staff competency and tangible results. NGO leaders are more likely to make that case among stakeholders and particularly donors, who are themselves knowledgeable about the intricacies of human rights work than among those who are not.

Results. As suggested previously, results command the attention of those intending to pass judgment on NGO performance. Results can be simply defined as *what is produced* rather than as the means of *production* (discussed previously) or rate of efficiency as *productivity* (to be discussed next). Dubnick adds that results are typically expressed in terms of the quantifiable or of popularity and demand (2005, 393). In the NGO setting, logframe planning and management tools align development project inputs with certain results based on appropriate intervention and implementation strategies.

Leaders in rights-based organizations confront a number of obstacles in demonstrating *results* to prospective donors and other external stakeholders, two of which merit particular attention. First, some NGOs enable others outside the organization to achieve sustainable results. Second, a focus on results, or the ends, typically discounts the value of instrumental efforts, or the means (like competence building), toward achieving results. But those committed to rights empowerment, particularly as understood in Sen's (1999) capacity-building approach, interpret the means of empowerment as both *ends and means*. In reality, some of the results claims that NGO leaders might assert straddle Dubnick's distinction between *competence* (or capacity building) and discrete *results*. For example, Uvin underscores the importance of building networks and forging alliances with other rights-sensitive organizations (2004, 165). Does success in establishing a network constitute a tangible result, a means of competence building, or a bit of both?

Productivity. Also known as cost-effectiveness, *productivity* is sweet music to the ears of reformers who would impose business-like efficiency criteria on organizations outside the private sector. Dubnick defines productivity simply as "the ratio of output to input for a given production unit under given conditions" and adds,

> From this perspective, performance is comprised of those actions that shape or determine the different factors in the production function. This can include decisions or acts regarding the mix of inputs, how they will be processed, what technologies will be used, where and when the production occurs, the disposition of outputs, and so on. (Dubnick 2005, 394)

Thus, productivity depends on limiting the production costs of benefits expected from the organization's efforts.

Can such a mechanical, bottom-line calculation work in rights-based organizations that have difficulty documenting results? Dubnick's continued discussion offers some clues: "Productivity performance has been a major issue in policing, for example, where competing views of the field's production function have generated considerable debate over the years. With regard to U.S. law enforcement, the debate in recent years has pitted advocates of the traditional professional crime control against supporters of community-based prevention" (2005, 394). At first glance, analogies between community policing and rights advancement appear misguided if for no other reason than because police actions sometimes threaten people's rights. However, some parallels stand out: both advocate changing beliefs and behaviors in the community, both need to stand accountable while holding others accountable, and both promise positive impacts but cannot necessarily demonstrate tangible *results* early on.

A recent newspaper editorial commends the efforts of two city police officers for collaborating with urban planners in advocating for community policing in the downtown business district. The editorialist relates that the officers advocate coupling tried-and-true safety and crime-prevention practices with efforts to create a vibrant downtown. Here's what they suggest: (1) Use inventive lighting of buildings, parks and other key downtown areas to create a sense of excitement and safety [and] (2) Install lighting, trim trees and fix sidewalks in areas that look unsafe to people. . . . [One of the officers comments:] "With relatively little money, their ideas could literally be transformational for the city. People tend to focus on the big-dollar projects. Sometimes the really big changes are right in front of us and don't cost a lot of money." (Riley 2009, A26)

In similar fashion, Uvin points out the economic advantages of rights-based development over traditional approaches that require heavy funding up front:

It seems that as the focus shifts from services to rights, the exclusive focus on money shifts as well. . . . In [the] traditional development approach, money is at the heart of the game. . . . There is no development relationship without significant injections of money. In the rights-based approach to development, money is much less crucial, at least in the first run. What matters are organization capacity, mutual influence, internal and external accountability, exchange of innovation and ideas, mechanisms of voice and control and redress, inclusive processes of decision making, increased availability of information, improvements in policy making and the legal environments of justice and the like. While none of these comes for free (and none comes easily or rapidly), none of them depends solely or primarily on massive injections of external funding. (Uvin 2004, 165)

Uvin's comments suggest not only that *productivity* as a mode of performance resonates in the rights-based organizational setting but also that it can validate rights advocacy and development in economic terms and, in so doing, offers leaders a platform for demonstrating accountability and integrating efforts. In terms of articulating a message (for both internal and external consumption), rights-based leaders can advance the cost-effectiveness argument that sustainable impacts, which underwrite capacity building and knowledge-based work, can be expected from relatively modest costs.

In summary, the performance question challenges NGO leaders to focus on the moral and monetary values of investing in rights-based advocacy and development to change circumstances that are well outside their control. Clearly, leaders cannot guarantee grandiose results (such as abrupt policy reversals on the part of repressive governments), but changes *do happen*—as with the curtailment of female genital cutting as an outcome of a Senegalese NGO's educational training program (see Easton, Monkman, and Miles 2003). Recognizing that "performance" embraces a variety of meanings relevant to NGOs, rights-based leaders can articulate cogent but realistic responses to those who question their potential to improve human conditions. As discussed previously, the leadership message to both external and internal stakeholders could convey any or all of the following: (1) the organization maintains and enhances essential competencies in terms of production; (2) competencies poise the organization to achieve significant, tangible results; and (3) rights-based NGOs are well situated to positively impact the poor, disenfranchised, and victimized at a comparatively modest cost.

Accountability in the Rights-Based Organization

What is *accountability*, and what responsibilities does it place on NGOs in general and on rights-oriented NGOs in particular? Leaders need to work through these complex and contentious issues in order to justify the legitimacy of NGOs that strive to affect behaviors and events in the absence of government authority. First, in regarding the "what is accountability" question, some administrative theorists treat "accountability as answerability," while others understand "accountability as managed expectations." Answerability keys in on the one-on-one relationship between the party demanding compliance (with some explicit or implicit criteria) and the "account-giver" obliged to respond. By contrast, the managed expectations approach suggests that organizations improvise to accommodate multiple demands in particular contexts (or conditions) to negotiate the diverse and/or conflicting expectations placed on them (see, e.g., Romzek and Dubnick 1987; Dubnick 2005; Romzek 2011).

Commentators on NGO accountability use similar terms, such as *formal* or *practical* accountability (generally implying answerability) and *strategic* accountability whereby NGOs deal with the problem of "multiple accountability"—or managing expectations (see, e.g., Edwards and Hulme 1996; Biggs and Neame 1996; Jordan and van Tuijl 2007). But as Jordan and van Tuijl (2007) assert, the broad issue of NGO accountability needs to be assessed within a political framework that stresses these organizations' vulnerability amid governments, corporations, and global trade organizations primed to discredit or dissolve NGOs. These power structures could then frame the accountability issue as a means to redirect NGO missions toward their own agendas and interests. Although accountability is critically important to NGO leaders, it must be understood within its broader political context.

These political issues become even more sensitive among advocacy organizations and development agencies committed to human rights advancement. By their nature, these organizations *need to demand accountability from others* and convince powerful forces that rights initiatives indeed serve their interests—namely, influence how others manage their expectations. Critical of the accountability mandates placed on NGOs, Uvin interprets appeals for NGO accountability as an extension of historical patterns of deprivation imposed on poor societies:

> The question of accountability lies at the very heart of development. Many of the governments of poor countries are not accountable to their citizens. This is in part because of their history of colonization: the state was created to extract resources for Europeans rather than be accountable to its citizens, and that model of state-society relations has been continued after independence. It is maintained by the practice of development aid, which . . . maintains outward-oriented systems of accountability—all the more so after a few decades of Cold War politics and "blind" development aid. No technical progress is sustainable or beneficial to the poor without improvements in accountability. The rights-based approach has the merit to force this issue onto the agenda . . . because once one begins speaking about rights and claims, one automatically ends up talking about mechanisms of accountability. (Uvin 2004, 131–32)

In essence, Uvin encourages rights-claiming organizations to demand accountability from governments, funding agencies, donors, and corporations. Their authority to reverse the answerability relationship stems from their own (universal) rights apart from any authority delegated to them or regulations placed on them. This view is shared by other commentators who assert the rights and authority of legitimate human advancement organizations (see, e.g., Jordan and van Tuijl 2007; Peruzzotti 2007).

The balance of this section divides NGO accountability into four discussions that reflect alternative understandings of accountability and the nature of the accountability relationship. The rows in table 5.2 show the distinction between the "answerability" and the "managed expectations" accountability perspectives. The columns differentiate between the traditional accountability relationship, whereby external powers hold NGOs accountable, and rights

Table 5.2

Modes of Accountability in Rights-Based Organizations

	Outward-oriented system of political accountability (development, public service, and civil society missions)	Rights-claiming accountability (rights-advocacy mission)[a]
Accountability as answerability[b]	Report to the individual stakeholder—usually an aid agency—using its measures and formats	Hold other actors accountable through legal processes (justiceability) or other means
Accountability as managing expectations[b]	Prioritize multiplicity of stakeholder expectations—use development as a lever for rights advocacy	Influence how other actors manage expectations; show how a rights focus aligns with their interests

a. See Uvin, Peter. *Aiding Violence: The Development Enterprise in Rwanda*. Bloomfield, CT: Kumarian Press, 1998.
b. See Romzek, Barbara S. "Accountability and Contracting in a Networked Policy Arena: The Case of Welfare Reform." In *Accountable Governance: Problems and Promises*, edited by Melvin J. Dubnick and H. George Frederickson, 22–41. Armonk, NY: M. E. Sharpe, 2011.

claiming that reverses the relationship by holding those forces answerable for their behaviors affecting human rights. Note that the boundaries between the cells (interpretations of NGO accountability) are depicted as broken lines that imply some overlap, since (1) organizations may find some advantages in adopting mechanisms "to make themselves answerable," a proactive strategy in managing expectations, and (2) NGOs may be moving toward more assertiveness in promoting human rights causes; thus, the right column (NGO demanding accountability) represents an ideal for development agencies, as well as an apt description of some rights-advocacy organizations.

Answering to Stakeholders

Nearly all NGOs are held answerable to institutional donors that support their work, and some are subject to the intensive scrutiny of host governments. Few would dispute that NGOs are obliged to answer to funding agencies, but differences arise as to *how* NGOs should respond. On an abstract level, "answerability" appears synonymous with "compliant reporting," but it could as well be the case that account givers (such as NGOs) answer in ways that attempt to explain specific circumstances, perhaps justifying their work, or even redefine the complexity, uniqueness, nuances, and so forth of the issue at hand (see Dubnick 2005, 383). Note that the compliance interpretation corresponds to the upper-left cell in table 5.2, while explaining and redefining fit in the lower-left cell as expectations management strategies. For example, Northern bilateral aid agencies could ask the funded grassroots organizations to document how their advocacy-related activities align with the donors' priorities within the country or region (see Hirschmann 2002, 23). Some donors demand accountability through strict compliance with imposed formats, while others solicit NGOs' inputs in developing appropriate protocols for accounting purposes. In the latter case, the aid agency offers the NGO some latitude in explaining the contextual circumstances of their efforts, leaving their partners room to maneuver in their work (see Biggs and Neame 1996).

Donors appropriately hold NGOs accountable to ensure against misuse of funds, excessive administrative costs, lavish spending, and follow-through from their planning and implementation processes. It is vital for leaders to meet their regulative obligation to stand answerable in order to preserve NGO legitimacy in a competitive funding environment. However, critics claim that donor demands for upward accountability, especially if based on projected logframe outcomes, bureaucratize development in rights-related areas such as HIV/AIDS prevention, gender equality, advocacy, and other participatory initiatives (Wallace, Crowther, and Shepherd 1997; Wallace 2007). By Wallace's account, compliance reporting coerces development in ways that reinforce the power of Northern donors over the poor in the South, or as "ties that bind" that frustrate development agencies. For NGOs, these frustrations are compounded if aid flows from several funding agencies, each demanding its own reporting formats. More generally, upward accountability forces NGOs to elevate their obligations to powerful stakeholders over their responsibility to the mission (see Jordan and van Tuijl 2007, 5–8).

Governments also hold NGOs answerable, sometimes as a pretense for discouraging development- or advocacy-related activities that threaten the political status quo. Some regimes go so far as to register, license, regulate, and monitor NGOs to keep them on the straight and narrow. In the absence of rule of law and due process, governments can arbitrarily enhance or relax scrutiny through abrupt policy reversals that lack transparency. For instance, the government of Bangladesh, where over 12,000 NGOs operate, controls NGO behavior by promoting a threatening climate of fear and vulnerability (see, e.g., Hashemi 1996; Karim 1996). Of course, NGOs heighten their risks if they depend on their host government as a source of funding. In this case, it is difficult for NGOs to have it both ways in providing the public services that the government needs (thereby benefiting from stable funding) while at the same time pursuing rights advancement. As Hashemi puts it, "This implies that NGOs have to make a clear choice—between the four-wheel-drive vehicle that comes with government licensing and donor funding and the much harder conditions involved in living alongside poor people" (1996, 131).

Managing Expectations

As depicted in the lower-left cell in table 5.2, NGOs can undertake strategic initiatives to manage the accountability expectations imposed on them in ways that emphasize the incongruity between straightforward compliance logic and the complexities of development. If successful, efforts to manage expectations can provide NGOs "more maneuvering room" in their work and opportunities to reformulate their bottom-line for assessing performance (see Biggs and Neame 1996; Fowler 1996). Two particular strategies of expectations management warrant attention: internalized accountability and negotiated accountability through stakeholder dialogue. First, NGOs can take the lead in "institutionalizing suspicion" (Moore and Stewart 1998) on themselves by adopting codes of ethics (adopted internally or as members of voluntary self-regulating associations) that elaborate on (in)appropriate behaviors or practices and identify procedures for addressing alleged violations. The leadership task here is to make sense of what accountability means as a cognitive symbol for both the organization's staff and its stakeholders.

Second, NGOs can manage expectations by facilitating dialogue among diverse stakeholders that grapples with what performance really means in the midst of diverse expectations. Dialogue might begin with each stakeholder's candid statements of interests connected with the NGO's work and how that interest relates to the complexity of development or advocacy efforts. Such an approach distributes some responsibility, or accountability, to stakeholders while also directing attention to NGOs' problems, perhaps failures, in attaining goals. For example, discussion could focus on a particular development project as a lever for subsequent human rights improvement—particularly if the latter is expected as a spin-off (second- or third-order) benefit of the project (see Uphoff 1996). How long should that take? What obstacles loom? How might changing conditions affect impact? NGOs with the audacity to pursue candid dialogue among diverse stakeholders bet that the parties will emerge with more realistic and nuanced understandings of accountability and performance.

It is no easy logistical task to assemble stakeholders in one venue for in-depth discussion. Fowler refers to an Oxfam (UK and Ireland) 1994 initiative to gather some 250 representatives of stakeholders "to deliberate and provide advice on the strategic issues facing the organization." Note that by asking for advice, Oxfam exposes the stakeholders to the diversity of each other's expectations, thus providing them a quick lesson about the conundrums of dealing with multiple accountabilities. Fowler relates that this approach

> concentrates on gathering and in some way reconciling the contending perceptions and measures which are specific and meaningful to the diverse actors involved, now increasingly referred to as "stakeholders." To do this, participatory methods are usually adopted, whereby people define what measures are significant to them and later assess the degree to which the NGO's support has contributed to change. (Fowler 1996, 60)

The Oxfam approach to managing expectations is aptly described as a *social audit*, or "a method of accountability that involves all stakeholders and is neither prescriptive nor bureaucratic" (Zadek and Gatward 1996, 233). In reference to Traidcraft, a UK-based fair-trade organization, Zadek and Gatward outline a sequence of social audit steps as follows: (1) identifying stakeholders, (2) identifying individual stakeholder aims and indicators they would utilize, (3) drafting social audits (by the agency's operations staff), and (4) circulating and signing off on revised drafts (p. 235). Significantly, the iterative process that mediates expectations preempts power politics whereby powerful stakeholders vote up or down based on vested interests. These analysts assert, "Social auditing offers a form of accountability that is integral to ongoing planning. It recognizes the intimate relationship between stakeholders' participation and the effectiveness of decisions made and actions taken" (p. 237). Nonetheless, this technique can be applied to endeavors other than planning, such as evaluation and impact assessment (see Roche 2000). As strategies of accountability, social auditing and related methods can contribute much to capacity building in human-development and rights-advocacy work not accruing from traditional compliance reporting. First, they promote transparency "about what is, and is not, possible and about what can be achieved in the future" (Roche 2000, 552), and second, they facilitate a "context-in" approach that concentrates on "the changes that are happening in people's lives, what is significant about those changes, and then assesses the usefulness or effect of any intervention in relation to these changes" (Kelly,

Kilby, and Kasynathan 2004, 697; also see Roche 2000; Willetts and Crawford 2007).

Holding Others Accountable

Characterizing Uvin's claim that rights-based organizations should demand answerability from powerful societal forces, the right column in table 5.2 moves us into unfamiliar territory. The usual interpretation of the term *organization accountability* suggests external control on and scrutiny of the organization under some legitimate base of authority instead of the organization itself demanding accountability. For example, of some 30 chapters included in two edited volumes on NGO accountability, only two consider the case of organizations seeking accountable behavior from others—the others focus on how NGOs account to external stakeholders (Edwards and Hulme 1996; Jordan and van Tuijl 2007). When organizations *do* demand accountability, particularly government law enforcement agencies and other regulatory bodies, they often do so under legal authority and/or constitutional framework. From Uvin's assertion that rights-based efforts should hold governments, corporations, and other powers accountable, the contentious challenge is bound to surface: *On what authority do you make demands?* or *Whom do you represent?* Although perhaps worded differently, the challenge attempts to discredit the humanitarian organization's justification to assert moral authority as a basis for demanding accountability.

The short answer to this legitimacy question is that *nongovernmental* organizations are by nature not accountable to public authority as representative bodies. Instead, they claim authority as *constitutive* agents acting in the absence of constitutionally protected rights or of their implementation on behalf of those deprived of their freedoms (see Peruzzotti 2007, 53–55). The longer answer connects this constitutive role with Sen's explanation of the constitutive and instrumental roles of freedom:

> The constitutive role of development relates to the importance of substantive freedom in enriching human life. . . . Within the narrower views of development (in terms of, say, GNP or industrialization) it is often asked whether the freedom of political participation and dissent is or is not "conducive to development." . . . This question would seem defectively formulated, since it misses the crucial understanding that political participation and dissent are constitutive parts of development itself. Even a very rich person who is prevented from speaking freely, or from participating in public debates

and discussions, is *deprived* of something that she has reason to value. (Sen 1999, 36–37; italics his)

Thus, in their constitutive role, NGOs demand accountability in advancing substantive freedoms. Such reasoning is unlikely to satisfy everyone, particularly those who accept their government (or the market) as the wellspring and guardian of all human rights, and that may be just as well. As Peruzzotti implies (2007, 55–57), legitimate organizations are obliged to impose checks and balances on themselves through their commitments to social accounting/auditing disciplines (such as those discussed previously) that incorporate external scrutiny and anticipate suspicion.

Uvin states his case for demanding accountability as follows:

At the heart of any rights-based approach to development are concerns with mechanisms of accountability, for this is precisely what distinguishes charity from claims. As the Human Rights Council of Australia states, "Accountability is the key to protection and promotion of human rights." Indeed, the very move from charity to claims brings about a focus on the mechanisms of accountability. If claims exist, methods for holding those who violate claims accountable must exist as well. If not, the claims lose meaning. (Uvin 2004, 331; his references omitted)

That said, instances when NGOs directly hold others answerable (as in the upper-right cell in table 5.2) are generally limited to issues of justiceability, or pressing legal claims through available adjudicative processes and placing scrutiny on rights violations (widely known as "naming and shaming"). Both tasks draw on particular NGO competencies, knowing how to operate within the legal machinery (or "lawyering") and how to utilize mass-communication technologies (respectively). With regard to the latter, in its workbook titled *New Tactics in Human Rights*, the Minneapolis-based Center for Victims of Torture offers tactics for sharing critical information, such as establishing an antiviolence mobile phone network and informing potential victims of the legal time limits for protecting their rights (Cornell, Kelsch, and Palasz 2004, 34–41). But, with the exception of these two problems calling for direct answerability, most of Uvin's rights claiming involves political and diplomatic capabilities (such as "collaboration and confrontation") in persuading others to recognize how rights and freedoms align with their interests (or to rearrange their own expectations consistent with the lower-right cell in table 5.2).

Managing Others' Expectations

Rights-based action influences other actors to place higher priorities on redressing conditions of deprivation and rights violation. In an idyllic world, NGOs could persuade powerful aid institutions to expand their understanding of NGO professionalism not only to matters of sound financial practices and technical competence but also to those of rights awareness. NGOs could, ideally, stretch donor vision to consider the systemic implications of conditions placed on aid and patterns of funding distribution across nations. In other words, as one commentary proposes, NGOs could persuade governmental, civic, and corporate donors to adopt more democratic approaches that interrelate downward- and upward-accountability obligations in ways that encourage local capacity building and flexibility. After all, most funding aid *is* a matter of public policy as (government) allocations or as outcomes of fiscal policy incentives in the form of tax breaks (see Bendel and Cox 2007).

Since few NGOs (if any) can rearrange the institutional agendas of donors, the question turns to what development agencies and advocacy organizations *can do* to influence others' priorities that impinge on human conditions. Uvin mentions that one path in dealing with the aid system "is the radical capacity building approach . . . which entails a transfer of power and initiative to local actors" (2004, 198). Large, international NGOs (or INGOs) may be in positions to facilitate local capacity building by reconceptualizing how they engage and interact with their affiliates in particular locales. Similarly, local NGOs can rethink how they relate to traditional adversaries (such as government agencies or corporations) and potential allies in the community.

Short of transforming the aid system, large NGOs can recognize themselves as effective intermediaries between global donors and their affiliates and allies in local contexts. In stressing the need to negotiate the "trilemma" of "aligning the different levels of planning and strategy; balancing global analysis and priorities against local realities; and identifying both measures that indicate progress and promote and encourage innovation," Beckwith, Glenzer, and Fowler (2002) provide an account of CARE International's Latin American Regional Management Unit (LARMU) depicting how middle managers can "lead from the middle" in reducing poverty. As background, these authors comment, "Most global NGOs have intermediate management structures that straddle and bridge global and country levels. Typically, these geographically based structures serve basic administrative and oversight functions, but their contribution can be much greater" (p. 412). As a (regionally based) middle-management structure, LARMU connected a global (OECD) 50% poverty-reduction target to *industry-wide* (rather than simply CARE) success in the region. In essence, CARE reorganized itself in a way that enhanced its capability to advocate for poverty reduction in Latin America among and with other NGOs.

Local NGOs can also advance rights causes by searching for opportunities to reframe their existing relationships with stakeholders or other actors. For example, NGOs can assist corporations by monitoring unintended outcomes associated with human deprivation, such as subcontractors that exploit child labor (see Husselbee 2000). Similarly, the Guatemalan-based Coverco—The Commission for the Verification of Codes of Conduct—contracts with multinational corporations to monitor labor conditions in their apparel supply factories (Cornell, Kelsch, and Palasz 2004, 131–32). Local rights organizations can redefine their relationships with traditional adversaries; for example, advocacy organizations can collaborate with police agencies to expedite the resolution of rights grievances and, in so doing, contribute to the professional image of law enforcement (see Cornell, Kelsch, and Palasz 2004, 128).

In summary, NGO accountability clearly obligates organizations to answer to aid institutions through compliance reporting and in some instances to the regulatory and control apparatuses of host governments. On the other hand, NGOs that prudently negotiate the multiplicity of accountability expectations placed on them can carve out sufficient "maneuvering room" to advance a rights dimension in their own missions and in the priorities of other actors. Rights advocacy calls on organizations not only to stand accountable but also to make accountability demands on others to address deprivations and violations. Sometimes this involves direct (naming-and-shaming) confrontation, but in other cases advocacy is better served through diplomacy that demonstrates the institutional advantages accruing from human rights concerns.

Impact Assessment and Rights-Based Leadership

Donor demands for NGOs to "stand answerable" and to demonstrate significant performance can place organizations and leaders on the defensive. Nonetheless, skillful leaders can capitalize on the accountability challenge as an opportunity to make sense of exactly what the organization accomplishes in terms of its impact on people's lives. As Roche relates in his discussion of impact assessment,

> All organisations, whether they are a community-based group, a
> local NGO, or an international agency, need to make sense of what
> they are doing. They also generally want to know what difference

they are making. This produces two key problems for any organisation: how to synthesise or summarise what they are doing—the aggregation problem; and how they discover the degree to which any changes they observe were brought about by their actions—the attribution problem. These issues are further complicated if the organisation has to communicate to many other people, both internally and externally, about their achievements. (Roche 2000, 550)

"Sense-making" forces rights-focused leaders to come to grips with several problematic realities. First, as Uphoff notes, "sustainable impact requires both the attainment of second- and third-order effects and the existence of many people who have a stake in some institution, technology, practice, or legislation, so that it maintains support" (1996, 33). This suggests that sustainable empowerment may emerge fortuitously beyond the principal scope of the development program (in forestry, public health, or disaster response) and that evaluations and limited project time frames could undercut sustainable human advancement (1996, 33–35). Second, donors expect that meaningful outcomes are quantifiable as measured against goals. Such a fiction overlooks the more likely variations of outcome consistent with the intricacies of contextual situations. In other words, effectiveness is unlikely to fall on everyone in equal measure (men and women, various ethnic groupings, the literate and non-literate), and it may be the variation that energizes the next stage of program improvement. This suggests that evaluation, even in the context of accountability and performance assessment, works better as a diagnostic tool that generates questions (as examples, "Why do the results vary?" and "How do we respond to these variations?") rather than simple before-and-after answers for funding decisions or program worthiness. Competent decision making in these matters requires qualitative judgments that take the intricacies of context into consideration.

Leaders can look to the conclusions of prominent management authorities such as Rosebeth Moss Kanter and Peter Drucker to justify linking accountability with diagnostic performance assessment. Fowler relates,

In 1979, Rosebeth Moss Kanter reviewed the wide range of conceptual dilemmas, practical difficulties, contending principles, and different methods adopted in attempts to determine non-profit effectiveness, productivity, and performance. She concludes:

- That the measurement of effectiveness must be related to a particular context and life stage of the organisation.

- That rather than seeking universal measures, the need is to identify appropriate questions reflecting multiple criteria.
- That the concept of assessing organisational goals should be replaced with the notion of organisational uses, in recognition of the fact that "different constituencies use organisations for different purposes."

A decade later, organisational guru Peter Drucker (1990) used a different analysis to reach essentially the same conclusions, namely that:

- Performance must be contextually determined and interpreted.
- Questions should form the basis of the assessment approach.
- Standards must derive from the various constituencies that the organisation serves.
- The process of organisational assessment should be participatory. (Fowler 1996, 61–62)

Strategically, rights-focused leaders can manage expectations by reframing accountability as diagnostic learning that takes stock of where the organization is and is not going in its human advancement efforts. Such an approach redirects the accountability question from assessment of numerous "results" indicators against preprogrammed goals to programmatic efforts in relation to impact. Strategic accountability that is focused on impact promotes transparency in inviting comprehensive reviews of mission, beliefs and values, policies and procedures, and even current interpretations of accountability per se (see Cavill and Sohail 2007, 246–47). Thus, virtually all aspects of the organization's operations and strategic orientation are open to review and reassessment. But it also directs attention to actors and forces *outside* the organization that affect development and rights-advocacy work. The diagnostic orientation frames development work as developmental, and therefore *iterative*, in seeking opportunities for refinement through accountability that seeks better impact strategies through reassessment (rather than one-shot determinations of success in meeting objectives). Leaders opting for managing expectations through learning need to be open and candid with stakeholders, even equipping them with "litmus tests" for impact assessment within funding decisions (e.g., evidence of effective strategic planning, operational planning, and how well they mesh—see Dale 2003, 59). The trade-off becomes clear for donors and other stakeholders—if they demand more impact assessment, they need to participate in that process.

Impact assessment in rights-committed organizations concentrates on improvement in human conditions within particular social and political contexts and, as such, embraces a wider scope of concern than performance outputs compared against planned objectives. The balance of this chapter introduces some strategies of impact assessment related to both development missions and advocacy organizations, with particular attention to capacities that support iterative learning and involve intended beneficiaries.

Impact Assessment in Development Efforts

Regarding NGO evaluation, a fundamental question centers on whether the logical framework can be modified to support impact assessment beyond merely comparing the results outputs to planned objectives. An expert on regional development answers in the affirmative, suggesting that it is helpful to reinterpret the logframe as a general *approach* instead of as a constraining *framework*. Thus, Dale (2003) introduces the possibility of expanding planning targets into a flowchart of ends–means relationships beginning with program inputs and extending to a statement of (intended) long-term impacts—for example, "Children enjoy better health than before implementation of the health promotion project." Dale's theoretical flowchart includes some 30 interrelated activity milestones associated with implementation tasks, outcomes, and immediate achievements. He also stipulates that planners identify assumptions underlying the various paths and sequences in the flowchart. In essence, Dale argues that more detailed mapping in logframe planning can be used to probe impacts.

Another commentator, however, maintains that logframes should follow Robert Chambers's participatory approach by including local beneficiaries in planning and analysis, first identifying the steps in the typical logframe format as follows:

1. Participatory analyses: identify the groups affected by the project. The main groups are analyzed with regard to main problems, interests, potentials, and linkages. A decision is taken on whose interests and what problems are to be given priority.
2. Problem analyses—identify a focal problem and establish cause/effect relationships through the use of a "problem tree."
3. Objective analyses—transformation of the "problem tree" into an "objective tree."

4. Alternative analyses—assess different options for the project. This assessment can be based on technical, financial, economic, institutional, social, and environmental feasibility.

5. Identify the main project elements—goal (long-term overall objective), purpose (operational objective), outputs (results that are guaranteed by the project), activities, and inputs.

6. Assumptions—describe conditions that must exist if the project is to succeed but that are outside the control of the project.

7. Identify indicators—the performance standard to be reached in order to achieve the goal, purpose, and outputs (Aune 2000, 688).

Aune argues that the participatory approach could be used "to identify vulnerable groups (step 1 in the LFA), local problems and their causes (step 2), to discuss with local stakeholders the goals of the project and which activities should be given priority (steps 3–5), to identify the external factors which can influence the project (step 6), and to define the indicators (step 7)" (2000, 688–89).

Other experts essentially agree with the premise that the logframe *can* be adapted to assess contextual issues and facilitate communication between stakeholders. Dearden and Kowalski attribute criticisms of the logframe to "the clumsy artisan" problem is this way:

> Why is it that it has received such "bad press"? Like any other tool, from an axe to a scalpel, its impact is not determined by its nature but by the way it is used. Chambers (1997) chronicles examples of the way the tool has been used to reinforce the power of the "uppers." It is in order to address what we see as such abuses of an otherwise very useful tool by clumsy artisans that we have written this paper. (Dearden and Kowalski 2003, 502)

Thus, these authors emphasize training within the organization (they are trainers, after all) as the key for recognizing the logframe as "the product of participatory planning that is user driven and objectives led" (p. 502).

Other community development researchers propose that traditional program monitoring techniques (such as the logframe) can add on impact evaluation measures to assess significant, positive changes in people's lives. Willetts and Crawford (2007) promote the value of "the most significant change" technique, a process that generates interview data affected by a community program in Laos. Kelly, Kilby, and Kasynathan (2004) report on similar interviewing approaches as means for measuring the impact of community improvement programs in India and Sri Lanka. Both of these accounts of identifying change stress the need for rigorous methodologies for ensuring appropriate selection (i.e., making sure the "right people" are interviewed, validating responses as authentic, and recording responses "in the voice" of the interviewee). In other words, they maintain that logframe approaches can be adapted to measure contextual matters associated with impact, in the form of interview-generated viewpoints, provided that the organization follows established standards of research methodology.

All of this presents a problem for rights-based leadership in developmental organizations. On one hand, the traditional logframe (or similar rational planning approach) commands legitimacy through the eyes of donors and technical experts in "break[ing] down a complex set of activities and enabl[ing] a snapshot view of what a project or program is hoping to accomplish, how it will do so, and why it is being done at all" (Grove and Zwi 2008, 71). In addition, if sound research methods are followed, these approaches can be modified to capture some insights on unexpected outcomes and context vis-à-vis interview-generated opinions of program-induced change. In other words, traditional approaches are safe, sought by powerful donors, and capable of monitoring certain contextual results.

On the other hand, Uvin associates right-based development with the capability to reconceptualize the overall aims of development agencies. He asserts, "One of the main advantages of a rights-based approach to development is that it can bring people to reframe the nature of problems they seek to address and the levers for change they can employ" (2004, 160). In this regard, Grove and Zwi outline initiatives to reframe the provision of health care as "bridges to peace" in the Solomon Islands, Sri Lanka, and Timor-Leste. Such a reconceptualization is based on "belief that health may be a 'connector,' as it is an issue of common concern, with characteristics that unite people because 'we all care about health,' and because in some very real ways (for example in relation to communicable diseases) our own health is dependent on the health of others" (2008, 69). Grove and Zwi relate how leaders developed a "peacekeeping filter," or statement of five principles (and component parts), that serves as the unifying document for leadership in place of a logframe:

- cultural sensitivity,
- conflict sensitivity (conflict awareness, trust),
- promotion of social justice (equity and nondiscrimination, gender),

- promotion of social cohesion (community cohesion, psychological well-being), and
- promotion of good governance (community capacity building and empowerment, sustainability and coordination, transparency and accountability).

Figure 5.1 shows how project impact information related to (one of the) filter principles was ascertained as a means for iteratively revising the nexus between health care and peacekeeping. While inferring that quantitative data may indeed be useful in corroborating efforts, Grove and Zwi argue that the logframe falls short in measuring "what matters"—relationships between people:

> The logframe contains a natural bias towards quantification. The matrix demands "objectively verifiable indicators," forcing projects to consider how they will measure progress towards intended outcomes. . . . This emphasis on the "measurable" represents a crucial weakness. The matrix becomes dominated by those issues that are easiest to define and measure, rather than those that are most central to success. In particular, relationships between people (both internal and external to the project) and process issues (how the project is undertaken) are likely to be neglected, with attention focused on the most tangible outputs, such as clinics built or vaccinations administered. (Grove and Zwi 2008, 71–72)

Expressed in Uvin's terms, logframe approaches generally assume "technical, expert-based perspectives" (2004, 161) that may, using appropriate research methods, provide some contextually pertinent data, but they typically *do not rethink, reformulate,* or *reframe.* In his introduction to *Development and Freedom,* Sen underscores the importance of connections between various types (political freedoms, economic facilities, social opportunities, transparency guarantees, and protective security) of freedoms (1999, 10). Grove and Zwi's account of the health and peace-building bridge provides an example of Sen's interconnections that are possible by reformulating the aims of development.

Impact Assessment in Advocacy Efforts

At first glance, the task of assessing advocacy could appear relatively straightforward—as in the case of interest-group lobbying, pressures exerted either

SA = Strongly Agree; **A** = Agree; **B** = Both Agree and Disagree; **D** = Disagree; SD = Strongly Disagree; **DK** = Don't Know; **NA** = Not Applicable								
Principle	**Indicator**	**Response**						**Comments**
	Trust							
Conflict Sensitivity	The project is sensitive to health-related issues that have contributed to mistrust in this community	SA	A	N	<u>D</u>	SD	DK	• Clinic was periodically occupied by rebel forces, disrupting services—patients now afraid to come • Low attendance rates by Tamils, prefer to travel to a clinic farther away where they feel safer • Staff refusing to do outreach in certain villages • Some intimidation of hospital staff by rebel forces reported in the past

Figure 5.1 Sample completed section from the Health and Peacebuilding Filter. *Source*. Grove, Natalie J., and Anthony B. Zwi. "Beyond the Logframe: A New Tool for Examining Health and Peacebuilding Initiatives." *Development in Practice* 18, no. 1 (2008): 75. Used with permission.

change things or do not. In reality, advocacy work is messy and subject to changing environments and a diversity of strategies (Coates and David 2002). Like political campaigns, the advocacy environment is typically adversarial wherein agenda-driven institutions, organizations, and movements compete to change behavior and win hearts and minds. And as with lobbying and political campaigning, advocacy may be more effective through alliances and coalitions than as the outcome of a particular agency. In this sense, the longer term advocacy potential of the alliance could be as, or more, significant as its immediate clout in changing outcomes.

Human rights work necessitates advocacy, whether as integrated within development programs or central to explicit advocacy missions. In either case, rights-based advocacy focuses on transforming power relationships on behalf of the poor, deprived, or victimized (Uvin 2004, 143–46). On occasion, NGO leaders may wish to shy away from roles that confront stakeholders (such as governments of aid institutions) that affect other development objectives (Edwards 1993). In other words, advocacy impact assesses the prudence of rights organizations, and particularly their leaders, in an environment of stark power inequality most often punctuated by institutional agendas in the North determining what happens in the South in the name of development. Uvin relates that the lion's share of advocacy activity takes place in the North and is directed toward Northern governments and institutions because, like the rationale for robbing banks, that's where the money is (2004, 144).

Except where circumstances dictate otherwise, an NGO leader is generally well advised to assess the advocacy impact of the alliances or networks her organization leads or facilitates and, secondarily, to appraise the organization's actions in tandem with the collective effort. In the absence of silver-bullet methods for assessing the totality of impact, it is reasonable for the leader to interpret impact as an overlay of effectiveness in component tasks such as (1) clearly defining and measuring that which is valued (see Coates and David 2002), (2) understanding the power relationships at work in advocacy contexts, (3) aligning strategies and tactics appropriate within power relationships, and (4) learning from iterative assessment activities.

First, the importance of clearly articulated advocacy objectives presupposes the NGO's commitment to advocacy that should not be taken for granted. Rights-based leaders must therefore champion advocacy as a strategic priority rather than let it retreat to the back burners of agency attention. Clark suggests that the organizational inertia tends to push advocacy aside: "Advocacy may be seen as important but it is not urgent. Consequently, it is easily squeezed out by the day-to-day dilemmas and crises arising from the project activities, from donor pressures and from media enquiries" (Clark 1991, 127). Leaders can track budget trends on advocacy work as a percentage of agency spending and staffing assignments related to these functions to guard against "advocacy slippage." In addition, care should be taken to conserve the advocacy mission amid pressures from donors or other stakeholders to soft-pedal it. Efforts to specify precisely what is valued as dimensions of advocacy accomplishment can add clarity to advocacy efforts (Coates and David 2002). In this regard, advocacy impact can be assessed in terms of more than one objective; for example, beyond scrutinizing only the explicit policy objective (Did the advocacy effort achieve its legislative goals or stop a particular project?), impact analysis might also consider the societal outcomes related to strengthening involvement of the poor in civic participation (see Covey 1996). Thus, advocacy impact could be viewed positively along one particular dimension but not others, provided that it reflects the ends and/or means of empowerment.

Second, since human rights work is inherently political (Uvin 2004, 134–37), impact depends on effectiveness in analyzing the political contours of advocacy work. In large measure, the presence of ongoing research programs devoted to contextual analysis offers evidence of effectiveness (see Fox 2003). Competent political analysis entails understanding systems of power (pluralist, elitist, or ideological) inherent in the government regime or other entity targeted by advocacy initiatives (Coates and David 2002, 538).

Third, advocacy impact depends on how well political astuteness informs choices among advocacy strategies (the "what") and tactics (the "how"). Of particular concern is the organization's ability to draw on a wide array of strategies and to match them with appropriate levels of action (whether international, national/regional, or local/grass roots) and target arenas (multinational organizations, industries, national governments, the voting public, families, and so forth; see Chapman and Fisher 2000, 153). The director of the Center for Victims of Torture speaks to the importance of strategic and tactical versatility in targeting forces that affect the circumstances of victimization:

> Rather than brittle and easily disrupted, systems that use torture are often highly complex, allowing the different institutions which benefit from torture's use to support each other. As one part of the system is attacked, other parts (such as the police structure, the system of prosecutors, the indifference of the judiciary) help protect the target and allow it to self-repair. We understood this to mean that the system will not yield to individual tactics. Rather, the system needs to be affected in multiple areas at the same time to create disequilibrium and prevent self-repair. This requires the use of multiple tactics working in conjunction as part of a more comprehensive strategy. (Cornell, Kelsch, and Palasz 2004, 13)

The breadth of advocacy tactics ranges from conventional lobbying activities suitable in democratized political systems to mobilizing underground opposition movements in repressive settings (see Coates and David 2002, 538; Cornell, Kelsch, and Palasz 2004). It is strategically important to identify situations that are "justiciable," where those suffering rights violations can seek redress through judicial or other governmental processes, apart from those who are not (Uvin 2004, 131–34: Chapman and Fisher 2000, 161–62). In cases of advocacy pressing for policy legislation, strategic competency mandates that tactics be aligned with particular stages (agenda building, formulation, implementation) of the policymaking process (Chapman and Fisher 2000, 156–57). Finally, impact can be assessed in terms of the organization's ability to tap into the strategic advantages that alliances and partnerships offer over a go-it-alone approach (see Uvin 2004, 180–81). Again in the context of victims' rights initiatives, Douglas Johnson (the director of the Center for Victims of Torture) argues,

> Most organizations in the field incorporate a limited number of tactics within their repertoire. Organizations tend to focus on a narrow set of tactics, and rarely cooperate or collaborate on them. Not only does this limit influence to very narrow sectors in a complex, mutually reinforcing system, but each organization is shaping its strategy based on this isolated capacity rather than on what is needed to affect the situation. We do what we can do, not what we need to do. We speculated that more coordination between tactics would make them more effective. (Johnson 2004, 13)

Fourth, impact in advocacy work relies on the NGO's willingness to learn from past impact assessments. Generally, advocacy effectiveness relates to ongoing capacity-building processes that, like Rome, "[weren't] built in a day" (Coates and David 2002, 535). The advocacy function must be framed in longer term objectives that leaders protect from the quick-results demands of logframe output monitoring or similar management and evaluation methods. Continual learning is critical if the advocacy mission is to incorporate the values and motivations of people at the grassroots level, not simply as recipients of advocacy messages or passive beneficiaries of outcomes but as advocates on their own behalf (Chapman and Fisher 2000, 163–64; Nyamugasira 1998).

Conclusion

For rights-based NGOs, institutional legitimacy depends on its record of performance, its accountability to those who support and benefit from its efforts, and its ability to impact human conditions in ways that sustain human empowerment. Taken separately, the multifaceted natures of performance and accountability are difficult to digest either in the abstract or as applied to organizations aiming to promote human rights. Although it seems logical to associate both with questions of NGO impact, those linkages are generally obscure and ambiguous. For example, one might expect NGOs that promise to impact people's lives for the better can demonstrate convincing evidence of performance along the way. But, as suggested, performance takes on various meanings, such as how tasks are performed (or production), how competent the people are taking on tasks, how cost-effectively those task are performed (or productivity), and what the results are of task performance.

Since results can typically be measured, they may stand out to some as the most convincing evidence of whether organizations perform. But in the NGO context, results that can be easily counted and measured (such as acres of forest replanted, number of training session attendees, or even income growth) do not necessarily translate to sustainable human development. As Powell argues, empowerment organizations may indeed deliver services, but they are typically "knowledge-based" rather than "service-based" (2006, 520). Thus, although results might constitute the gold standard of performance in service organizations, competence is of utmost importance in organizations that can judiciously marshal knowledge to empower people and advocate for their rights. Given this reality, NGO leaders can look to the centrality of competent performance as critical within organizations that attempt to alter behaviors and counteract societal forces largely outside of their control.

As the case with any organization, rights NGOs stand accountable to conserve their legitimacy and credibility among their stakeholders and attentive publics. In particular, many NGOs are obliged to prepare detailed reports for donors as criteria for continued funding amid the intense competition for financial support in the development industry. Beyond this, however, organizations need to manage accountability or prioritize among the diversity of stakeholder expectations placed on them from program beneficiaries, governments, their own personnel, donors, and others. However, given their essential role in making claims against human rights violators, they also need to hold others—often powerful institutions and actors that exert power over the poor and victimized—morally accountable for their actions or inactions.

As discussed in this chapter, impact assessment offers leaders the occasion to work with stakeholders and the organization's staff to take stock of rights-directed efforts in reference to particular contexts and human situations. As a juncture for iterative learning, impact analysis can provide a supportive but realistic forum for determining strengths, limitations, and the next steps to be taken in improving human conditions.

Discussion Issues

1. "Conventional wisdom" leads some to judge humanitarian NGOs by their "overhead expenses" as a percentage of total costs—the lower the better. Presuming that "overhead" includes costs for salaries and training, how would highly competence-based organizations "rate" according to this logic? Explain.

2. Are the overhead-expenses criteria more reasonable (or "fairer") when applied to an organization primarily committed to long-term advocacy or to another focused on short-term disaster relief? Explain.

3. How can voluntary leadership efforts to "be more accountable" (1) promote learning within the organization and with its donor agencies and/or (2) enhance its stature as an advocate for human rights?

4. Some could argue that a leader who needs to "make sense" out of "what's going on" in the NGO ought to be replaced by someone better qualified. Do you agree? Explain why or why not.

5. Suppose that you are changing jobs, leaving your position as executive director of an environmentally focused development agency to assume a similar role in a human-rights-advocacy NGO. Discuss if and/or how your approach to impact assessment would change.

Notes

1. Even in government, elected-official policymakers appraise agency accountability and use performance reporting as a basis for subsequent budget appropriations. This is analogous to the donor–NGO relationship in that funding aid depends on evidence of performance. But clearly, the donor–agency relationship excludes the opinions of the poor and disenfranchised whose well-being and autonomy supposedly matter in human rights initiatives. And it is debatable how closely donors in the developed North can relate to the contexts of deprivation in the South and if performance data can directly speak to those contexts. Nonetheless, NGOs need to be recognized as accountable and effective in terms that resonate with donor institutions if they are to compete successfully for funding.

2. For example, administrative theorists Dubnick and Yang argue, "Accountability can be taken as a multiplicity of definitions that serve many purposes and is therefore difficult to conceptualize" (2009, 3). Their comment that definitions can serve many purposes, or can be agenda driven, relates directly to the ideological mind-sets of "appropriate change" discussed in chapter 3.

3. In government, the objective usually is to achieve top-level management coordination and integration across numerous agencies through reliance on a single measurement and evalua-

tion scheme (Epstein 1996, 56). But the processes for institutionalizing standardizing protocols (such as those needed to implement the 1993 Government Performance and Results Act in the United States) are politically contentious and protracted.

4. In other words, these initiatives reduce complexity through selectively designed systems that circumscribe issues deemed important while excluding a host of other factors that affect outcomes concerning how a government agency delivers services or how an NGO promotes human development.

5. A prolific scholar in the areas of public sector accountability and performance, Melvin Dubnick is widely regarded as a preeminent authority on issues of accountability in public organizations.

6

Organization Learning and Knowledge Management as Foundations of Rights-Based Accomplishment

Presumably, all organizations "want to learn," and most leaders "value learning." It is not surprising that much of what is written about NGO management in one way or another associates "organization learning" with program effectiveness, success in local participation, or other good outcomes. Moreover, exemplary NGO executives have been recognized as "learning leaders" (Hailey 2000; Smillie and Hailey 2002). All of that said, it is necessary to cut through the learning rhetoric to critically examine what is actually required of a learning NGO. Compare these "learning" scenarios:

A. The much-revered founder of an international development organization that values local participation wants to learn why her subordinate who manages the Ghana office is ineffective in dealing with community leaders. That management is summoned to the international office to explain.
B. Representatives of an NGO's regional offices meet to learn how to manage fieldwork in accordance with the organization's guiding principles.
C. An NGO dedicates workshop sessions to determine why actual program outcomes depart significantly from logframe projections.

Scenario A "learning" (calling the area manager in to account for her actions) will likely lead to a confrontational dialogue of defensive behaviors that will drown out astute analyses of either expectations or the political context surrounding the area office. Scenario B "learning" endeavors to establish causal (X causes Y) standards of "what works" that could be used to evaluate subsequent fieldwork (that could lead to future confrontations such as that in Scenario A). By contrast, Scenario C aligns most closely with Korten's (1980) recommendation to "embrace error" by focusing on the discrepancy between the actual and the expected as effective problem solving in the absence of "self-fulfilling, self-sealing, and error-escalating processes" (Argyris 2002, 214).

Chris Argyris's distinction between "single-loop" and "double-loop" learning adds clarity to what organization learning entails in terms of "embracing error":

> *Single-loop learning* occurs when errors are corrected without altering the underlying governing values. For example, the thermostat is programmed to turn on if the temperature in the room is cold, or turn off the heat if the room becomes too hot. *Double-loop learning* occurs when errors are corrected by changing the governing values and then the actions. A thermostat is double-loop learning if it questions why it is programmed to measure temperature, and then adjusts the temperature itself. (Argyris 2002, 206; italics his)

Organization learning therefore occurs in a questioning (rather than defensive) atmosphere in which all participants (including leaders) "say what they know yet fear to say" and advocate their ideas "in a way that invites inquiry into them" (p. 217).

Organization learning also involves "incorporating information technology into the developmental plans and daily practice of organizations in a way that generally facilitates productive learning" (Argyris 1994, 350). In the contexts of development and rights advocacy, Argyris's reference to "information technology" calls for broad interpretation that encompasses a number of sources (internal documents, research, websites, program beneficiaries, other programs, and so forth) and conveys varying levels of meaning (from data to information, knowledge, understanding, and explanation) as related to the NGO's mission. The emerging study of "knowledge management" offers guidance for understanding the complexities of information technology as it affects action learning and is therefore utilized in this chapter as a helpful framework for understanding how knowledge translates into action.

The first section surveys the information environment of NGOs and discusses the strengths and limitations of various information sources in facilitating organization learning. The second section applies knowledge-management tools for learning in building various organizational competences such as strategic planning, (particular) management techniques, and internal coherence, as well as sharing and capturing knowledge. In part, knowledge management involves "knowing what you know" and being aware of what is not known (rather than being "unaware of unawareness"; Argyris 2002) and distinguishing between "tacit knowledge" (that internalized within the organization) and "explicit knowledge" that is recognized as valid but has yet to be embraced. The last section focuses on how rights-oriented NGOs can interpret the meaning of knowledge as justification for persuasive efforts and how they can leverage those efforts in collaboration with other organizations in networks and partnerships.

The Information Environment

Human rights and development agencies, like all organizations, depend on various information sources to guide action learning. From a knowledge-management perspective, information can be described as a *message* having a sender and receiver. Davenport and Prusak contend that information is typically intended to influence the judgment (or reshape the tacit knowledge of) the receiver (1998, 3). Their argument corresponds to the observation that policy analysts do not so much help government officials solve problems as to produce interpretations of issues that "help policymakers to gain a better understanding of the world around them" (Gormley and Balla 2004, 37; see also Feldman 1989, 106–14). Referring to the persuasive intent of the informational "message," Davenport and Prusak argue,

> The word "inform" originally meant "to give shape to," and information is meant to shape the person who gets it, to make some difference in his outlook or insight. Strictly speaking, then, it follows that the receiver, not the sender, decides whether the message he gets is really information—that is, if it really informs him. A [message] full of unconnected ramblings may be considered "information" by the writer but judged to be noise by the recipient. (Davenport and Prusak 1998, 3)

In development and rights-based contexts, persuasive information flows from many sources (funding agencies, governments, researchers, consultants, Internet clearinghouses, etc.) dispensing "true knowledge" to organizations. In his article "Which Knowledge? Whose Reality?" Mike Powell emphasizes,

The crucial point that needs to be made about "knowledge" in relation to development is that there is no universal understanding of what it is. . . . The issue for anyone working on development issues cannot be simply how to deal with "knowledge," but how to act effectively in an environment of multiple "knowledges." How can this be done? What relationships are possible between different "knowledges"? (Powell 2006, 521)

Powell believes that development organizations are not adept at understanding and using knowledge, specifically arguing that "current trends in information, knowledge, and communications management practice within the sector are making matters worse, and that strategic opportunities offered by new technologies and new models of information exchange have not been properly understood, let alone exploited" (2006, 518). In some cases, he suggests, senders base their messages on the erroneous premise that development organizations are service providers as part of "a billion-dollar industry . . . in the growth of the global service economy" (p. 519). Rather, rights and development organizations, although they may in fact offer services, are essentially knowledge based, and as such they need to know what information exists and whether it "makes sense" within the context of the organization's rights-making and empowerment effort.

Powell identifies five common sources of (internally and externally generated) information available to development organizations: program information, formal research, organizational knowledge-management processes, information and communication technology systems, and voices (or participatory stakeholders). Each of these key components of the information environment is discussed in the following section in regard to the strategic opportunities it provides, as well as the problems it presents, for rights-focused NGOs.

Program Information

As Powell suggests, the information that an organization gathers through its program experiences can be invaluable in supporting subsequent activities, assuming that (1) people in the agency know that particular records exist and where they might be found and (2) they are cognizant of the historical context that surrounded how and why that information came about (2006, 525). He offers the following as an example of valuable information in the institutional memory of a development organization: "The knowledge gained—that one particular type of truck breaks down a lot in muddy conditions—may not be profound, but it is certainly essential if you are planning a relief programme in a rainy season" (p. 525).

The problem of "knowing that information exists and where to find it" takes on added significance within "vicious cycles" facing development agencies and likely human rights organizations. First, organizations need to preserve institutional memory, given the rapid turnover of staff, the geographic distances between "home" and field offices, and the succession of discrete programs over time. Nonetheless, "short-term" employees have few incentives to build organization memory by keeping records or documenting observations in the midst of other demanding pressures. Thus, a "chicken and egg" conundrum arises in that records and documents exist only *if prior steps have been taken* to promote documentation and record keeping. In addition, the information most easily accessed—for example, logframe output data or accounting information required by funding agencies—may not always prove as qualitatively useful as knowledge for subsequent decisions.

With regard to the "chicken and egg" problem of encouraging habits of sound documentation, some argue the need to design explicit information systems that will build memory over time. Referring to Oxfam's gender programs in Uganda, Payne and Smyth (1999) attest to the importance of "designing reliable systems" to channel relevant information. Similarly, Coward and Fathers (2005) review alternative system design models used in the private sector as compatible with the information needs of development organizations. By contrast, others approach the issue of encouraging documentation from a more organic perspective in keeping with commitments to organization learning and participative management. If staffers (whether "long-timers" or "short-timers") value organization learning, they need to take the time to document significant "lessons learned" for the benefit of their successors (e.g., see Richardson 2006). Similarly, people who are invited to participate in decision processes may have greater incentive to record their observations than those who are not (Hailey and James 2002).

The historical context and purpose for generating a particular stream of information may affect (and in many cases limit) its value in current situations. Thus, to the extent possible, it is helpful to recollect how various stakeholders reacted to the information at the time it was generated. As suggested, it is questionable how valuable accountability and financial reporting information (that development organizations provide donor agencies) may be as knowledge bases for either. Survey research on donor (Department for International Development [DFID]) and development agency relations in Uganda and South

Africa conducted by Tina Wallace and her colleagues indicate tendencies among donor organizations and development agencies alike to discredit information flowing from reporting. NGO officials in these African settings complain that (1) accountability reporting is too time-consuming, (2) rigid accountability formats make it difficult to raise real problems and program complexities, and (3) little feedback is provided. On the other hand, donors indicate that (1) they need the accountability reports to satisfy government policymakers, (2) they are overwhelmed by all the reports submitted to them, and (3) information is lacking about what's most important—impact and program change (Wallace 2007, 112–13). Given these disconnected informational perspectives, it is questionable how much bilateral funding agencies can learn from each other or benefit within their organizations by information generated in conformance with accountability protocols (see Takahashi 2006). Context is important as well in ascertaining the current value of information that was generated from those who participated in a past development or empowerment program. That information could have reflected the particular political outlook or agenda of key actors involved at the time (Musyoki 2002).

To sum up, program experiences can yield valuable information to enhance organization memory. Nonetheless, valuable information may be difficult to access unless leaders make concerted efforts to cultivate the virtues of documenting lessons learned among development workers. Historical records need to be understood within the contexts of original purposes and political interests at play.

Formal Research

Can rights-based organizations depend on research as a source of information to create knowledges (the plural here refers to a diversity of understandings) that can support policies of empowerment? Powell is somewhat skeptical of formal research as a support for rights-focused development because (1) much of it is funded and/or published by Northern development institutions and therefore is intended to advance those agencies' agendas and (2) research typically assumes an academic or institutional format that practitioners find difficult to use (2006, 523). His first criticism is substantiated in a number of commentaries that take Northern aid agencies to task for conveying a dogmatic "message" of neoclassical economic and structural adjustment remedies for all development and human empowerment problems. In this regard, it is ironic that a chief economic advisor at the World Bank (a main target of these criticisms) likens that institution to a church, a propagator of "official views" or dogma. Specifically, Ellerman comments on the

World Bank's "rage to conclude" or supply "ready-made solutions" to development professionals:

> The puzzles that development agencies face about inducing economic and social development are perhaps the most complex and ill-defined questions confronting humankind. . . . Yet one must marvel at the tendency of the major development agencies to rush forward with universal "best practices"—a tendency based not on any methods resembling social science but on a bureaucratic need to maintain elite prestige by "having an answer" for the client. In contrast, every field of science is populated by competing theories, and scientists do not feel the need to artificially rush to closure just to "have an answer." (Ellerman 2002, 289)

In their discussion of "norms entrepreneurs" (discussed in more detail in the following section), Finnemore and Sikkink attribute the World Bank's "doctrinal purity" to its professional training:

> Studies of the World Bank similarly document a strong role for professional training in filtering the norms that the bank promotes. In this case, the inability to quantify many costs and benefits associated with antipoverty and basic human needs norms created resistance among the many economists staffing the bank, because projects promoting these norms could not be justified on the basis of "good economics." (Finnemore and Sikkink 1998, 899–900)

Other critics probe the political motivation of Northern institutions as information providers—for example, Broad suggests that the World Bank foray into knowledge management should be understood as a goal-succession strategy to maintain the authority of its message when its role as a major lender was waning (2007, 701). Furthermore, Broad argues that its new research role served its "paradigm-maintenance" purpose in propagating its neoliberal global ideology (p. 702). Interestingly, corroboration for Broad's arguments can be found in a working paper on knowledge management published by the Overseas Development Institute, which quotes Steve Denning, a World Bank official, as follows:

> We were drowning in information, managing it very inefficiently, and if we cleaned it up we would save a lot of money. But it occurred

to me that we'd still not be a very relevant organization. The World Bank had been a lending organization most of its life, and we were facing private-sector banks that were lending much more than we were. At that time, people were asking themselves if we had a future at all. So I started to ask myself a different question: Suppose we were to share our knowledge? We had over 50 years' worth of know-how about what works in development and what doesn't. (Ramalingam 2005, 59)

The working paper adds, "Denning was named Programme Director and assigned the task of making the Bank a knowledge organisation. The programme caught the attention of the leadership of the Bank, and saw the Bank being re-branded 'the Knowledge Bank' in the 1996 inaugural speech of Bank President James Wolfensohn" (Ramalingam 2005, 59). Another commentator concurs, explaining that the World Bank's structural adjustment discourse deflects the research focus away from the political toward technocratic and economic "wisdom" that "can only be perceived as neutral with respect to those who already accept liberal principles" (Storey 2000, 366).

It *is* the case, however, that these Northern funding agencies employ "anthropologists" (referring to noneconomists, most often social scientists) ostensibly to reflect a diversity of viewpoints. Nonetheless, critics charge that such scholars often find their work compromised by the oversight of their bosses. Broad (2007) indicates that World Bank officials are inclined to censor research that diverges from economic dogma and even to misrepresent the thrusts and contexts of empirical findings. In reference to the DFID in the United Kingdom, Panayiotopoulos relates that social scientists must often operate within restrictions of institutional confidentiality, such that "any work paid for by the [agency] remains our 'property,' but [that] in most cases we would not object to report contents being used for teaching purposes, and indeed saw this in a positive light" (2002, 48). Since scholars (especially, social scientists) in funding agencies are tethered on a short institutional leash, there is reason to question the independence of their work as a basis for knowledge generation within the rights-based organizations. This donor dominance in restricting and "owning" research hardly appears conducive to the goal of empowerment—or assisting people in "taking ownership" of their life circumstances.

Powell's comments about the difficulties practitioners encounter in working with (academic and institutional) research formats strike a responsive chord with two Danish researchers who have developed a comprehensive approach to putting research into practice (or RintoP). Specifically, Aagaard-

Hansen and Olsen (2009) value research activities that (1) involve a long-term relationship between researchers and development professionals, (2) serve multiple audiences in broadly accessible formats (such as "policy briefs"), and (3) encompass a variety of modalities. The multimodality component of their approach focuses on developing an effective RintoP process by

- forging long-term links between researchers and practitioners in the form of partnerships and informal communications channels,
- facilitating the reformulation of research priorities whereby end users identify the knowledge gaps that research should address,
- training university students how to connect research to practical application,
- disseminating "dormant research" that has never been published but is useful within the organization, and
- "training practitioners in the basics of research methodology" (Aagaard-Hansen and Olsen 2009, 382–83).

Referring back to Davenport and Prusak's image of the information message (1998, 3), it appears that the burdens for making research more useful fall both on the receiver (practitioners) and on the researcher.

Issues bridging advocacy research with practice appear less problematic than that supporting development initiatives. Fox indicates that advocacy activists have followed two complementary but alternative traditions for spanning the research–action divide—grassroots participatory action research (discussed in this section as a separate information source) and power-structure research using strategies that (1) "follow the money" and/or (2) "expose injustice in ways that make invisible problems visible" (2006, 28). The power-structure tradition corresponds closely with Uvin's notion of a rights-based approach as a framework for analysis: "A rights framework provides a mechanism for reanalyzing and renaming 'problems' like contaminated water or malnutrition as 'violations' and as such, something that need not and should not be tolerated. . . . Rights make it clear that violations are neither inevitable nor natural, but arise from deliberate decisions and policies" (2004, 130). But going a step further, the power-structure tradition works to elicit emotive moral passions in analysis through this two-step process:

> The first goal is get people to say "ah-hah!—so that's what's really going on." . . . The hope is that revealing injustice and hypocrisy will provoke the anger that is so crucial for motivating action. But

anger is not enough—it can motivate people to want to make a difference, but it is not enough to show how they can do so. Here power-structure research contributes a crucial second step—it also serves as a guide for how to be strategic about public action by revealing where the pressure points in the system are. (Fox 2006, 28)

As a conduit of applied research, the Minneapolis-based Center for Victims of Torture is particularly adept at finding the pressure points of victimizing systems and then recommending specific advocacy tactics for practitioners' use in comparable situations (Cornell, Kelsch, and Palasz 2004). In essence, this center looks to practitioners on the front lines of advocacy organizations to share effective advocacy tactics to assist others in rights work.

Organizational Knowledge-Management Processes

Although this chapter incorporates "organization learning" within a "knowledge-management" framework, it is unclear exactly how these two endeavors relate. In an influential article on "community organization and rural development," David Korten understands the learning organization as agile, serendipitous, and adaptive:

> Achieving fit through the learning process approach calls for orga-nizations that have little in common with the implementing orga-nizations geared to reliable adherence to detailed plans and condi-tions precedent favored in the blue-print approach. Its requirement is for organizations with a well developed capacity for responsive and anticipatory adaptation-organizations that: (a) embrace error; (b) plan with the people; and (c) link knowledge building with ac-tion. (Korten 1980, 498)

With regard to "embracing error," Korten goes on to suggest that "preplanned interventions into varied and constantly changing socio-technical systems will nearly always prove to be in error" and thus provide the impetus for learning by the errors they cause. Nonetheless, as knowledge management has come into vogue, some organizations "preplan" deliberate interventions to structure knowledge-management systems intended to make "learning" routine.

In NGOs, discussions about "learning" are sometimes enveloped within overarching concerns related to other issues, such as sustainability (Johnson and Wilson 1999), vision and mission (Beckwith, Glenzer, and Fowler 2002), and program implementation (Rodríguez-Carmona 2004). Accounts of these experiences sometimes elaborate on particular "learning-action" processes as prescriptions for reformulating NGO thinking regarding the problem at hand. For example, Scott-Villiers (2002) discusses the effectiveness of ActionAid's "Accountability, Learning, and Action System" in reframing its obligations to the poor. Similarly, Beckwith, Glenzer, and Fowler (2002) report on CARE International's Latin America Regional Management Unit as a means of "leading learning" from the middle (i.e., the intermediate region-specific level) of a large organization to revise strategic planning principles and processes. In essence, "knowledge-management systems" have been designed to generate information related to significant initiatives to re-evaluate priorities and procedures. Nonetheless, some of these accounts associate organization learning with frustration and dissonance encountered in organizations rather than with "learning systems" per se. For example Scott-Villiers concludes his article on ActionAid's experiences as follows:

> Confusion and exasperation seem to play an essential energising part in the learning process. It took more than a decade of trying to change before ActionAid managed to put a congruent set of changes in motion. Procedures in particular often endure long after the conditions and aspirations for which they were created have moved on. Many people in many development organisations are aware that their procedures for dealing with partners, funders, and the poor are sending out messages that are contradictory to their own current thinking. (Scott-Villiers 2002, 434–35)

It can then be surmised that NGO professionals should distinguish information generated from organization-driven systems (even those designated as "learning systems") from action learning that recognizes errors and incorporates those experiences into tacit knowledge (Korten 1980).

Information and Communication Technology

As Powell suggests, it stands to reason that development and advocacy organizations should exploit information and communication technologies (ICTs) to the extent possible within their financial and human resources constraints. Since ICT refers to a means of accessing (and disseminating) information rather than a particular *source of information*, not much can be said about the (in)appropriateness of computer-generated information per se with regard to development or rights work beyond the practicalities of costs, training needs,

and equipment availability. One such practical issue concerns whether organizations should buy off-the-shelf software or "build their own" by acquiring
open-source programs (Powell 2006, 529; Bryant 2006, 561–62).

Nonetheless, Bryant raises an intriguing, substantive question of whether
the appeal of ICT may in fact be as much *symbolic* (amid the backdrop of
globalization discourse) as *instrumental* in actual task accomplishment. As a
case in point, he quotes a 2005 *World Disasters Report* published by the International Federation of Red Cross and Red Crescent Societies:

> Looking back over the events of 2004, it is striking how many of
> the year's disasters could have been avoided with better informa-
> tion and communication. For tens of thousands of people, disaster
> arrived suddenly, unannounced. (International Federation of Red
> Cross and Red Crescent Societies 2005, introduction)

On this, Bryant comments,

> The authors of the report, however, are at pains to point out that
> their concerns do not begin and end with the Internet: the type
> of information, its form, and the ways in which it is gathered and
> broadcast are of paramount importance. In many instances the for-
> mal, official, centrally controlled information channels are far less
> effective than the informal, dispersed, locally generated ones. (Bry-
> ant 2006, 559)

He points out that person-to-person communications within the context of
community appears as (or more) effective in responding effectively to tsunamis
and other disasters as use of high-technology systems, an argument that advocates of participatory inquiry would likely embrace. Nonetheless, ICT utilization is important in maintaining lines of communication within development
and advocacy networks, as discussed later in this chapter.

"Voices" of Participation

In the context of information, Powell poses the classic dilemma of adapting
Robert Chambers's participatory methods to development: which comes first,
the authentic voice of the people or program strategies designed to elicit "participatory" involvement (2006, 529)? In Chambers's Participatory Rural Appraisal, information is "owned, analyzed and used by local people" and can be
revealed through a variety of approaches led by locals, such as

"Handing over the stick" and they do it: basic to PRA is facilitating, handing over the stick, chalk or pen, enabling local people to be the analysts, mappers, diagrammers, observers, researchers, historians, planners and actors, presenters of their analysis, and then in turn facilitators. (Chambers 1997, 117–19)

Chambers is especially critical of consultancy work, which he derides as "development tourism," whereby "uppers" rely on conventional ways of "doing NGO business" instead of listening to the marginalized (Chambers 1981; Hirschman 2003). On the basis of his work in Mozambique, Hirschman argues that consultants on short-term assignments *can* in fact take deliberate steps to capture authentic participatory information, for example, by "using rhetorical space" (subjecting donor rhetoric to local people's scrutiny) and relying on local organizations for guidance (2003, 497–98). Similarly, Debebe recounts how an "outsider" consultant recalibrated his understanding of Navajo tourism initiatives by reassessing his perspectives on economic development in relation to local values (2002, 364). According to Seeley and Khan (2006), large NGOs such as PROSHIKA in Bangladesh can draw on qualitative research techniques to determine "issues to be addressed" that align subsequent activities to authentic information. At minimum, it is important for NGOs to recognize factors that compromise the authenticity of participatory information.

A Ugandan economist elaborates on relationships among voices of the poor, information flows between Northern and Southern NGOs, and NGO credibility in advocating for the poor. Specifically, Nyamugasira argues that governments can easily discredit the advocacy claims made against them as unrepresentative of those for whom NGOs purportedly speak:

Northern NGOs must be held accountable for the advocacy agenda they pursue. . . . If the desire is to inject the voice of the traditionally voiceless, then this voice must be clearly heard before it can be clearly articulated. . . . NGOs need to stop being preoccupied with their own narrowly interpreted bureaucratic mandates and get down to the business of seeking out and listening to the poor in order to secure a mandate to speak clearly and with conviction on their behalf. The poor live in the so-called culture of silence from which they must be liberated. (Nyamugasira 1998, 302–3)

Although some (such as Powell) suggest that authentic voice can be heard only through the efforts of Southern organizations, Nyamugasira suggests that Northern NGOs can exert authority in human rights advocacy so long as they can convincingly ground their claims in authentic participatory information.

Knowledge(s), Knowledge Management, and Organization Learning

An expert on NGO management bluntly asserts, "Unless NGOs learn, they are destined for insignificance" (Fowler 1996, as quoted in Smillie and Hailey 2002, 70). To lead a learning organization is to subject its management values, structures, and strategies to continuing scrutiny from within (Smillie and Hailey 2002, 69; Padaki 2002). Although success in learning correlates with effective change in turbulent circumstances, it seldom comes about easily. Rather, organization learning derives from knowledge-based processes, as Smillie and Hailey explain:

> Knowing what works and why is essential to the success of NGOs, and knowing what does not work is equally as important. Knowledge involves awareness, memory, and familiarity that develop with experience and learning. Knowledge is the product of information, experience, and judgment. It is of little use, however, if it is not disseminated, applied, and above all, used for learning. Knowledge and learning are therefore inextricably linked. (Smillie and Hailey 2002, 70)

But as Powell suggests, it is preferable to use the plural *knowledges*, implying that there is no universal consensus of what constitutes *knowledge* (singular). Thus, "the issue for anyone working on developmental issues cannot simply be how to deal with 'knowledge,' but how to act effectively in an environment of multiple 'knowledges'" (2006, 521).

If a learning organization is the ideal, leaders need to put development processes in motion to attain it. Although Powell connects the term *knowledge management* (KM) in development with the "World Bank's definition of itself as a 'knowledge bank'" (2006, 521; also see Broad 2007), it is nonetheless appropriate to view KM more generally as a particular set of organization tactics to foster learning. Certain paradoxes arise since some measure of management direction is required to cultivate bottom-up cognitive discernment and judgment. Thus, tensions need to be regarded as inevitable and healthy within learning organizations. As Padaki expresses it, refined thinking understands these tensions not as polar opposites but rather as "complementarities" or organizational balances between "the need to hold together" (i.e., to conform and converge through regulatory process) and "the need to be different" (i.e., to innovate and diverge through the developmental process; Padaki 2002, 330). But with regard to structure, it follows that the creative tensions are workable to the extent that organizations rely on mutual adjustment (rather than top-down control) as the principal means of coordinating action (see Mintzberg 1993, 253–81).

The balance of this section examines particular knowledge-management strategies that development and rights organizations can pursue to promote organization learning. Drawing from Ben Ramalingam's working paper *Tools for Knowledge and Learning: A Guide for Development and Humanitarian Organisations* published by the Overseas Development Institute (2005), five organization competencies emerge as platforms for promoting learning: strategy development, management techniques, collaboration mechanisms, knowledge sharing and learning, and capturing and storing knowledge. Each of these competencies corresponds to principal areas of inquiry in the general study of KM (see, e.g., Davenport and Prusak 1998; Prusak and Matson 2006).

Strategy Development

For Ramalingam, strategy development represents an organization competency that "relates how an organization might start to look at its knowledge and learning in a strategic manner" (2005, 4). He outlines five tools, or methodologies, that "can be used to plan, monitor, and evaluate knowledge" within a strategic context: knowledge audits, social network analysis, most significant change analysis, outcome mapping, and scenario testing. Elaborating on each, Ramalingam offers detailed descriptions of processes involved. All of these methodologies aside, development and humanitarian organizations can experience difficulty grasping what it is that they actually know in relation to particular contexts of action. KM experts Leigh Weiss and Laurence Prusak describe the problem as one of "seeing knowledge plain." They refer to a case in the business sector where a group of executives used the same words, but their meanings were obviously different with regard to competitors, threats, and opportunities:

> Before long it was clear that there was very little consensus or agreement. . . . These differences only emerged by literally drawing the competitive landscape on a chart. The words were significantly misleading until they were represented visually. As this story

demonstrates, there is an increasing realization that can be an extremely potent tool and method for working with knowledge. (Weiss and Prusak 2006, 323–24)

Making knowledge visible is just as essential in development and human rights work in general and in facilitating participative inquiry in particular. Regarding the former, Scott-Villiers's account of the British NGO ActionAid's frustration in developing a learning strategy appears similar to Weiss and Prusak's executive group:

> The mission and goals had been transformed, decision making had shifted away from the centre, new people had joined, and after a number of attempts to adjust what had become entrenched procedures, the organisation's systems began to align. . . . There was a tendency to "add on" rather than to make strategic choices. ActionAid was neither transparent, as claimed in its strategy, nor did it account to the poor and its partners. [An external evaluation] pointed out ActionAid's complacency. In the words of an ActionAid staff member in London, "We realised we had been patting ourselves on the back." (Scott-Villiers 2002, 431)

With regard to participative inquiry, Robert Chambers makes knowledge visible throughout *Whose Reality Counts?*, a book that he illustrates with hand-drawn diagrams rather than professionally produced tables and charts. The chapter "Learning to Learn" within this book reverses conventional development roles in that the rural poor become analysts and so-called "professionals" become learners (1997, 104). Drawings and maps (on paper or in the dirt) become the media for seeing knowledge plain.

Weiss and Prusak make the case that "knowledge visibility" can help professionals such as those in their business executive example and Scott-Villiers's ActionAid setting "better navigate a knowledge environment and act on it." For them, making knowledge visible offers several distinct advantages:

- creating a rich picture of what is known so that knowledge connections are visible and comprehensible;
- better communicating complex relationships;
- showing time, space, and activities in a multidimensional setting;
- showing multiple levels of relationships and causations;

- stimulating new knowledge—the act of making knowledge visible creates new knowledge, so it is just not the output but the process that is valuable;
- exposing what is not known;
- displaying patterns that were previously not known; and
- creating common symbols to foster group coherence (Weiss and Prusak 2006, 327).

Although each of Ramalingam's five tools for using knowledge "makes knowledge plain," two of them—the most significant change analysis and outcome mapping—poignantly demonstrate the advantages of making knowledge visible in complex development efforts. A critical review of the most significant change technique used in two development programs in Laos asserts that this tool achieves success if an enabling context (of senior management support, team leader commitment, staff–villager trust, and a learning culture) exists. Specifically, Willetts and Crawford explain,

> The primary benefits identified by management staff were that it "forced in-depth development thinking"; "created deep changes in people's thinking among the staff"; and "helped us learn what actually happens, at least for some cases." Field staff made similar observations, captured in statements such as: "We can measure if work done is fruitful or not. Did they understand? Did they practice or not?"; "We can work up close with villagers, not get shy, we open minds together"; and "It gives us time to look at our work and see what we have done." (Willetts and Crawford 2007, 369)

These reactions are indicative of new knowledge generated, recognition of what was not previously known, and a renewed sense of group coherence.

Oriented toward performance and impact evaluation, outcome mapping is especially useful in negotiating the *aggregation* (adding up all that the agency accomplishes) and the *attribution* (isolating one agency's particular role in bringing about change) problems discussed in chapter 5. This methodology is premised on the assumption that development and rights organizations interact with others amid a number of contextual factors that affect human conditions. Two evaluation specialists with the International Development Research Centre explain how outcome mapping helps agencies learn about their own efforts in collaboration with others:

By considering the myriad actors and factors that contribute to development processes, it focuses on how a programme facilitates rather than causes change and looks to assess contribution rather than attribution. Outcome Mapping encourages a programme to link itself explicitly to processes of transformation and provides it with the information it requires in order to change along with its partners. (Earl and Carden 2002, 520)

Earl and Carden's additional comments show how outcome mapping makes knowledge visible in ways that correspond to making connections comprehensible, as well as to the other advantages listed previously.

It is particularly valuable for monitoring and evaluating development programmes, whose results and achievements cannot be understood through quantitative indicators alone but also require the deeper insights of a qualitative, contextualised story of the development process. (Earl and Carden 2002, 523)

At its essence, outcome mapping assesses how participation in collaborative efforts affects positive behavioral changes within (and among other) organizations. In this regard, the technique enables the NGO to learn about the outcomes of its own (and other groups') involvement in networks, coalitions, and donor–aid recipient relationships (Earl et al. 2001, 1–3; Ramalingam 2005, 20).

In summary, it can be said that by examining learning and knowledge strategically, organizations take the initiative to "look inwardly" as Peter Uvin recommends: "All development agencies would benefit enormously if they managed to create an atmosphere of critical internal debate about human rights among their own staff and direct partners" (2004, 154). In this regard, an organization's candor in "making knowledge plain" can help maintain its strategic bearing on human empowerment and rights affirmation.

Management Techniques

At its core, the issue of knowledge creation depends largely on managerial attitudes and behaviors related to learning and to human factors that influence it. In their book about leadership in Asian NGOs, Smillie and Hailey identify BRAC's executive director F. H. Abad as especially adept at setting the stage for organization learning:

He saw himself acting as teacher to his staff, while in turn learning from his colleagues and the communities with whom he worked: "I made a point to go into the field, at least for four to seven days, live there, and talk to BRAC staff. The staff would congregate in one place, and we would then discuss and analyze strategies and problems, and then make vital decisions on the spot. This is how we learned . . . in fact, BRAC started learning while doing things, and the excitement was that everybody was learning too. It was like a 'little university.' " (Smillie and Hailey 2002, 75)

Along these lines, empirical research intent on discovering "what knowledge managers really do" finds that effective KM leaders are much more focused on human resources issues than on technical concerns related to data and information systems (Asllani and Luthans 2003). Stated in the negative, KM "can be seriously hampered by narcissism and self-aggrandizement that are deeply rooted in individuals and the institutions they build" (Bhardwaj and Monin 2006, 82).

Ramalingam prefaces his compilation of six management techniques for facilitating learning on the Native American proverb "Tell me, and I'll forget. Show me, and I may not remember. Involve me, and I'll understand," indicating that his methodologies are grounded in the human dimensions of organization. One technique, the SECI approach, promotes interplay between tacit (internalized) and explicit (codified) knowledges to facilitate "effective knowledge and learning in ongoing projects and programs" (2005, 28–29). In essence, leaders encourage staff to "open up" by relating stories and anecdotes that reveal knowledge interlaced with values and beliefs. Such collective revelations allow the organization to mobilize tacit knowledge proactively in problem-solving contexts (Bhardwaj and Monin 2006). The acronym SECI—standing for socialization, externalization, combination, and internalization—derives from Nonaka and Takeuchi's (1995) influential book *The Knowledge-Creating Company*, which rejects Western traditions that separate "pure knowledge" from a person's beliefs and values. In its focus on interaction between tacit and explicit knowledge, Ramalingam's SECI technique promotes "the need to be different in development" that Padaki (2002) balances with needs for regulation as a healthy tension within action-focused organizations.

Four of Ramalingam's management techniques can be characterized as rather simple workshop tools that either analyze knowledge requirements or apply that knowledge. First, the "blame versus gain" technique helps people recognize their own defensive behaviors that inhibit "embracing error" as a means of organization learning (Korten 1980). Specifically, this tool illustrates how "blame responses" (e.g., blaming people for getting it wrong—"You should have never let this happen.") can be transformed into "gain responses" (focusing on the process that allowed the mistake—"What could you have done differently?"; Ramalingam 2005, 31). In emergency relief work, for example, it is crucial not to overlook mistakes but at the same time to value the individual's morale. For these situations, Raymond-McKay and MacLachlan propose a critical incident analysis, a variation of "blame versus gain," whereby an interviewer asks,

> "What led up to the incident?", "Why did the incident occur?", "Who was involved?", "What were you thinking/feeling?", "How did you attempt to deal with . . . ?", and "If the incident occurred again how would you deal with it?" (Raymond-McKay and MacLachlan 2000, 677)

This critical incident technique provides a clearer picture of how relief workers function in crisis situations because it focuses on fluid, adaptive abilities rather than on more conventional job-related skills.

A second technique applies Kurt Lewin's force-field analysis to encourage people to identify contextual forces that work either "for" or "against" proposed changes in the form of a program innovation or improved human condition. This management tool supports an open, democratic mode of decision making that promotes transparency elucidating the context of the issue at hand. Ramalingam introduces a third tool, "activity-based mapping," that encourages people to think systematically about inputs and outputs of related activities that are linked and ordered. Maps (or diagrams) of these activity systems can then be used to "invite participants to analyze the map, raising such questions as: 'What knowledge seems most critical to this process? What knowledge is missing?'" Then maps can be used to "brainstorm how the knowledge maps can be used to improve activities across the organization" (Ramalingam 2005, 34). Ramalingam refers to a fourth tool as a reframing matrix, a diagnostic that encourages participants to visualize a problem (e.g., a program that does not promote fund-raising) from a variety of internal and external stakeholder perspectives. As he explains, "In humanitarian and development work, it may be useful to think through the potential perspectives of different internal and external stakeholders" (p. 39). In this regard, the reframing matrix is effective to the extent it moves participants to visualize problematic issues from other stakeholder perspectives.

An additional management technique, structural innovation, is especially adaptable to human-rights-advocacy settings. This tool leads people to think about alternative programming possibilities connected with different program attributes. Ramalingam offers the following example:

> In order to develop activities to be undertaken as part of a communications strategy for mainstreaming a social development programme at Swiss Development Cooperation (SDC), [a] team undertook this process. The attributes we identified were as follows:
>
> - Reason/benefit: Why is the client communicating?
> - Content: What is the client communicating?
> - Audience: To whom is the client communicating?
> - Channel: How is the client communicating?
> - Frequency/timing: When and how often is the client communicating? (Ramalingam 2005, 37)

He then arrays various program options, including "awareness raising" (content = political and social conditions, audience = policymakers, channel = publications, and frequency/timing = monthly) and "influencing and shaping public debate" (content = vision and mission of the project, audience = beneficiaries, channel = Internet/e-mail, and frequency/timing = weekly). Structural innovation stimulates new and creative thinking by visualizing how alternative combinations of program attributes can spur on beneficial change.

In reference to their study of South Asian NGOs, Smillie and Hailey find support for Peter Senge's argument that "the leader of a learning organization should have a facilitative role rather than an inspirational or technical one. The leader should be a designer, a steward, a teacher" (Senge 1990, quoted in Smillie and Hailey 2002, 135). Managers with strong interpersonal skills can draw on creative knowledge-centered tools (such as those discussed previously) to facilitate organization learning in ways that reframe or extend future possibilities.

Collaboration Mechanisms

Among other reasons, organization learning is vital because knowledge by nature is a group undertaking, or a matter of group cognition (see Nosek 2004). Moreover, as a network knowledge expert deduces,

- knowledge is a human activity,

- human knowledge is driven by the need for sense-making,
- sense-making takes place within a contextual framework, and
- context development takes place within a community or network (Shariq 1998, 11–12).

In particular reference to the private sector, Gupta and Govindarajan assert that social ecology *is central* to KM, despite the allure of the supposed rationality of information technology. Although it is directed toward a business audience, their explanation can temper the rationalistic biases of NGO and governmental managers as well:

> Because all knowledge starts as information, many companies regard knowledge management as synonymous with information management. Carried to an extreme, such a perspective can result in the profoundly mistaken belief that the installation of a sophisticated information technology infrastructure is the end-all and be-all of knowledge management. Effective knowledge management depends not merely on information technology platforms but more broadly on the social ecology of an organization. Social ecology refers to the social system in which people operate. It derives from an organization's formal and informal expectations of individuals . . . and affects how people interact with others. (Gupta and Govindarajan 2006, 230)

In addition, the collective learning experience is important because (1) fairness in the *processes* of engagement, explanation, and expectation is just as crucial as a good outcome (Kim and Mauborgne 2006) and (2) outcomes depend on collectively knowing "what we know" and "who knows what" (Cross et al. 2006).

If organization learning is to generate creative options for development and rights-advocacy organizations, knowledge development needs to be cultivated "through a set of practical ground rules and techniques" (Prusak and Matson 2006, 5; Leonard and Swap 2006). Ramalingam prefaces his presentation of collaboration-inducing tools by introducing a developmental framework for team building (applicable to both face-to-face and virtual teams). This framework approaches team development as moving the group through successive stages, starting with a collective of withdrawn individuals, working through hostile interactions, and ultimately achieving a supportive environment of shared responsibility. Each of the stages connotes significant differences in regard to the following group characteristics:

- atmosphere and relationships,
- understanding and acceptance of goals,
- listening and information sharing,
- decision making,
- reaction to leadership, and
- attention to the way the group is working (Ramalingam 2005, 42).

In addition, Ramalingam refers to two techniques that can facilitate organization learning in rights-focused agencies. First, "action learning sets" consist of "between six and eight people who meet together regularly over a reasonable time period and 'present' and collectively work on problems faced in ongoing practice" (2005, 48). This technique is particularly useful for involving participants to affect program outcomes and addressing issues warranting improvement in the work context. The ground rules call for explicit steps governing group interaction:

1. Start by one member presenting the problem.
2. Other members offer constructive questions to coax out alternative views and perspectives.
3. New understandings (if generated).
4. Test in workplace.
5. Bring results back to the group.
6. Draw conclusions about new learning; put it into practice or revert back to step 1 (Ramalingam 2005, 48).

Second, Ramalingam refers to Edward de Bono's work *Six Thinking Hats* (1999) as a source of a technique that assigns group members different-colored hats to induce varying styles of thinking about the same problem as follows:

- White hat—objective, rational, factual thinking;
- Red hat—emotional, suspicious, intuitional thinking;
- Black hat—negative, pessimistic thinking;
- Yellow hat—positive, optimistic thinking;
- Green hat—creative, alternative-generating thinking; and
- Blue hat—summary thinking about the thinking of everyone else (Ramalingam 2005, 50–51).

Ramalingam recommends this technique as a way to put skepticism on the table in what might otherwise result in a linear, rational discussion, implying that the wide range of perceptions (including pessimism) stimulates knowledge development as organization learning. As a case in point, he refers to a learning process among those working on housing and resettlement in Sri Lanka in the aftermath of a tsunami:

> The German government, through its Federal Ministry for Economic Cooperation and Development (BMZ), is supporting key Sri Lankan governmental organizations in facilitating and implementing the housing and reconstruction process. The Sri Lankan and German counterparts jointly conducted the planning of the entire project, including its outcomes and key activities. The joint project planning sessions commenced with the six thinking hats methodology, which was used to generate a shared sense of the key issues in the reconstruction process that needed to be further explored and practically addressed. (Ramalingam 2005, 51)

According to Peter Uvin, capacity building is paramount as it "encourages development actors to broaden the range of their potential partners and work with local human rights organizations" (2004, 140–41). Thus, organization learning can facilitate capacity building by enhancing the agencies' abilities to collaborate in ways that generate knowledge.

Knowledge Sharing and Learning

If political analysis, reframing, and reflection are critical within a rights perspective (Uvin 2004), then knowledge-sharing issues arise as challenging leadership issues. Data and information retrievable from available records or logframe analyses can be useful only if they can contribute understanding and explanation to organizational memory. In a "pyramid of meaning" developed by Laszlo and Laszlo (2002, 405), "knowing what" (through data and information) is no substitute for "knowing how" (understanding) or "knowing why" (explanation), both essential for agencies intending to improve human conditions. But, as discussed earlier, development and rights agencies face particular difficulty preserving organization memory given high rates of staff turnover, or what Kransdorff and Williams (2006) call the "swing door and musical chairs" problem. Thus, it is important that an NGO's memory resides in teams and groups rather than with individuals such as technical experts or high-ranking managers. As with all organizations, knowledge reflecting higher-level meaning (i.e., understanding and explanation) needs to be shared in order to be embedded into memory.

Among others, Ramalingam offers two particular "knowledge sharing" techniques that are used as well in the business sector: "stories" and "after action reviews." He suggests that "stories" (or narratives) can be used in a variety of development contexts, such as

- team- or community-building exercises,
- within multidisciplinary or multicultural teams to break down barriers,
- workshop warm-ups,
- trip debriefs,
- personal project reviews,
- entertainment and fun, and
- monitoring systems (2005, 58).

In each of these situations, narrative telling encourages individual and group reflection on significant events and experiences. Ideally, these narratives "need to be simple and powerful . . . [and] targeted at people with the power to make a decision and change things" (p. 59).

As former World Bank executive Steve Denning explains, stories "provide a vehicle for unveiling unseen tacit knowledge [that] draws on deep-flowing streams of meaning to catalyze visions of a different and renewed future" (2000, n.p.). A story (or parable) works *not* because it conveys factual information but because it serves as a springboard initiating conversation about predicaments or stumbling blocks that keep people from acting justly or reaching consensus within an organization (e.g., about what type of software is needed). Stories work to facilitate participative learning and decision making because they (1) rely on verbal expression, (2) encourage opportunistic development through iterative thinking, and (3) focus on the "big picture" rather than distractive detail (Cohn 2004, 145–56). Effective human rights campaigns depend heavily on stories that incite emotions as much as or more than transmitting information. As Chapman and Fisher comment,

An effective campaign is based on stories and the extent to which these are accepted by different parties. Heroes or heroines are created whose actions and exploits become mythologised, and so serve to motivate supporters. Thus, an essential characteristic of campaigns is their fluidity, though this dynamism creates difficulties in assessing and managing them. Campaigns cannot be understood as a linear, mechanistic, or logical sequence. (Chapman and Fisher 2000, 155)

In essence, stories promote collective problem solving to surmount organizational problems in achieving humanitarian goals.

Ramalingam characterizes "after action reviews" (AARs) as similar to oral debriefings in business organizations (see Argote 2006) but as considerably more extensive and elaborate. A facilitator develops a number of questions to "establish a common understanding of the work under review" and "generate reflections about successes and failures" in the project (Ramalingam 2005, 64). It is incumbent on the facilitator to design these questions purposefully so that expected responses can be significantly meaningful to contribute to organization learning. As a case in point, Ramalingam shows how this tool was used in a workshop attended by NGO professionals from Indonesia, India, Sri Lanka, and Thailand who convened following the 2004 tsunami:

> [The AAR] presented an opportunity for participants . . . to discover what happened and why, and how to build on strengths and improve on areas of weakness . . . and collaborate more effectively together. Of the best practices discussed over the two days, five were selected as having been most crucial to improving response time and effectiveness:
>
> • Having existing capacity to respond,
> • Making linkages at the community level with local structures and community leaders,
> • Having consistent leadership in the development of strategic plans,
> • The existence of a longer-term planning and fundraising strategy, and the use of humanitarian standards. (Ramalingam 2005, 65)

These best practices served as the basis for action planning among the NGOs represented at the table. Thus, after action, reviews offer insights about the factors accounting for strengths and weaknesses of program initiatives. Conducted appropriately as learning events rather than performance evaluations or fault-finding inquiries, AARs work because participants feel free to be open and candid in a nonthreatening setting (Collison and Parcell 2004, 147–70).

Capturing and Storing Knowledge

Learning NGOs need to preserve generated knowledge, insights, and "lessons learned" to maintain program continuity amid high staff turnover. In the vocabulary of KM, the challenge is to convert *tacit knowledge* embedded in individual or group experiences to *explicit knowledge* that can be codified and easily retrieved. Knowledge researchers refer to the location where explicit knowledge is stored in the organization both metaphorically as "bins" or "cupboards" (Mulder and Whiteley 2007) and literally as files and folders in an electronic data system or even written records. Although high turnover in development and rights-advocacy organizations necessitates codification, managers must take measures to structure knowledge retention procedures with some caution. The Chinese proverb "the palest ink is better than the best memory" (used by Ramalingam 2005, 73) suggests that overly structured protocols may exaggerate the significance of past observations and/or dull the edges of new learning experiences by requiring them to conform with standardized formats.

Ramalingam introduces a number of techniques for capturing knowledge, several of which involve electronic data storage. As an example, he recommends using shared computer network drives to support electronic folders corresponding to pertinent topics such as programs, communities, or activities. Other folder systems, however, could be more encompassing, such as that used by the NGO Tearfund:

> During 2001, Tearfund established a shared drive on its server with the purpose of supporting learning. The shared drive is organised with a folder for each of Tearfund's 15 departments, in which there are five sub-folders: "About," "Policy," "Strategy," "Learning," and "Archive." All activities, projects, and correspondence are organized within the sub-folders and each department has an assigned activity administrator responsible for ensuring the folders are correctly and consistently used across departments. (Ramalingam 2005, 86)

Clearly, shared network drives allow for wider accessibility to pertinent documents among collaborating organizations, but in addition, they facilitate network integration by introducing a common terminology among participating groups and formalizing liaison mechanisms among those responsible for records keeping in each agency (Ramalingam 2005, 85).

Although the "exit interview" is a conventional face-to-face learning instrument used in many organizations, high-turnover NGOs can rely on it as a strategic tool to preserve knowledge if the individual leaving the organization does so voluntarily. The interview session(s) can be especially adept in capturing and transferring knowledge if all who can benefit are included and discussions focus on the explicit (recorded) knowledge assembled by the departing individual, as well as her or his observations, viewpoints, and experiences. As Ramalingam puts it, development leaders do well "to outline a handover procedure that allows relevant knowledge to be preserved without a disproportionate amount of working time taken up" (2005, 77). Conducted well, the exit interview offers NGO leaders a significant learning opportunity that can improve the quality of "handovers" (from the departing to the successor) in development and humanitarian sectors known for high employee turnover. As with the other four knowledge-related organizational competencies, "knowledge capture and storage" (making knowledge easy to access) depends on judicious planning and leadership support.

Knowledge, Learning, and Networks

The cliché "knowledge is power" resonates forcefully in the business world where effective KM is recognized as a competitive advantage. Writing primarily in the context of business, Laszlo and Laszlo (2002) argue that KM *evolves* and that so far three generations of KM have surfaced, each embodying the previous but extending further. For them, first-generation KM involves knowledge sharing that has in essence occurred throughout time, long before "knowledge management" was in vogue as an area of inquiry. For example, Frederick Taylor's "scientific management" entailed the transmission of information from "efficiency expert" to the worker applying that knowledge to improve performance. If, as Laszlo and Laszlo assert, first-generation KM is about *imitation*, then it can be said that "best practices" used elsewhere constitute an exercise in first-generation KM (p. 401). By contrast, second-generation KM embraces knowledge sharing as well but extends beyond that to learn for the sake of generating knowledge for *innovation*. In particular, business organizations have been able to create knowledge for innovation by "learning through collaboration, which in the business world has been adapted and applied as 'organization learning'" (p. 402).

But it is the third generation of learning that "can foster business knowledge . . . for the expansion of a corporate citizenship agenda and the emergence of evolutionary learning corporations" (p. 402) that has profound implications for human rights advocacy. After explaining how third-generation KM evolves from a "paradigm of participation" in which people collaboratively interrelate varying levels of meaning (from data to information, knowledge, understanding, and then wisdom), Laszlo and Laszlo define it in this way:

Third-generation KM is about the democratization of knowledge, about citizen involvement, and the expansion of boundaries of what traditionally has been considered education in order to design an authentic learning society. It is not so much about knowledge and know-how any more but about *meaning* and *know-why*. It is based on a new way of thinking informed by a planetary ethic and a different way of living from what is now favored by mass-media commercialization. KM has both the potential and responsibility to contribute to the emergence of a sustainable global civilization. (Laszlo and Laszlo 2002, 408; emphasis added)

In other words, it interprets what data, information, and knowledge *mean* within the context of societal betterment. In that it requires the collaboration of external actors, third-generation KM is at the core of Peter Uvin's call for "choos[ing] new partners" as vital in a rights-based perspective:

One of the major—and by now totally evident—consequences of a rights-based approach to development is that it encourages development actors to identify different partners. In an RBA, development actors are no longer limited to traditional development partners, namely, organizations that locally reproduce discourse, aims, and strategy of the foreign agencies themselves. Indeed, throughout the world a large array of organizations exists that does what human rights are all about . . . promoting human dignity through the development of claims that seek to empower excluded groups and that seek to create socially guaranteed improvements in policy (including but not limited to legal frameworks). These groups, often without saying so, "do" human rights. They do it differently from the usual manner of human rights NGOs—the "naming and shaming" approach. They do it through grassroots organization, collective mobilization and bargaining, changing values throughout society, pushing for change in laws and policies and institutions, and confronting discrimination (not only by governments but also by non-state actors, whether for profit or not). . . . Improving their capacities for learning and networking, their degree of internal democracy and representativeness, and their impact on other actors is part of rights-based development work. (Uvin 2004, 163)

In this context, advocacy networks may become what Finnemore and Sikkink call *norm entrepreneurs* that attempt to convince a "critical mass" (of governments, corporations, or other entities) of their altruistic convictions that challenge prevailing views by managing meanings. As knowledge managers, norms entrepreneurs engage in third-generation KM, apparent in this explanation:

> Norm entrepreneurs are critical for norm emergence because they call attention to issues or even "create" issues by using language that names, interprets, and dramatizes them. Social movement theorists refer to this reinterpretation or renaming process as "framing." The construction of cognitive frames is an essential component of norm entrepreneurs' political strategies, since, when they are successful, the new frames resonate with broader public understandings and are adopted as new ways of talking about and understanding issues. (Finnemore and Sikkink 1998, 897)

In short, networking builds capacity for effective rights advocacy not simply by "sharing knowledge" (although it certainly should do that) but also by leveraging its multiorganizational legitimacy to (re)interpret what information, situations, events, and circumstances *mean* in the language of rights and human dignity.

Multiorganizational partnerships and networks offer political opportunities to advocate for rights claims on a global stage, appealing to international bodies that can pressure those repressive forces obstructing those rights. As Keck and Sikkink explain, transnational advocacy networks provide rights seekers the opportunity to shift venues to advocate their cause to authoritative entities that hold political sway over oppressors:

> We call the feedback that comes from this kind of venue shifting "the boomerang effect" and producing it is one of the most common strategic activities of advocacy network. When the links between state and domestic actors are severed, it initiates the "boomerang": domestic NGOs bypass their state and directly search out the international allies to try to bring pressure on their states from the outside. (Keck and Sikkink 1998, 221–22)

In regard to knowledge and meaning creation, transactional advocacy networks embody the paradigm of participation (underpinning third-generation

KM), a "worldview that sees human beings as co-creating their reality through participation: through their experience, their imagination and intuition, their thinking and their action" (Reason 1994, 324).

Keck and Sikkink (1998) explain that international networks can exert pressure through their ability to build a cognitive frame, or (re)interpret issues, in ways that resonate and become embedded in the political culture. Sperling, Ferree, and Risman (2001), for example, discuss how Russian women activists used international proclamations (affirming the universal rights of women) to address the deteriorating status of Russian women in the post-Soviet era by crafting the slogan "Democracy Without Women Is No Democracy!" These researchers argue that the local, grassroots action of these women took on international significance (hence, "the boomerang effect") given the recent history of Western funding supporting the rise of civil society in Russia and the roles of US foundations empowering these women through seminar training. In suggesting that women's advocacy "has become increasingly professionalized and 'NGO-ized,'" Sperling, Ferree, and Risman touch on Uvin's inference (in his quotation) that a rights-based perspective should avail itself of more sophisticated alternatives than simply "naming and shaming." Thus, NGO leaders need to recognize the importance of knowledge management and meaning management as an effective means of translating information into advocacy power, particularly if channeled through collaborative networks and partnerships that offer multiple venues for political action.

Keck and Sikkink also reiterate the connection between development work and rights advocacy by emphasizing the power that can be unleashed by reframing technical, supposedly nonpolitical, issues in terms of human circumstances:

> The tropical forest issues issue is fraught with scientific uncertainty about forests' role in climate regulation, the regenerative capacity and the value of undiscovered or untapped biological resources. By reframing the issue, calling attention to the impact of tropical forest destruction on particular populations, environmentalists have made a call for action independent of the scientific status of the issue . . . [and by doing so] turn the cold facts into human stories intended to motivate people to action. (Keck and Sikkink 1998, 225–26)

In this regard, technical data and information take on different meaning in the face of people's testimonials and life experiences.

By shifting the focus from advocacy networks themselves to *campaigns* in which they are involved, the power of collaboration can be seen in broader perspective beyond just the principled motives of rights organizations. Specifically, rights organizations can "choose partners" that are motivated by diverse interests beyond altruism and empathy. For example, in their discussion of "bridging the double divide" of Northern and Southern trade unions and NGOs, Anner and Evans account for the formation of complex collaborative relationships that depart somewhat from Keck and Sikkink's transnational advocacy model:

> This whole organisational matrix is knit together by a set of internationally oriented labour activists, some of them inside the labour movement, some in the NGO world, many shifting back and forth between the two. . . . The fact that the basic rights complex is able to integrate principled ideas and values with everyday interests is arguably its most exciting characteristic, both practically and theoretically. . . . [Especially] interesting is the logic of organisational relations—a logic that forces groups and leaders to adopt a broad vision, even those whose natural tendencies might be to pursue their own interests in a more pedestrian, immediate way. (Anner and Evans 2004, 38–39)

The campaign lens can also show relationships between grassroots forces, such as the Russian women activists (discussed previously), in concert with nationally or internationally focused NGOs. In reporting on effective campaigns promoting breast-feeding in Ghana and opposing child labor in India, Chapman and Fisher conclude,

> The case studies thus highlight the essential links between policy and project work. International development NGOs first took up advocacy work which drew upon their practical experience on the ground ("practice-to-policy"). This developed into a trend of moving resources from development projects into advocacy, although recently this trend has partly gone into reverse, with NGOs increasingly identifying the need to inform macro-level policy proposals with concrete micro-experiences. These findings close this loop, not only confirming how closely linked advocacy and project work are, but also the need for long-term work at the grass-

roots even after policy changes have been achieved. (Chapman and Fisher 2000, 163)

Again, Uvin's case for development work and rights advocacy as two sides of the same coin finds corroboration. Agencies that can use knowledge management have the potential to translate facts and information into human meaning as influential rights advocates.

Conclusion

Organization learning is sometimes characterized as "double-loop learning," a logic whereby people can examine the sense and logic of their workplace from a critical distance. To the extent that double-loop learning and embracing error (Korten 1980) are possible, those capacity-building processes depend on (1) a disciplined understanding of exactly what "knowledge" means relative to rights-oriented missions, (2) deliberate prompting to stimulate shared learning, and (3) an action-learning focus to leverage learning for human empowerment. In regard to the first, it can be said that although data and information abound, meaning is in short supply. Nonetheless, organizations should resist urges to "grab information by the throat and demand it to speak." Alternatively, rights agencies can tap into the emerging field of knowledge management to anchor organization learning on a systematic understanding of knowledge as a basis for action. Through a focus on knowledge management, NGO professionals can find their own authority as active interpreters of what information may or may not mean with respect to organization values and mission—in essence, what "makes sense." As *institutional leaders*, NGO professionals have no more pressing responsibility than to make sense of the ambiguities and uncertainties surrounding conditions of oppression and deprivation. Second, NGO leaders not only need to model learning but also must take deliberate measures to integrate it within a range of agency activities to accept the realities of lessons learned as guidelines for action. Organization learning is by no means a "stand-alone" exercise but instead interrelates with other competencies such as strategic planning, management techniques, internal cohesion, knowledge sharing, and capturing knowledge. In cultivating diagnostic orientations in strengthening these (or other) competencies, managers need to maintain a delicate balance between initiating learning and biasing its outcome. With regard to the former, leaders can rely on a variety of tools (such as those discussed in this chapter) to initiate organization learning and knowledge-management inquiry. As for the latter, it is important for them to develop sufficiently thick skin to deal with the consequences of "knowledge made plain" and the friction it causes.

Third, organization learning should be premised on the expectation that its outcomes will build on the agency's capacities to empower people. This chapter asserts that development and advocacy organizations can marshal knowledge-management skills in crafting sophisticated strategies that leverage influence on behalf of human rights. In that regard, KM involves not only the dissemination of knowledge but also the management of its meaning within contexts of human circumstance. Thus, by creating new knowledge partnerships, NGOs can leverage the legitimacy of multiorganization networks and partnerships in pressuring powerful actors to abandon policies and practices that compromise human dignity.

Discussion Issues

1. How can leaders motivate volunteers and "short-time" personnel to keep detailed records and accounts of "lessons learned" to support organization memory?
2. In your own words, explain the problems encountered in dealing with "multiple knowledges" both in personal life and in leading advocacy organizations.
3. Why might rights-focused agencies resist "making knowledge plain"? What could account for that reticence? How might leaders deal with this problem (or *should* they)?
4. A skeptic could argue that third-generation "knowledge creation" is nothing more than propaganda and indoctrination. Would you agree—generally? Within the specific context of human empowerment? Explain.
5. Identify particular networks or organizations that as "norm entrepreneurs" have effectively challenged prevailing ideas of human fairness. At what point (event or situation) did a critical mass of society's thinking appear to shift?

7

Gender and Rights Advancement

Fundamentally, it is not about sex[1] or necessarily women per se but about roles and power relationships between men and women. The issue at hand is *gender* as it relates to human empowerment and development. According to the World Health Organization, "Gender refers to the socially constructed roles, behaviors, activities and attributes that a particular society considers appropriate for men and women."[2] This issue of *social construction*, a term used by social theorists, implies that mortal humans themselves define "appropriate" power relationships between women and men in communities, religious enclaves, families, and other social contexts. But what does all of this mean for a rights-oriented NGO? Is it the case, for example, that

1. oppression based on gender is more inhumane and destructive than that based on race, nationality, religion, class, or other depriving factors?
2. gender is a distinct personal identity unto itself?
3. rights deprivation in its many forms and contexts usually relates (either directly or indirectly) to gender?

The best response (3) implies that rights-focused leaders need to focus on gender concerns in order to diagnose conditions of disempowerment in their agencies and within the populations that they serve. Transformative changes that empower *people*—whether women *or* (and) men, lower caste in relation to upper caste, disabled to able-bodied *or* other personal identity criteria—require an organizational resolve to delve beneath the superficial to address the "deep structures" that account for the power dynamics that privilege some and marginalize others (Plantenga 2004). To follow one commentator's analogy, it is as though the rights-sensitive professional studies a detailed, complicated map of oppression on which numerous personal and social identities (gender, race, class, and so forth) intersect. The map reader can establish her bearings by locating one particular highway, not necessarily the most important one (as suggested in response 1) but one that is easily recognizable—in this case, *gender* (Crenshaw Williams 1991, 2000, cited by Hankivsky 2005, 979–80). By following where the "gender highway" leads and how it converges with other identities that marginalize people, one can better grasp the underlying nature of deprivation. In this analogy, gender is *not* isolated as a fundamental issue separate from other identities (as suggested in response 2) related to rights deprivation, but instead it offers a powerful *lens* for analyzing the messy contexts of social inclusion and exclusion and of privileges and vulnerabilities (Plantenga 2004). In the words of prominent experts in gender and development,

> We understand gender to be a primary building block in the construction of power and power relations, and a primary arena through which power is manifested. Thus, gender is an opening to discussing and questioning power constructions deriving from other bases such as age, class, ethnicity, and religion. (Rao and Kelleher 1998, 182)

In this regard, "learning leaders" need to prioritize gender as an underlying and sensitive issue in development work not only to rectify gender disparities within their organizations (see Hailey and James 2002, 405) but also to utilize gender *as a lens*, or analytical tool, that can elucidate the complex textures of oppression and rights deprivation.

Beyond benefiting from gender as a *lens* that moves rights indignities into clearer focus, rights-based NGOs can also extend their effectiveness by relying on gender as a *lever* for improving human conditions. Gender is an especially sensitive issue in the "international development community" not only because global institutions have so strongly promoted women's empowerment as a global governance norm but also because the empirical linkage between improving women's lives and progress in other life quality areas is so widely acknowledged. For example, economist Amartya Sen makes the case that women's agency (or control over their lives) reverberates positively for children, men, and ultimately the whole of society:

> The lives that women save through more powerful agency will certainly include their own. That, however, is not the whole story. There are other lives—men's and children's—also involved. Even within the family, the lives affected may be those of children, since

there is considerable evidence that women's empowerment within the family can reduce child mortality significantly. Going well beyond that, women's agency and voice, influenced by education and employment, can influence the nature of the public discussion on a variety of social subjects . . . and environmental priorities. (Sen 1999, 193)

As evident in specific circumstances (some discussed later in this chapter), women tend to demonstrate particularly strong interpersonal competencies and a developed ethic of caring (compared to men; see Gilligan 1982) that can be instrumental in protecting and empowering others. For example, the staff of the Center for Victims of Torture calls attention to Machsom Watch, a human rights initiative that "uses the presence of Israeli women to protect Palestinians [on the West Bank] passing through the Israeli checkpoints and ensure that their rights are respected" in its workbook *New Tactics in Human Rights: A Resource for Practitioners* (Cornell, Kelsch, and Palasz 2004, 33). In this regard, it can be said that Machsom Watch makes use of gender as a *lever* for protecting the rights of marginalized Palestinians entering and leaving an intimidating environment.

The reader is cautioned *not* to interpret the inclusion of this chapter linking "gender" with "rights advancement" as implying that gender-based oppression is any more (or less) appalling or critical than treatments of refugees, displaced persons, indigenous peoples, or other marginalized identities. Instead, the intent here is to elaborate on gender concerns, not simply to highlight issues of disparity and abuse but to explore how rights-sensitive organizations can engage gender as a *lens* for analyzing oppressive contexts and as a *lever* for improving human conditions. The first section places primary emphasis on the "gender lens"—that is, the analytical strengths that NGOs can accrue by focusing on power relationships within the organization or program initiatives related to gender—but also refers to how gender issues serve as "levers" of empowerment in particular situations. The second section examines "gender mainstreaming" as a lens to analyze rights disparities in organizations and programs and as a lever to promote human rights.

Gender Awareness as a Lens: Analyzing Interests and Power Relationships

In emphasizing that a rights-based approach is inherently *political* in nature, Peter Uvin (2004) refers to a policy paper published by CARE, a US-based

NGO that focuses on poverty with special attention to women who are "at the heart of CARE's community-based efforts to improve basic education, prevent the spread of HIV, increase access to clean water and sanitation, expand economic opportunity and protect natural resources." Uvin quotes that policy paper as follows:

> A rights-based approach deliberately and explicitly focuses on people achieving the minimum conditions for living with dignity. It does so by exposing the root causes of vulnerability and marginalization and expanding the range of responses. (CARE 2001, in Uvin 2004, 135)

If Uvin's proposition that "human rights is a political matter" (2004, 134) is valid, then it is the case as well that NGOs working for women's empowerment need competent analysts capable of discerning the range of women's interests in particular contexts and predicting how programmatic efforts actually affect gender politics. The following discussions stress the imperatives of (1) recognizing the heterogeneity of women's interests and concern regarding specific situations and (2) anticipating how characteristics of programs intended to "advantage" women may actually (for better or worse) impact gendered relationships in families or the community.

Disaggregating (and Reconciling) Women's Interests

NGO professionals need to engender a mind-set recognizing that initiatives intending to "empower women" will differentially impact particular groupings depending on a host of factors related to status and setting. Such a presumption serves to scrutinize the gender narratives crafted by funding agencies and other power actors (typically in the North) that support their ideologies and interests. For example, a 1997 Micro-Credit Summit (of UN and development bank officials) touted the gender-empowering potential of microfinancing in hyperbolic terms of its ability to "initiate an 'upward virtuous spiral' of women's economic, social, and political empowerment" (RESULTS, as reported in Mayoux 1998, 235). Thus, Mayoux maintains that empowerment impacts should be examined on a disaggregated basis in a manner that relates program design to the varied circumstances of women affected. In other words, a rights-based orientation to gender empowerment needs to be premised on the assertion that women's interests are by nature heterogeneous and diverse. Such expectations guard against wholesale representations of women's "helplessness" or "victimhood" or of lumping together the plight of "womenandchildren" as monoliths (see Eade 2003, 147) or as *gender myths and feminist fables* (the title of a recent book; Cornwall, Harrison, and Whitehead 2008). To the contrary, it may be the case that particular subgroupings (e.g., Himalayan mountain women) enjoy more independence and agency than their counterparts (non-mountain inhabitants in Bolivia or Ecuador; see von Dach 2002). Analyses of workers' rights in the horticulture industry, for example, differentiate between ethical trading code protections for women employed as formal, permanent workers and those employed as informal (temporary, seasonal, or casual) laborers (see Barrientos, McClenaghan, and Orton 2001; Tallontire et al. 2005, 564). That said, differences in women's circumstances related to particular inequities, crises, or deprivations can sometimes bring about synergies that reconcile diverse interests to mobilize rights-claiming power.

An ability to change gender relations—often interpreted as a litmus test of NGO impact (Feldman 2003, 6)—may, in fact, subject women to *contradictory forces* that advantage *some* women in *some* respects but detract from freedoms in other ways. In some circumstances, the paradoxical nature of these crosscutting gender effects result from NGOs' efforts to adapt to changing funding environments and role expectations imposed on them. For example, one analyst examines how neoliberal funding pressures cause NGOs in Bangladesh to bureaucratize and, in doing so, impose contradictory forces on women participating in microcredit programs. Specifically, Feldman shows how the intense competition for funding led NGOs to adopt microfinancing program strategies that treat women as individuals and potential free-market entrepreneurs rather than as a relevant grouping of poor women. Furthermore, the self-selection of "poor" (or, better, relatively less-poor) women coming forward to participate offer NGOs justification for claiming "success" with gender empowerment. But Feldman maintains contradictory outcomes may loom beneath the surface of these "success stories":

> NGOs are frequently credited with providing resources and services that transform the daily lives of poor programme participants. This transformation is indicated by the frequently drawn association between women's access to credit and dramatic increases in their decision making, participation in the marketplace, increases in children's education and health, and reductions in fertility. These interpretations of NGO and participant interest highlight . . . contradictory programme relations: women may have greater decision-making authority in the household, participate in the marketplace, and reduce fertility while they are simultaneously involved in more

complex relations of dependence in their communities and in NGO programmes. (Feldman 2003, 14)

Another account of microcredit programs in Bangladesh depicts a perverse portrayal of women's deprivation and rights abuse within these gendered power dynamics of families as institutions. A development consultant on microfinancing reports on the violence against women inflicted by husbands who either object to or expect to "cash in" on their wife's participation in microcredit borrowing from the Grameen Bank. Beyond that, the bank knowingly exacerbates this abuse by using social coercion by mandating regular "borrowers' circle" meetings as a means of enforcing loan repayment. Specifically, Mallick quotes a corroborating account of the rights-depriving logic of how borrowers' circles work:

> When a woman fails to make her installment on time, she experiences humiliation through verbal aggression from fellow members and bank workers in the loan centre. . . . In an extreme case peers may take the defaulter to the bank office. For a man, if he is locked inside the bank building for several days it would mean almost nothing to other people in the village. But if this happens to a woman then it will bring [public disgrace] to her household, lineage and village. People in other villages will also gossip about it. (Rahman 1999, as quoted in Mallick 2002, 154)

As Mallick suggests, income empowerment for women involved in the Grameen Bank's program may well be offset by the contradictory effects of mental and physical abuses.

On the other hand, what may *appear* as contradictory gender relations could in fact be attributable to Western gender expectations inappropriately imposed on other cultures. One observer appeals for a better understanding of the transformative roles that women assume in Islamic society, principally by capitalizing on the seeming contradictions between abusive practices tied to religion and Islamic teachings that bestow agency on women. Haleh Afshar explains the tactical logic, which is derived from Qur'an passages that grant inalienable rights to everyone because there are no intermediaries between people and God:

> The successful battle for Islamic rights by women has had unexpected outcomes. . . . They are fighting for Islam. Nevertheless,

> what they are doing is opening up a path towards much greater participation in Islamic politics. They have refused to be browbeaten by the more misogynistic of the religious leaders and have insisted that the revolution should pay them their due for both supporting it from the beginning and for becoming an exemplar to the rest of the Islamic world. Iranian women have constructed a multifaceted Islam which is increasingly delivering what elsewhere could have been called feminist demands. (Afshar 2000, 532)

Here, the strategy of articulating the contradiction between divine authority and aberrant practices that abuse women constitute a subtle variation of "naming and shaming" typically associated with human rights advocacy. Afshar's assessment of women's transformative role in the face of a repressive regime illustrates how gender can serve as a *lever* for advancing human rights.

In addition, the rights of children—and specifically those of girls as distinct from boys—tend to be contradicted, or at least masked, by NGO poverty-reduction programs aimed at serving women and/or families. An official with the Children's Environments Research Group appeals to donor organizations to adopt children's well-being as a programmatic focus. Specifically, Bartlett (2001) keys in on some basic, technical issues in development—such as water, sanitation, drainage, and family waste management—that impinge on children's living environments, given their particular vulnerabilities related to physical and mental health. Indeed, research on a Save the Children poverty program in Uganda indicates that "children have a different perspective on poverty from that of the adult key informants. . . . They have a positive view of their own potential role in mitigating poverty, and are highly critical of the current performance of local government" (Witter and Bukokhe 2004, 645). Here again, as well as in the contexts of Bangladeshi microcredit and Islamic gender relations, there are compelling reasons why gender issues related to development should be disaggregated in ways that anticipate diverse effects given the heterogeneity of women's and children's interests.

Development NGOs need to decide whether to actively differentiate among women's interests or simply to enable them to emerge. In large part, this quandary reflects philosophic differences between the "women's welfare" orientation and a commitment to self-empowerment (discussed in reference to the differences between the Women in Development and Gender and Development approaches for attending to gender concerns in development organizations). But beyond this, it focuses on whether and how organizations rely on participatory approaches to encourage women to articulate their interests.

At the "structured or rational" end of the scale, NGO leaders may rely on particular interactions within the project planning-management-evaluation cycle as adequate vehicles for bringing women's interests forward. In their analysis of natural resources management in Kenya, Thomas-Slayter and Sodikoff (2001) depict an "information pyramid for enhancing gender-inclusion" wherein interest articulation can occur at various levels of interaction in a partnership between the development agency and the local community group—for example, in the initial data collection used for "social/gender analysis," "local participation and analysis," and "evaluating the enabling conditions of the program" (p. 54). Throughout their discussion, these authors stress the importance of gender-disaggregated data (in the sense of disaggregating accounts of women versus men in farming roles rather than disaggregated among various categories of women). Thomas-Slayter and Sodikoff comment,

> After the evaluation is complete, it is time to assess the current context. Have social changes in the community occurred as a result of the activity? Interviews and other tools can be employed and the data can be re-analysed. Depending on whether the situation has changed, with objectives met or prevented, the participants can reformulate objectives and strategies once again, always with an eye to monitoring and evaluating indicators of impact, process, and sustainability. (Thomas-Slayter and Sodikoff 2001, 58)

Thus, it can be said that these researchers value gender inclusion in natural resources management and trust that rational management systems can be adjusted to accommodate the articulation of gender-pertinent interests.

On the other end of the scale, NGOs may themselves experience discovery as gender interests organically evolve through normal programmatic interactions with constituencies. Operating in West Africa, the NGO Tostan characterizes its gender-focused mission as employing a strategy of "organized diffusion" (Tostan 2006, 6), aptly described as "an attempt to devise non-formal education and literacy programming for rural Senegalese women grounded in their own perception of problems and based on their own learning styles" (Easton, Monkman, and Miles 2003, 446). Easton and his colleagues explain how this NGO reveals diverse interests through participation:

> A curriculum for the programme was devised in a highly participatory and iterative manner. Designers held a series of workshops with rural women to identify their felt needs, to develop and test

curricula that reflected their concerns and used language and cultural forms familiar to the participants, and to anchor the approach
in a Senegalese version of "women's ways of knowing." . . . Tostan
staff [broke away from] the then-traditional approaches to literacy
programmes that had little practical application in their lives. The
Tostan model that emerged used a problem-solving approach based
on the women's perception and prioritisation of their own needs.
(Easton, Monkman, and Miles 2003, 447)

As discussed in chapter 3, Senegalese women self-mobilized through Tostan's
educational offerings to curtail the practice of female genital cutting in their
village that in turn motivated those in neighboring communities to do the
same.

In comparing the two (systems-focused and emergent) strategies to induce gendered interest-articulation, it is hard to ignore donor influence as a
determinant of how NGOs process gender concerns. Tostan's initial successes
occurred during the late-1990s with UNICEF support. Since then, more donors have come forward (see the listing of Tostan donors in chapter 4) to underwrite efforts to scale up the Tostan model for effectiveness in a multiplicity
of settings. As apparent in the NGO's *Five-Year Strategic Plan: 2006–2011*,
Tostan (2006) has taken on the responsibility to formalize its procedures (and,
in doing so, pushing its model closer to the systems-focused approach). It follows then that NGO leaders need to reconcile receptivity to diverse gender
interests with the policy and management parameters required by funding
agencies.

Although women's interests often diverge, there is evidence that women
(more so than men) draw on an ethic of caring and relationship building (see
Gilligan 1982) in ways that connect their diverse interests. In other words,
women share the motivation and capability to build social capital, which
promotes individual empowerment and a collective resolve to address rights-
depriving situations. In her research project "Hidden Voices: Working Through
a Culture of Peace," Ann Jordan interviews 14 women who work in various
peace-building capacities—for example, in Bosnian postwar reconstruction
and with Colombian human rights victims. With regard to social capital, relationship building, and the melding of diverse interests, Jordan points out,

All the women I interviewed mentioned the importance of working collaboratively and in solidarity with others—in other words,
developing good solid relationships and understanding. The main

values underpinning all of these include trust, acceptance, good-will, respect, forgiveness, compassion, and humour, with trust as the underlying key factor. Much was made of reaching out to others and finding common ground by recognising our mutual humanity. One woman stated that whatever you do individually is part of the larger picture. The need for active listening was also widely expressed. (Jordan 2003, 243)

An official in a Scottish bilateral NGO probes the deeper psychology of women's relationship building through her interviews with Malawi women volunteers working in a nursery feeding project in that West African nation. Specifically, Uny reports that the majority of these women described their motivations for volunteering as a "safety-net investment," as expressed by one interviewee:

I saw that it was a good thing to do this work to help the children in the village, because I thought it may affect me also in the future, that I might also need help from friends, so I thought I should help, so that in the future, if people help me, it won't be a hassle to them either, and they should also help my children. (Uny 2008, 442)

This woman's stated rationale parallels the general finding in Uny's study "that women give their time and effort out of their concern for others in greater need than they are themselves . . . but motivations [are also] driven by bonds of reciprocity" (2008, 443). Again, gender serves as a *lever* for rights empowerment.

As the requisites of social capital, concern for others and reciprocity can reach far on behalf of rights work, which becomes evident in Povey's (2003) compelling account of Afghan women's organizational efforts to move reconstruction forward amid conflict and violence against women in this war-torn setting. She explains how women's coping strategies led to the founding of secret women's organizations, in which prominent women empowered those who lacked education and status, which over time transitioned into women's NGOs that exerted pressure on the government. Povey explains,

Throughout the violent conflict, women's NGOs also remained in touch with each other and with female members of the community through networking and solidarity groups. In the post-Taliban era, these organisations have become important agents for reconstruction. In a post-conflict period in which the state does not yet exist in any real sense, women's NGOs are playing a crucial role, particularly in relation to education, training, and skills to create opportunities for women to have access to income-generating activities, thus contributing to household well-being. (Povey 2003, 274)

But to reiterate, these NGOs are built around concerns for other women and their diverse situations, as one interviewee relates: "There are 136 women working in our NGO. We work with the refugees; we work as health workers in the hospitals. We have literacy classes in poorer areas and we teach women handicrafts in order to generate incomes for themselves and their families" (Povey 2003, 274–75). A question that arises from Povey's research, and from a similar study of women's empowerment in a religiously conservative province in Pakistan, is whether success in activism within challenging environments depends on skills and aptitudes of particular women (see Paterson 2008).

Relying on their coping abilities, prominent women in Kabul were able to draw in others from different circumstances and social statuses to establish social cohesion and to mobilize in order to claim rights from government. In this regard, Sen discusses the reach of women "as active agents of change; the dynamic promoters of social transformation that can alter the lives of *both* women and men" (1999, 189; italics his). In her work in moral cognitive development, Carol Gilligan (1982) argues convincingly that women speak in a different voice than men do—a voice that calls for relationship building and unity. Regarding gender empowerment, NGO professionals need a general awareness of the heterogeneity of women's interests at play in particular settings. Furthermore, rights-based organizations need to hear the voices of women unable to speak because of linguistic problems or even physical disability (see, e.g., Thurston et al. 2004). But along with that, NGO leaders should where possible draw on women's strengths in building social capital in promoting human dignity.

Anticipating Programmatic Effects on Gender Politics

Does success in gender empowerment vary with particular *types of programs* implemented? Perhaps the Grameen Bank's microcredit and Tostan's continuing education programs serve as contrasting program types in terms of gender politics. With microcredit, money (along with access to it) becomes the logical "change agent" in terms of its presumed potential to promote entrepreneurial behavior in women. But, as discussed, the Grameen program (unintendedly but perhaps not unpredictably) offers men access to an additional source of money available by exploiting wives' participation in microlending. On the other end of the scale, Tostan's program involves interactive adult education—rather than approving loans or funding assistance—to foster conscious raising among women and some men that in turn creates space for women. Like Tostan, the Indian NGO Gram Vikas provides interactive educational programming for the rural poor and achieves success in creating space for women by changing men's perceptions of gender roles. Jayapadma offers the following example of changing attitudes:

> A village leader once famously commented, "So now women will wear pants and go out of the house, and men will wear bangles and stay at home." His wife went on to become the leader of the women's group. Questioned again on his comment after a few years, he refused to admit to what he had earlier said, and stated: "This is a village and a hundred people will say a hundred different things. This is the 21st century after all—women should have the same opportunities as men. You see, the root of all problems is illiteracy—once that is addressed, things will change." (Jayapadma 2009, 153)

In between but closer to microcredit, technical assistance in the form of *direct funding* for a community need or improvement may reinforce the political (and often patriarchal) power structure with influence over and access to funding agency representatives. In this regard, Makhoul and Harrison focus on patriarchal client–patron relationships in rural Lebanon villages as the means of accessing direct funding from government agencies and NGOs like Save the Children for sanitation and infrastructure improvements. These researchers explain how gendered worldviews translate into opinions about community "needs":

> One of the interesting findings of this study was the different ideas people have about the development status of their village and the language they use to express this. Rather than using abstract definitions, they tend to define development by comparing their village with others. . . . The more educated men, such as the school principal in Ain Zeitoun and the sheikhs (religious leaders) in Dar el Lawz, see both the people and their villages as backward and in need of improvement. (Makhoul and Harrison 2002, 617)

But by contrast, women see themselves

> as recipients of development rather than as active participants or
> initiators. The changes which have taken place in the village are
> presented as influenced by God who, according to the women, has
> already helped them in many ways. There is an element of fatalism
> in their perspective: "We will live as God has written for us to live."
> (45-year-old woman in Ain Zeitoun; Makhoul and Harrison 2002,
> 618)

Makhoul and Harrison conclude by suggesting that men recognize NGO funding assistance programs as part of the client network that in turn perpetuates the gendered status quo in these Lebanese communities (2002, 621).

A fourth program type, occupational training for women, can be positioned near the Tostan (educational) end but nonetheless distantly related to money and income generation as well. In reference to an aquaculture training program for Thai women supported by the Asian Institute of Technology and the government, Kusakabe's research validates the findings of another study:

> As Chen points out, the amount of knowledge and access to and
> control over resources that women have has as much to do with
> "ideology." The whole process is thus a negotiation between women
> and men within the household, and between women and the wider
> community, over access to and control over material resources and
> knowledge. (Kusakabe 2003, 336)

In other words, "the critical factor [in women's success] is the resources and knowledge that women have relative to their husbands. Even when they have more resources, their choices to use them are restricted by 'ideology'—the socially defined roles and responsibilities placed upon women. Conforming to these ideologies is necessary to avoid conflict in the household, which most women cannot afford to create" (Kusakabe 2003, 342).

Although a small sample, these four cases offer some support to the proposition that the type of program intended to improve women's status can (positively or negatively) affect gender politics within the family and community. From a women's empowerment perspective, there is cause for apprehension when access to money is at the core of a program's "empowerment" logic. Such programs tend to reinforce patriarchal patterns of resource acquisition that compromise women's standing in marital and community politics.

As distinct from program type, an organization's *goal* orientation can affect gendered relationships within the family and other institutional settings. In regard to the Grameen microfinancing program, Mallick is of the opinion that the bank's operative goals were self-serving in nature. He quotes another source who characterizes the parameters of microcredit for women as banking "business as usual":

> It must also be recognised that providing financial services to poor people is expensive and building sustainable financial institutions to do this requires patience and a keen eye for costs and risks. Most formal financial institutions in low income countries currently avoid providing these services for sound commercial reasons, and commercial sources of informal finance are able to offer loans only by charging relatively high interest rates. (Mallick 2002, 162)

Mallick asserts that the bank plays it both ways by taking full credit for its social contribution while turning a profit:

> Grameen is also a political chameleon. It has the ability to affirm beliefs that both conservatives and liberals hold dear. From the right, Grameen can be seen as an entrepreneurial institution that makes the case for less government; from the left, it appears to be an enlightened social welfare program that argues for the value of government involvement. (Bornstein 1996, as quoted in Mallick 2002, 157–58)

Shortsighted or unrealistic development goals can disrupt gender relationships *even if* men are generally supportive of women's endeavors. A microfinancing project in southern India intended "to develop women's skills and confidence in managing all aspects of silk-reeling and enable them as entrepreneurs to earn three to four times their present income" (Leach and Sitaram 2002, 577). The (unidentified) NGO instituted a 28-day intensive training session to instill technical and management skills that also involved husbands' buy-in to support success. Nonetheless, this program fell short of providing women the business acumen to navigate the extreme volatility of the silk market. Subsequently, frustration and disillusionment set in among both women participants and their husbands.

By contrast, other organizations are inclined to *adjust* goals in order to be more effective in empowering women. Such an orientation can be found in

NGOs that, like Tostan, support women's leadership and self-empowerment through interactive participation. Still other more technically focused organizations can be successful in adjusting goals by pursuing organization learning to counteract unintended outcomes that complicate gender relationships. For example, the Southern Highlands Dairy Development Project in Tanzania, supported by the Tanzanian and Swiss governments, promotes women's ownership of milk-producing cows. Initially, men became the "real" owners of livestock in the social-vocational environment of dairy production. Mkenda-Mugittu reports,

> In many cases, both the social environment and the project culture favoured men. In the project locations, the distribution of income and control over benefits derived from farming are heavily controlled by male household heads, and women's rights over land and other valuable assets are very limited. These cultural norms inhibited women from benefiting from dairy cow ownership. Local people were very clear about the problems related to female ownership of dairy cattle: how can a landless woman think about buying a dairy cow? Where will she build the shed? Where will she cultivate fodder? (Mkenda-Mugittu 2003, 461)

Professionals in this joint project responded by reviewing the various constraints to equitable gender outcomes (e.g., polygamous households, competing household responsibilities, and lack of control of resources; Mkenda-Mugittu 2003, 467) and then charting an array of behavior changes amenable to gender empowerment ("increase women's ability to get access and control over products like milk, manure, offspring, etc."; p. 465). This organization learning process yielded adjustments that ultimately accounted for women's empowerment through dairy entrepreneurship. Thus, NGOs intending to promote gender rights would do well to scrutinize the logics and motivations underpinning program goals and monitor outcomes that warrant goal adjustment. Nonetheless, programs that promote women's occupational advances do not necessarily facilitate gender equity unless specific measures are taken to intervene in ways that address women's social capital in communities (see Gotschi, Njuki, and Delve 2008).

In his popular textbook on public administration, Nicholas Henry refers to *implementation*—the delivery and execution of programs—as "the most hands-on facet" in government management (2004, 303). Some policy analysts cite the problems of multiple objectives and the multiplicity of participants with competing agendas and priorities as barriers to effective program implementation (see in particular Pressman and Wildavsky 1973). By contrast, the NGO literature uses the term *implementation* more generally as program execution, sometimes in reference to problematic issues but more often not. Still, the problems that public management experts associate with government programs apply to gender empowerment as well. Development and human rights programs, like governmental services, are driven by multiple objectives—such that the gender-empowerment goal can be "crowded out" by other priorities such as economic growth or good governance. On the other hand, the problem of "too many participants" for effective governmental implementation is often recognized as a *tactical advantage* in a human rights context, especially if the victimized or marginalized can experience self-empowerment through meaningful participation. Thus, implementation problems arise when NGOs overlook opportunities to involve experienced and knowledgeable women to oversee monitoring efforts to alleviate gender inequities and deprivations. More specifically, this complaint can be directed toward NGOs that rely on in-house staff to monitor gender outcomes rather than on more astute women who are available to provide richer interpretations and insights (see Barrientos, McClenaghan, and Orton 2001; Corrin 2003).

Gender Mainstreaming: Lens and Lever

The term *mainstreaming* refers to deliberate efforts to institutionalize gender equity into development and rights-advocacy organizations and the programs they implement (Goetz 2002, 389). Thus, mainstreaming integrates a concern not merely for women per se but for the quality of gender relations into how organizations function and programs are designed. Specifically, this emphasis on evaluating whether or how gender is *integrated* into programs reflects what is known as a Gender and Development approach (GAD) to gender analysis— reflective of the Beijing Platform for Action as the consensus of those at the Fourth World Conference on Women held in 1995 and at the Beijing at Ten follow-up conference there a decade later. In its focus on integration or "gender mainstreaming," the GAD approach to gender as a development and rights issue differs markedly from an earlier Women in Development approach that merely addressed "women's concerns" or women's welfare typically as an "add-on" or additional program component or organizational consideration rather than as a primary focus of identity and analysis.

From a GAD perspective, it is generally safe to assume that most any proposal to change gender relations will be met with resistance by those preferring the status quo (quite often men) who are likely to invoke "biological differences" as a first line of defense and "traditional beliefs" as the second (see Alim 2009). Thus, mainstreaming strategies intend to *transform* or *redistribute* resources and responsibilities within the politics of gendered relationships. As Ahmed explains, the transformative nature of mainstreaming differs significantly from *instrumental* policies (to meet women's specific welfare needs) and *ameliorative* efforts (to allocate specific resources such as microcredit loans to women) without the prospect of redistributing or transforming power (2002, 302). This section elaborates first on gender mainstreaming as applied to various phases of program development and then proceeds to leadership issues relating to gender mainstreaming within organizations.

Mainstreaming the Gender Perspective in Programs

From a programmatic standpoint, NGOs that are committed to gender mainstreaming willingly subject their own programs to in-depth gender assessment and pressure other institutions—particularly government agencies—to do the same. More specifically, in the language adopted at the 1995 Fourth World Conference in Beijing, gender mainstreaming requires

> assessing the implications for women and men of any planned action in order to make their respective concerns and experiences an integrated dimension of the entire project cycle so that women and men benefit equally and inequality is not perpetuated. The ultimate goal is to achieve gender equality by transforming the mainstream. (United Nations 1997, as quoted in de Waal 2006, 209)

Two generalizations help clarify the significance of gender mainstreaming as applied to program planning and management: (1) as a general rule, the logical framework (at least, as it is typically formulated) does not, and probably *cannot*, accommodate the depth and scope of the impact that mainstreaming demands and (2) the importance of rigorous and intricate evidence-based analysis *cannot be overstated* in reference to the various phases of the project management cycle.

The intent in the first generalization is to emphasize what gender mainstreaming as a development strategy requires rather than to discredit logframes (although they are often criticized). Conceptually, a logical framework consists of a matrix wherein the project is represented in terms of its *goals*, statements of *purpose* underpinning those goals, *outputs* expected to be reflective of goal attainment, and particular program-initiated *activities* pursued to bring about desired outputs. If mainstreaming simply involved achieving gender parity—that is, equal numbers of men and women participating in or benefiting from a particular program (de Waal 2006, 209), then the logframe protocol might work since "head counts" of men and women could suffice as indicators of goal attainment, and specific program activities might be specified as means of reaching parity indicators. But in seeking out an equality of opportunity or a "level playing field," mainstreaming obligates program planners to identify *barriers* to achieving gendered equality of opportunity (relative to the technical nature of the project, whether forestation, aquaculture, infrastructure improvement, etc.) and then to introduce measures to eliminate those barriers. In a nutshell, logframe analysis is by design too succinct, linear, and superficial to capture the complexities of the cultural and institutional impediments that tilt the playing field toward gender inequality. Gender mainstreaming requires one to think in terms of impacts—rather than outputs and activities—that account for barriers to equality in the first place and then how to surmount them programmatically.

The second generalization, stressing the need for evidence-based analysis in each phase of the project cycle, reiterates how professional competence is at the heart of an NGO's gender empowerment and advocacy capability. With regard to the *planning phase*, a physician and a gender specialist discuss the linkage between "gender and evidence-based planning" in terms of the critical roles of planners in documenting barriers to gender equity as rationales for program interventions and advocacy efforts (Andersson and Roche 2006). Making a case (to funding agencies or governmental authorities) to allocate resources to "level the playing field" for women is difficult, among other reasons, because the circumstances leading to gender inequalities are unrecognized as policy priorities in the absence of hard, gender-specific data. At an intuitive level, for example, the relationship between violence against women and poverty (of women *and* men) may appear obvious (see Terry 2004), but advocacy requires empirical evidence to substantiate that link and to support appeals for action. Planners in NGOs and in government agencies can make those cases, provided that they (1) enjoy the institutional backing to focus on gender issues (and the planning environment *itself* is not patriarchal or abusive [see Olufemi 2004] nor dominated by "grim resisters" of gender mainstreaming [see Howard 2002]) and (2) have access to gender-sensitive data that can measure the contours of gender inequity. Furthermore, women as planners and participants should assume significant stakeholder roles in developing the planning framework (Howard 2002, 165–66).

The hard reality, as Andersson and Roche (2006) explain, is that gender-sensitive information that can inform resource allocation decisions is typically scarce. These analysts emphasize that routine data collection on the part of public agencies or even humanitarian organizations dealing with the "status of women" is often inadequate to identify impediments to gender equality or to assess the actual impacts of gender-related program initiatives. With regard to the latter, Andersson and Roche point out,

> For example, if we measure the change in incidence of low birth weight among women who attend antenatal clinics, we may be measuring effectiveness and not effect (impact). The women who received antenatal services may be in better health and have better access to resources and therefore nutritional care than those pregnant women who did not attend antenatal clinics. Planners need to know the effect that antenatal care has for the whole population of pregnant women, not simply among those who benefit from the service. (2006, 143)

Furthermore, they suggest that planners and managers need to develop a common framework, or "language," of analysis that interrelates three fundamental concepts in an integrated gender-information system: impact, coverage, and costs. These indicators can capture the actual (rather than theoretical) gender effects of programs and identify the factors that constitute barriers to gender empowerment and that pose risks to women.

> A social audit of the gender gap in primary education in Pakistan found that a girl whose mother had no education was about three times as likely not to be enrolled in school as a girl whose mother had some education. Many mothers also believed that their daughters should not receive formal education. The mothers' lack of education and belief about their daughters' rights were risk factors that predicted girls not attending primary school. The relevance is the predictive value: increasing female education and changing what mothers believe about education might reduce the gender gap in primary education. (Andersson and Roche 2006, 145)

In gender mainstreaming, the planning process is critical in "facilitating collective consciousness raising" (p. 151) that documents the causality of gender inequality in providing gender-sensitive evidence and urging public agencies to refine data collection to seek gender-specific information.

Second, program mainstreaming requires that the gender implication of intricately researched benefits and costs inform budget and resource-allocation processes within NGOs and public agencies. At the macro-level, for example, Sen demonstrates the societal benefits accrued by nations that invest in education and literacy for females (1999, 195–98). With regard to macro-level costs of violence against women, Terry comments,

> So far, most attempts to count the public cost of VAW have focused on domestic violence and have been confined mainly to rich countries such as the USA, New Zealand, and Canada, although there have also been some studies in Latin America. Estimates differ widely depending on what costs are included in the calculations. One study for the London Borough of Hackney estimated that the cost to the borough of dealing with domestic violence during 1996 amounted to £5,130,000 (approximately US$8,708,000). (2004, 473)

By contrast, gender mainstreaming more often obligates NGOs to document their own program budgets—or advocate for governments to expend resources—at the micro-level in terms of gender-disaggregated costs and benefits. Public agencies, even when attending to gender-pertinent issues, are inclined to measure only direct costs and benefits, thereby skimming over the complexities and nuances of how programs affect (and do not affect) women. Terry identifies the direct costs of violence against women as medical treatment, counseling, police services, criminal justice, and "safe" shelter provision, but

> there is also a range of indirect socio-economic costs flowing from VAW. These arise from decreased participation by women in the labour market, lower earnings, absenteeism, and staff turnover. Women who are less productive earn lower incomes, and these lower incomes in turn mean lower spending and lower economic demand. There are also inter-generational effects, such as the impact of domestic violence on children's future earnings. (Terry 2004, 474)

Even time expended constitutes a significant gender cost, as Andersson and Roche relate:

In the health sector, those visiting private or traditional health services waited an average of 57 minutes, while those visiting the hospital waited close to two hours per visit. This was in addition to time spent traveling back and forth to the health facility, which was often a great distance from their residence. The cost of time is disproportionately borne by women, who are the primary caregivers in households and communities. (Andersson and Roche 2006, 146)

In addition, mainstreaming requires organizations that advocate for gender equality to cite evidence of the cost of initiatives *not provided*, such as immunization services not available or water infrastructure projects not prioritized (Andersson and Roche 2006, 146). NGOs can advocate for gender in their budget proposals to funding agencies and their advocacy appeals to governments to the extent they support their proposal with gender-specific benefits and costs information.

Third, the implementation of gender mainstreaming can, as Moser and Moser (2005) relate, be understood in terms of both institutionalizing it and making it operational. At the institutional level, NGOs might anticipate grappling with an organization culture that resists committing to an overarching gender perspective. In this regard, NGOs can take deliberate steps to phase in their mainstreaming policies and to incorporate gender training and establish mechanisms for accountability along the way (Dawson 2005, 85; Moser and Moser 2005, 16). By contrast, implementation at the operational level involves the program mechanisms set in place to achieve gender equality in particular settings, particularly in terms of enabling women's participation and monitoring the status of gender relationships.

Fourth, the evaluation stage in gender mainstreaming can and should stimulate organization learning not only by assessing specific indicators of women's progress but also by appraising what the organization is learning about its collective self with regard to (1) its progress in instituting a gender framework, (2) what it has learned about gender relationships and barriers to women, and (3) its general ability to facilitate women's empowerment. For an NGO to "study itself" by virtue of its commitment to gender mainstreaming is akin to what Peter Uvin describes as "the inward look," which is integral to a rights-based perspective. "Gender empowerment" could reasonably substitute for "human rights" in Uvin's appeal for organizational introspection:

All development agencies would benefit enormously if they managed to create an atmosphere of critical internal debate about human rights [and gender empowerment] with their own staff and direct partners. . . . If agencies managed to do this, they could radically reinvent themselves: people may begin reporting the truth to their superiors (orally in cases where the written word is too scary), create explicit ethical bases for joint action, develop with senior foreign staff strategies for advocacy and protection of their employees, and learn to think in advance of the likely human rights [or gender empowerment] impacts of various scenarios of action. All of these would be breakthroughs—truly new ways of living a rights-based approach to development in a daily way. (Uvin 2004, 154)

Some of Oxfam GB's criteria for institutionalizing gender mainstreaming (associated with three phases of institutionalization) are illustrative:

- Female and male beneficiaries participate equally in decision making in planning, implementation, and evaluation of projects, and their voices are reflected in the way program decisions are made (Phase 1).
- There is a balance of women and men in senior and middle management, or the organization is actively seeking to redress an imbalance in order to reflect more equitably its beneficiary population (Phase 2).
- The organization challenges gender-stereotyped beliefs and discriminatory attitudes toward women, both in its internal practices and externally (Phase 3) (Dawson 2005, 85).

As did professionals with the Southern Highlands Dairy Development Project in Tanzania, project personnel can pose specific questions that glean what has and has not been learned about gender relations in the program context: "Are male and female bargaining strategies understood? What are they?" and "How do women and men experience and value outcomes/benefits from project activities?" (Mkenda-Mugittu 2003, 469). Last, the NGO's candid assessment of its actual capability to facilitate gender empowerment may be sobering in view of Desai's general finding that

despite commitments to gender mainstreaming, NGOs have insufficient understanding that they can facilitate the process of empowerment of women in such a context. . . . My experience of working with NGOs suggests that they rarely evaluate their interventions in the context of the wider economic, social, and cultural changes to which they respond. (Desai 2005, 90, 96)

Nonetheless, even such an unflattering assessment of gender empowerment progress can help clarify the organization's potential for subsequent action. In this regard, an NGO's willingness to confront its weaknesses and impediments through an "inward look" can be taken as a sign of organizational maturity.

Assuming some success *has been* achieved in facilitating gender empowerment, an NGO can evaluate the benefits accruing from such empowerment, especially as it relates to project sustainability—in other words, probing if women's involvement as leaders or participants has placed (or, in the future, will place) project outcomes on a firmer footing than otherwise would have occurred. Thomas-Slayter and Sodikoff ask this question in reference to five natural resources management projects (respectively) in Kenya, Nigeria, Malawi, The Gambia, and Rwanda and find "ample evidence to support the assertion that prospects for achieving livelihood security and sustainable environments in Africa will be improved if women have a more central role in resource management decisions" (2001, 59). But just as revealing in their comparative case studies are the enabling conditions (such as extension and training, local participation and organization, and partnerships and linkages) that contribute to project sustainability through women's empowerment (p. 57). Thus, it follows that gender mainstreaming in program development not only attends to women's empowerment but also provides a lens for strengthening organization learning that aligns actions with values and integrates gender concerns within human rights missions.

Mainstreaming the Gender Perspective in Organizations

Regarding gender mainstreaming in organizations, Anne Marie Goetz toys with structural adjustment rhetoric about "getting institutions right for market efficiency" to coin the phrase "getting institutions right for women" (2002, 389). From a leadership perspective, tough questions arise as to how rights-based organizations intent on mainstreaming, or integrating, a gender perspective into program management first "turn themselves around" to align organization structures and management systems with gender equality program values (see Padaki 2000). A professor of planning offers glimpses of (government) planning organizations that clearly "have it wrong" for the women planners they employ and that aptly serve as "basket-case" counterexamples of the gender-sensitive organization. According to Olusola Olufemi, the everyday life of women working in Sub-Saharan African planning agencies is frustrating and humiliating. Olufemi documents this male-dominated institutional setting through her interviews with professionally trained women currently working in these organizations, as well as others who have abandoned the profession in disgust. Some of the comments refer to men's perceptions of women's technical capabilities, for example,

> At meetings or during fieldwork, women planners constantly face comments such as: "She is a woman" (meaning she can't do any better, she can be undermined and she is supposed to be voiceless). (female planner and lecturer; Olufemi 2004, 415)

Other remarks reflect the gender politics at work within these African planning organizations:

> Older male colleagues think you don't matter or you can be manipulated for various purposes or they are doing you a favour by including you in projects. (female planner in a research organization; Olufemi 2004, 416)

Still other reactions can be linked to professional gender relations based on cultural expectations:

> Women are expected to add the feminine touch in the meetings or gatherings either by taking notes or serving tea; there is silence when you contribute in meetings (consensual or non-consensual, not sure); no response so you are not even sure if your contribution is meaningful or not. (Olufemi 2004, 416)

These comments are indicative of three levels at which gender relations are perceived within an organization (technical, political, and cultural)—each of which warrant attention in organization mainstreaming (see Sprenger 2002, 414; Ahmad 2002, 299). Rights-based leaders need to be analytical in distinguishing among these levels of gendered perceptions, but so too must they master the political sophistication to recognize resisters' tactics to undermine gender equality by redirecting agency discourse toward other issues that reinforce the patriarchal trappings of the organization. In other words, by steering discussion toward overt technical issues such as formal rules, procedures, precedents, and results imperatives, resisters can covertly appeal to the hierarchal norms embedded in the organization culture to override competing values related to gender equality (Longwe 1997). Sara Longwe, a consultant in women's development, refers to the tendencies of gender policies in development agencies "to evaporate in a patriarchal cooking pot" since

> although the policy goals are concerned with women's increased "participation and control over resources," project objectives have re-interpreted this as "increased access to resources." The (bottom-up) strategy of women's participation and empowerment has been reversed into a (top-down) strategy of service-delivery. (Longwe 1997, 150)

One approach to gender equality—advanced by Gender at Work, an international collaborative for equality and social justice—offers NGO leaders a strategic guide for gender empowerment that accommodates (1) varying stakeholder (technical, political, cultural) points of view, (2) tactics of covert resistance, and (3) key organization elements, all combined in four change imperatives stated in figure 7.1. By distinguishing between needed changes in the informal and formal organization (horizontal axis) and between individual change and systemic change (vertical axis), figure 7.1 depicts gender empowerment as functions of individual consciousness in men and women (cell 1), access to resources (cell 2), institutional norms (cell 3), and overt rules and policies (cell 4). A mong other insights possible, this Gender at Work guide alerts leaders that issues concerning proposed changes to the technical nature of the organization (cell 4) contends with individual consciousness (cell 1) and deeply structured norms (cell 3).

The logic in the guide offers a choice of alternative "entry points" (e.g., starting with changing leadership's commitment to gender empowerment; see cell 1) as a platform for embarking on significant change—despite pockets of misgivings and skepticism about gender equity at various levels of management. In this vein, Rao and Kelleher (1998) chronicle the Bangladesh Rural Advancement Committee's (BRAC's) efforts implementing its Gender Quality Action Learning (GQAL) Programme exploring the gendered relationships in this extremely large NGO. As background, Rao and Kelleher explain,

> BRAC is an organization in transition from a collective to a corporation pursuing empowerment goals in a volatile socio-economic and political environment. Externally, it is grappling with an enormous expansion in area coverage, and an increasing complexity

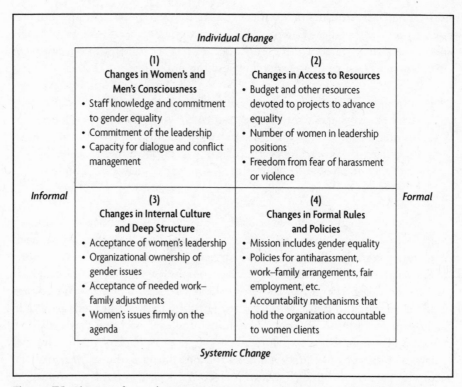

Figure 7.1 Objectives for gender mainstreaming in organizations. *Source*. Adapted from Rao, Aruna, and David Kelleher. "What Is Gender at Work's Approach to Gender Equality and Institutional Change?" *Gender at Work*. Used with permission.

and technical sophistication in programme content. Internally, organizational complexity is enhanced by a series of features: a management style geared toward target achievement which militates against the search for lasting solutions to the difficult problems of women's subordination and gender-equitable change on the ground [and] a brewing conflict between traditional patriarchal norms and behaviours and a nascent culture of gender equity. (Rao and Kelleher 1998, 177)

The researchers' linkage of gender issues relating to BRAC's significant organizational transition exemplifies what Shelly Feldman calls a "paradox of institutionalization" whereby NGOs tend toward corporatism, bureaucratization, and self-reliance that "means that gender inequality and other structural conditions that reinforce poverty are left unchallenged by most NGOs; and that opportunities for a self-representative politics are no longer central to the mobilizing strategies of the NGO movement" (2003, 23). Nonetheless, Rao and Kelleher indicate that BRAC was able to use the GQAL methodology through which large numbers of staff members learned about gendered patterns both in the regional office and in the field, and some "resisters" eventually adopted supportive attitudes toward gender equality—although not without its share of logistical problems in implementation. Alim's (2009) subsequent research associates BRAC's GQAL efforts with positive changes in "villagers' knowledge, perceptions, and attitudes toward gender roles over time" (p. 300) indicating that the program "registered some success in shaking traditional norms, beliefs, and customs" (p. 309; also see Goetz 1997 for a more critical account).

It could be prudent for NGO executives to delegate a significant share of gender-equality leadership to advisory committees composed of a wide diversity of individuals within—and perhaps external to—the organization. Thurston et al. find that an advisory committee within a community education NGO raised individual consciousness with regard to concern for nonverbal women affected by physical disabilities. These researchers report,

> Members found it to be an educational experience. . . . For example, one [nondisabled] respondent said: "A lot of the discussions we have had have been beneficial just on a personal level. . . . I always come out of there feeling like I've gained some knowledge." Listening to and learning from others was thought to make their own work richer. . . . Members from professional communities stated they had learned a great deal about the problems of people with disabilities. The women with disabilities, however, found that they were used principally to enlighten others on the obstacles to the recognition, communication, and reporting of abuse. (Thurston et al. 2004, 489)

Parallel with the imperative to change individual consciousness (see cell 1 in figure 7.1), the advisory committee stimulates dialogue that in turn enriches staff knowledge related to a marginalized gender status and empowers disabled women by depending on them as educators. That said, Thurston et al. indicate that some committee members experienced frustration since it was unclear how some of the more intangible committee contributions (e.g., sharing perspectives and giving advice) would find their way into routine decision-making processes in the organization (p. 491). However, if applied to Gender at Work's logic in figure 7.1, the committee's efforts to change men's and women's consciousness (cell 1) could offer leaders justification to initiate gender-related changes in accessing resources (cell 2) and/or formal rules and policies (cell 4).

In regard to Thurston et al.'s analysis of how one gender advisory committee functions, it is revealing that the committee's gender focus leads to concern departing from women per se to target power inequities between the physically able and the physically disabled. Thus, the role of the gender perspective as a lens for exploring power relationships is fundamental to organization (or, for that matter, program) mainstreaming. Rao and Kelleher emphasize this understanding of gender in reference to BRAC's experiences in implementing the GQAL Programme to promote gender equality:

> The question of where gender is suggests particular understandings of gender itself. If one conceptualized gender as meaning women, then gender was lost. If instead one conceptualized gender in terms of the relationships between men and women, then to some extent, gender was found. . . . We understand gender to be a primary building block in the construction of power and power relations, and a primary arena through which power is manifested. Thus, gender is an opening to discussing and questioning power constructions deriving from other bases such as age, class, ethnicity, and religion. (Rao and Kelleher 1998, 182)

Stated another way, a gender perspective appears more apt to expose leaders to the deep-structured, institutional roots of power than other diagnostic approaches—notably, organizational development (see Plowman 2000)—directed toward issues of efficiency and effectiveness (presumed to be "gender neutral") at the technical level.

Clearly, mainstreaming depends on gender sensitivity among those who serve in key leadership positions and who influence organization values and management styles (Ahmed 2002, 303). But in addition to negotiating the internal forces that affect gender relationships (as characterized in figure 7.1), NGO leaders may be challenged to reconcile their commitments to mainstreaming with external obstacles that could dampen resolve to pursue gender equality. Managers of development agencies working in highly patriarchal settings may confront human resources problems in recruiting and hiring women, particularly in fieldwork positions that require mobility and attendance at evening meetings, which encroach on the norms of marriage and family life (Ahmed 2002, 304–5). These cultural sensitivities test even the most committed human rights advocates with the dilemma of balancing insistence to include the traditionally excluded against the need to work within context. NGO leaders may confront this conundrum in interacting with other organizations having vested interests in maintaining their patriarchal status quo. In creating a hypothetical scenario of a relationship between a Northern bilateral agency (in the "SNOWDIDA" government) and a Southern ("Sundia") planning ministry, Longwe caricatures interorganizational cooperation as an opportunistic rationale for reinforcing each other's male-dominated culture:

> Here we have to understand the common patriarchal interest between SNOWDIDA and its cooperating Ministry, the Sundian Ministry of Planning (MOP). . . . The Sundian MOP has exactly the same problem as SNOWDIDA. It also has a government which, at the political level, has handed down policies on women's equality and advancement. . . . The Sundian government policy on gender equality would challenge the customary laws and traditions which have always maintained male domination of Sundian society. Whereas the North-South relationship has many underlying conflicts and tensions, common patriarchal interests can provide the basis for brotherhood. (Longwe 1997, 152)

Although perhaps overstated, Longwe's parody "gets at" the fundamental human rights problem of respecting culture while advocating for human rights, as Peter Uvin explains: "The human rights edifice provides us with little support to deal with many of these questions. Its language is one of absolutism, neither allowing much room for choices and trade-offs nor providing much in the way of specific operational tools for social change" (2004, 30). Thus, the unsettling question is whether leaders committed to gender mainstreaming paint themselves into an absolutist corner or alternatively apply their concern for gender relations pragmatically as a diplomatic tactic to redirect negotiations with other interests.

Conclusion

In his assertion that human rights is a political matter, Peter Uvin points out, "When one begins moving beyond charity and assistance to the realm of claims and rights, one also begins focusing much more on social structures of inequality, exclusion, and oppression" (2004, 135). Logically then, rights-based organizations are strategic in positioning their gender-pertinent efforts in the political framework of men's and women's relationships—a GAD perspective—rather than as benevolent welfare initiatives. Strategically competent organizations understand that definitive interests have the potential to drive change, so it is essential to scrutinize generalizations (such as a wholesale acceptance of tradition by women) that justify the gendered status quo. It is more realistic to assume that women's interests are by nature diverse within cultural settings and that rights-based development efforts should help clarify and accommodate those interests aligned with equality. Put metaphorically, the strategically competent organization can channel its commitment to gender empowerment as a *lens* that guides analyses of deprivation in particular settings and as a *lever* that extends the organization's influence to address rights-abuse situations. Nonetheless, women generally share an ethic of relationship building that can mobilize and empower other women (and men). Thus, organizations that can assist women to leverage social capital are especially well positioned to promote gender equity goals.

Politically astute organizations should cultivate some predictive capabilities to anticipate how programs may affect gendered relationships in particular settings. For example, development officials should recognize that programs designed to channel money as (microcredit) loans or direct development assistance (whether intended to benefit women specifically or improve conditions generally) are apt to reinforce patterns of male control over family or community resources. By contrast, initiatives that promote interactive, continuing education for women (and men) appear more reliable as programmatic vehicles for empowering women. Organization learning that monitors program effect on gendered relationships can facilitate gender equity if program goals can be adapted to reflect that learning.

Gender mainstreaming implies a commitment to understand agency programs, organization structure, management systems, and institutional cultures in terms of the pattern of the gender relationships that they perpetuate. With regard to programs, such a commitment focuses on identifying impediments and barriers to gender equity (and then addressing them) rather than simply relying on quantitative outputs suggestive of parity between men and women. Often these barriers are difficult to document in the absence of gender-specific data—seldom collected by government agencies. But to reiterate, rights-based organizations can be effective advocates of gender equity to the extent they can rely on evidence-based data to substantiate gender-based deprivations in particular settings.

Mainstreaming also obliges rights-focused leaders to take stock of the quality of gender relationships within the organization itself in terms of its technical operations, political processes at work in allocating resources and rewards, and the "deep structure" of its institutional culture. Claims of "gender neutrality" associated with technical necessity warrant particular scrutiny as covert justifications for the male-dominated status quo. Leaders can utilize gender-mainstreaming initiatives as tactics not only to probe gender-equity concerns but also to examine power relationships that account for marginalization or rights deprivation due to a variety of discriminatory circumstances.

Discussion Issues

1. A development organization intends to shift its program focus from "improving women's welfare" to "empowering women." Discuss how this change could affect (1) relationships with funding agencies and (2) program planning strategies.
2. The Ministry of Transportation plans to build a highway linking isolated, rural villages to a major urban center to stimulate the nation's economy. How might women's interests related to this project differ from men's? Could a diversity of interests arise among women within a particular village? Explain.
3. What historical evidence could be marshaled to either support or challenge the proposition that *women are more capable of building social relationships than men* in human development work?
4. Discuss the relevance of *coverage* as a component in a gender-information system as important in planning a program to shelter and counsel victims of human trafficking.
5. Twelve of 25 management positions are held by women in Agency X as compared to 4 of 17 in Agency Y. Thus, it follows that *Agency X has been more committed to gender mainstreaming than Agency Y.* Do you agree or disagree? Explain.

Notes

1. I am indebted to my colleague Natalie Florea Hudson for this observation.
2. From www.who.int/gender/mainstreaming/en/index.html, accessed May 29, 2010.

8

Human Resources Management in Humanitarian and Development NGOs

One of the world's largest and most prestigious international NGOs recently posted a job advertisement on its website[1] for a human resources (HR) administrator to "assist with our personnel records, pay and benefits for our senior international staff and to help our busy reward team on pension caseworks and insurance claims." The advertisement lists a number of formidable responsibilities, including

- providing administration for expatriate and senior staff,
- assisting with international pay components including gross and net pay calculations and tax reimbursements,
- liaising with regional HR and payroll to ensure that agreed service standards are met, and
- working flexibly as part of the reward team (among other responsibilities).

The annual gross salary for this position approaches US$27,000.

In his casebook on public management, Robert Watson characterizes personnel issues as follows: "Organizations are made up of people and many organization problems ultimately end up being people problems. As such, management tasks like recruitment, selection, and training are vitally important to the health of the organization" (2002, 43). For a variety of reasons (discussed in this chapter), humanitarian and development organizations typically confront "people problems" that in some cases compromise capabilities to implement programs. But unfortunately, many NGOs find it difficult to support a viable human resources operation on a par with the INGO that is clearly searching for an *additional*, mid-level human resources specialist in a well-established personnel system. Indeed, some NGOs would be hard-pressed even to justify the modest sum of US$27,000 to support a single HR manager in the organization.

This chapter directly addresses the human resources dilemmas of smaller NGOs that experience more difficulty supporting proactive human resources development than larger, well-funded organizations such as the one referenced previously. The first section elaborates on some contextual factors that generally characterize human-resource-related needs of humanitarian and development organizations. The second section elaborates on how four specific human resources functions (staffing, compensation, training, and promotion) relate to the capacity building in these organizations.

The Context of NGO Human Resources Management

The extent to which NGOs can undertake human resources activities that complement capacity building, organization learning, and empowerment missions depends on factors such as (1) the changing nature of state power and conflict, (2) the changing nature of humanitarianism, (3) the alignment of mission and HR purpose, and (4) the varying perceptions of HR within the organization. First and especially important to humanitarian organizations with global missions, the changing international context affecting both interstate relationships and the nature of conflict requires NGOs to take "a look inward" at themselves and the skill requirements of their staffs (J. V. Henry 2004, 43). With regard to interstate security, the erosion of state sovereignty since the cold war has hastened military interventions linked to humanitarian objectives, for example, in Somalia, Kosovo, and Afghanistan (p. 48). Thus, NGO personnel risk losing their impartiality and becoming targets of belligerents. As a result, conflict becomes increasingly intrastate in nature, requiring NGOs that value local-community participation to be especially astute in mastering the complexity of local conflict and avoiding actions that could inadvertently aid aggressors (see Anderson 1999).

A World Vision program officer tells of that INGO's hiring dilemmas in selecting nationals to distribute food aid in civil-war-torn Sudan in the late 1990s. Specifically, Riak reports that, as the second-largest employer in the region after the army, World Vision found itself entangled in the conflict by hiring locals:

A conflict was identified between the community and the local authorities that had developed out of a hiring procedure. The analysis showed that WV was inadvertently contributing to this conflict through a recruitment and hiring policy that depended almost entirely on the [army] and was, therefore, subject to abuse. Ways to address this included recruitment through churches, open advertising, and committee interviews. These changes provided the community with the opportunity to participate in staff selection, to seek employment, and to represent to a greater extent the diversity of [the region]. (Riak 2000, 502)

Human resources issues arise here in terms of both staff competence to analyze the effects of hiring procedures and World Vision's ability to recruit individuals with the potential to develop those skills.

Second, the rapid growth of the humanitarian sector in the twenty-first century has affected donor policies in ways that severely limit NGOs' abilities to invest in HR development. In recent years, diverse groups of organizational actors (such as civil society organizations and human rights agencies) have stepped onto a crowded stage with development NGOs and emergency relief agencies to compete for donor funding. As a People in Aid study of NGO human resources management reports, "The aid policies on which humanitarianism depends have also changed, with increasing pressure on budgets affecting many, and the realignment of policy affecting others" (J. V. Henry 2004, 44). Large bilateral donors, for example, USAID, have thus adjusted their aid policies to reflect national interests and political ideologies, which in turn intensify pressure on the humanitarian sector by directing aid to relatively few INGOs (pp. 45–46). In addition, the bilateral agencies have become less willing to fund capacity-building efforts like those related to human resources development.

Political scientist Michael Barnett argues that the purpose of humanitarianism has become more political and its organization more institutionalized:

Once upon a time humanitarian agencies used to define themselves largely in opposition to "politics." . . . [But during the 1990s those] agencies and states began to share agendas. States became more willing to act in the name of humanitarianism, fund relief operations, use their diplomatic and political power to advance humanitarian causes, authorize military troops to deliver relief, and consider the legitimacy of humanitarian intervention and the protection of civilian populations. (Barnett 2005, 723–24)

Barnett concludes by asking the question of whether "principled actors have changed world politics by pressuring states to take the high road and redefine their interests" or "global politics has reshaped the nature of humanitarian action" and answering in terms of the latter (2005, 733). Given this apparent inversion from a principle of caring to a utilitarian political outcome, Hugo Slim wonders if NGOs should draw on moral exemplars—such as El Salvador's Archbishop Romero or South Africa's Steve Biko—as role models for human resources training (1997, 255).

Third, the human resources management *orientation* of rights-based and humanitarian organizations should be distinctly developmental or focused on capacity building, in contrast to the regulatory purposes of HR in public organizations. Padaki argues that if the HR function is truly developmental, then its management cannot simply consist of a "bag of (control) tools" but must instead emerge from "a sound body of theory and methodology" related to how HR management builds NGO capacity (2007, 66). On the basis of her research on community health-care projects in Tanzania, Robinson elaborates on the problems civil-society organizations confront in mediating the regulatory orientation of public HR management with their (NGO) capacity-building needs:

> There are significant problems in moving from a state-centred, hierarchically managed view of public policy based on notions of control, to a more decentralised and pluralistic system. In the current health management system in Tanzania, the district government role has not been conceived of as a policy role. There is little emphasis in practice on information analysis, team work, or strategic thinking. . . . Finally, non-governmental actors of all kinds often fail to think through their own roles vis-à-vis government systems and policy. What is commonly missing is an appreciation and analysis of interdependence. (Robinson 1999, 85)

However, Hailey and James's study of effective NGO leaders such as those in BRAC and PROSHIKA (both in Bangladesh) shows how strong leadership can link organization learning with HR management to build capacity: "The research suggests that effective learning is a hard-won goal, which depends as much on formal training, effective information systems, and human resource management strategies as on informal, participatory processes" (2002, 398–99).

Fourth, human resources development is sometimes perceived more as a liability than an asset within humanitarian organizations because of its costs in relation to scarce resources and the burdens it places on operational managers (J. V. Henry 2004, 57–58). Human resources' reputation as an excessive administrative cost can be understood by reviewing the scope of obligations that "good practice in the management and support of aid personnel" entails. For example, People in Action's model *Code of Good Practice* includes the principle that "the security, good health, and safety of our staff are prime responsibilities of the organization." When broken down into component activities, that principle translates into numerous expenditures, such as the costs of

- assessments of security, travel, and health risks for workers and their dependents at regular intervals;
- health clearances before international postings;
- record-keeping on work-related injuries, sickness, and accidents; and
- available health care, personal counseling, and career advice during a worker's assignment (2003, 20).

The availability of personal counseling emerges as especially important for development workers given common occurrences of role stress in the forms of alienation, emotional load, responsibility load, and work–living imbalances during assignments (Padaki 2007, 71–72).

But, as Padaki suggests, the accompanying costs of staff well-being pose an ethical dilemma for humanitarian agencies *"spending on themselves . . .* made possible by *spending somebody else's money"* donated to assist distressed people outside the organization (2007, 71; italics his). Advocates of vibrant human resources programs (such as People in Aid) regard the pervasive attitude associating NGO efficiency with minimal personnel (e.g., under 5% of total) costs as "a simplistic perception by evaluators of the use of human resources in humanitarian action. . . . [Instead] human resources should be the starting point from which to calculate the capacity to respond to needs" (J. V. Henry 2004, 58). As stated by an official of the International Federation of Red Cross and Red Crescent Societies, "Budgets are upside down. We should put human resources at the top, and then work out what we can do with the available resources, not the other way around" (M. Fortier, quoted in J. V. Henry 2004, 58). This logic, however, may not always compute among operations managers who consider their personnel-related responsibilities as added burdens and view them with disdain. Such perspectives appear understandable among agencies lacking specialists with HR expertise. But ultimately, these tensions can be reduced if and when donor institutions recognize the importance of human resources development in humanitarian work and become more willing to fund it.

Human Resources Functions in NGO Settings

Generally, human resources management can be understood as a set of particular personnel functions including (1) staffing, (2) compensation and classification, (3) training and development, (4) employee advancement and promotion, and (5) handling of grievances and disciplinary action (Watson 2002, 43). The following discussions of HR functions as related to NGO workforces basically follow this scheme with just a few departures. First, NGO staffing issues arise in the context of high employee turnover trends and the corresponding need to retain the most-valued people. Second, employee classification seldom surfaces as a significant concern linked to compensation (as is the case with government employment) because most NGOs lack the resources to maintain classification systems based on comprehensive job analyses. Furthermore, it is unclear whether job classification would promote workflow in organizations more often characterized as team-based adhocracies (see chapter 4) than hierarchal bureaucracies. Third, disciplinary concerns have yet to emerge among NGO human resources priorities, except in occasional reference to "involuntary turnover" more often attributable to inept human resources practices in the agency rather than to workers' failings (see Vale 2010, 15).

Staffing, Turnover, and Retention

Estimates show that more than 19 million people worked in NGOs at the beginning of the twenty-first century (Wheat 2000, 55), and related statistics reveal strong public enthusiasm toward the prospect of working in humanitarian organizations (International Health Exchange/People in Aid 1997, 2). One could reasonably expect rights-focused agencies to empower their employees and volunteers just as they empower their program beneficiaries. But the evidence suggests that some NGOs treat their employees shabbily. According to an NGO management trainer, realities of how workers are treated fall short of these expectations:

> NGOs generally have a poor record of providing decent social security benefits for their staff. Development work being noble, staff are not expected to grumble. . . . Consider the irony of the case. An NGO grows in stature for its commendable work in the non-organised sectors of employment—organising domestic work-

ers, truck loaders, coolies, and casual labourers into associations to press for their basic rights to minimum wages, decent working conditions, social security, and so on. However, when the staff get together with other like-minded people to discuss working conditions in the development sector, they are firmly discouraged. (Padaki 2007, 74)

At the extreme, shocking accounts of sexual abuse against females employed in lower-level NGO positions raise the specter of a hypocritical double standard, especially where NGO managerial misbehavior violates government laws concerning sexual harassment in the workplace (Vasan 2004, 2197–98). But more often, inconsistencies between espoused empowerment values and actual management practices contribute to workers' disillusionment because of an inability to find self-actualization and career development opportunities, which in turn lead to staff turnover as a principal NGO management concern (see, e.g., Eade 1997).

In general, the human resources conundrum related to turnover lies in the paradox that despite voluminous applications submitted for position openings, NGO jobs are hard to fill (Richardson 2006). One survey of NGO recruitment experiences reports,

> With agencies receiving over 3,000 enquiries *per week* about work opportunities, there is clearly huge public interest in helping developing countries. Yet a third of the agencies were unable to fill 372 posts. The problem appears to be that the help offered by people interested in working overseas is often not the right kind. (International Health Exchange/People in Aid 1997, 2; italics theirs)

Donor pressures on recipient NGOs to hire professional experts have turned NGO recruitment and selection into a competitive seller's (i.e., qualified candidate's) market. In responding to the recruitment survey mentioned previously, an official in one agency commented, "There is still a perception that organizations want unskilled volunteers—the vast majority of enquiries we receive are from people with no relevant professional skills or qualifications" (International Health Exchange/People in Aid 1997, 5).

NGOs that have instituted coherent human resources development strategies are better equipped to function effectively in competitive skilled-labor markets and to adopt measures that help retain those most important to the agency's long-term success. With regard to turnover, a prudent HR development program acknowledges the inevitability—and the desirability—of people leaving the humanitarian sector, but it also takes a systematic approach that differentiates among recruitment markets and types of candidates attracted to NGO work. At a fundamental level, NGOs need to monitor their *internal markets* consisting of those currently employed somewhere within the organization. The NGO's command of its internal market allows it to accommodate the career development aspirations of the key employees targeted for retention. Second, an effective HR development plan distinguishes between *national* (or in-country) and *international* (expatriate) *markets* and anticipates factors that impinge on turnover-related human circumstances associated with each. Many NGOs hire liberally from within the countries they serve to negotiate cultural settings and language problems often confronted in the field. But those placements can exact substantial human burdens (especially for women working in remote areas where they are subject to ridicule and even harassment for living outside of a family setting) related to social ostracism (in the work setting and in home communities), physical danger of violence or disease, or burnout-inducing boredom during the nonworking hours (see Goetz 1995, 1997; Ahmad 2002). By contrast, expatriate employees can experience acculturation problems leading to social isolation. Padaki maintains that this social isolation takes a particular toll on young people entering development or human-rights-related professional service:

> They have family and friends who don't quite understand it: "he should have studied for the civil service"; "she could be married into a nice family by now"; "look at his classmates"; "what sort of life is she leading?"; and so on. Over time the young person is distanced not only from family and old friends, but also from the community and the larger middle-class constituency itself. The price to be paid for such isolation is both emotional and intellectual. (Padaki 2007, 71–72)

Moreover, NGOs should distinguish among various types of workers, each of which is able to contribute to the agency mission but nonetheless merits different levels of consideration with regard to turnover and retention strategies. The "occasional," or short-term, worker—usually with a much-needed technical or professional background—enters humanitarian work periodically as a departure from a regular career path. A recruitment handbook (based on the survey mentioned previously) remarks, "One surgeon in France has two CVs—one which lists international humanitarian experience and another which does not refer to it" (J. V. Henry 2004, 32). A second type, also non-permanent, includes those who do not seek full-time employment, in some cases volunteers (or as the French call them, *cooperants*), attracted by the challenge of assignments. In contrast to these temporary classifications, a third "permanent" category includes those who are most likely to advance to senior management levels and embody the memory of the organization. This third grouping of (at least potential) "old hands" is especially important to retain in preference to hiring management expertise from the outside; the People in Action recruitment handbook uses a survey response to explain why prior experience in other NGOs is not always a career asset:

> Those who have solid experience with several different organizations often lack the ability to adjust to and adhere to the mandate of our particular organization. Indeed, we often find that the best people for top management positions have been working internationally in other sectors and have solid management experience, and for whom we are the first humanitarian organization for which they have worked. (J. V. Henry 2004, 32)

A strong HR development strategy both recognizes that lifestyle issues are associated with each worker type and focuses as much on the informal nature of interpersonal relationships as on formalized policies. Regarding the latter, it is especially prudent to scrutinize the quality of manager–employee relationships as a "push factor" that if strained could push a valued employee to leave the organization (Vale 2010, 11). As such, NGOs usually exercise more control in ameliorating push factors in retention initiatives than over "pull factors" that lure employees to more attractive positions in other NGOs.

A 2009 survey of humanitarian programs serving people in the horn of Africa explains that staff retention programs work best where (1) managers approach staff issues collaboratively rather than as individuals with personal agendas, (2) managers know who needs to be retained, and (3) the agency negotiates flexible understanding of mutual obligations between the worker and the agency on a case-specific basis (Vale 2010, 10–11). In essence, it is recommended that NGOs depend on *psychological contracts* to surmount the push factors that lead to worker dissatisfaction. In *Psychological Contracts in Organizations*, Denise Rousseau defines the term as follows:

> *The psychological contract* [involves] individual beliefs, shaped by the organization, regarding the terms of an exchange agreement

between individuals and their organization. Psychological contracts have the power of self-fulfilling prophecies: They can create the future. People who make and keep their commitments can anticipate and plan because their actions are more readily specified and predictable both to others as well as to themselves. (Rousseau 1995, 9; italics hers)

The author of the 2009 retention report concludes by intimating how these exchange agreements could lead to positive futures:

To obtain significant improvements in retention would require the organization to be recognized as a "great employer of professionals." This may require a commitment to addressing the office or the team's culture. Behaviors and attitudes would need to be underpinned by the belief and conviction that an organization's added value in any humanitarian situation is their highly performing and professional teams. Ultimately people are the first priority because only through them can an I/NGO succeed. (Vale 2010, 11–12)

Effective human resources development, according to this conclusion, reflects the primacy of human competence as an NGO performance standard (as discussed in chapter 5) and the managerial imperative to balance the informal culture with the organization's formal structure (chapter 4).

Compensation and Related Issues

Modern government organizations typically link employee compensation to elaborate job classification systems, and business firms often combine comparative industry standards with individual performance appraisals. Although some large humanitarian agencies may base pay on job classification, many NGOs simply lack the unrestricted funds needed to invest in human resources management. As Padaki suggests, agencies may be better advised to invest their limited funds in proactive development (HRD) practices that promote effective "people-organization fits" than on regulatory schemes such as job classification systems:

HRD may be viewed as a sub-set of HRM [management], dealing specially with its developmental objective—the enhancement of effectiveness in the person–organisation fit. . . . Herein lies the catch. Enhancing an effective fit between person and organisation calls

for two complementary tasks: fitting the person to the organisation, and fitting the organisation to the person. A preoccupation
with the former is simply regulatory [personnel management] with
a new label . . . Organisational Development. [That] refers to the
process of strengthening the capability of a single organisation or
group. The stress is on the performance of the organisation as a
whole. (Padaki 2007, 67–68)

All of that said, the 2004 survey evidence indicates that many humanitarian
agencies "do HR on the cheap" by relying on operations managers, rather than
HR specialists, to make personnel decisions that not only affect careers but
also compromise the physical safety of professionals (J. V. Henry 2004, 58).

Clearly, the inadequacy of human resources support looms as an over-
riding problem associated with compensation, not only in monetary terms
but with intrinsic job satisfaction as well. Beyond this, NGOs confront other
personnel issues linked to compensation, including the length of overseas assignments, nonsalaried compensation for volunteer workers, compensation
for field-workers, and contract variations in a multinational workforce. First,
survey data show that only about 10% of humanitarian workers in both the
salaried and the volunteer ranks seeking overseas assignments actually secure
them. Some large INGOs, such as the International Federation of Red Cross
and Red Crescent Societies and Médecins Sans Frontières (Doctors Without
Borders), screen applicants through rigorous testing, training, and orientation courses. The majority of those who do land overseas stints find their stays
cut back because of the short-term nature of project funding, staff rotation
practices, need to deploy elsewhere, or other reasons (J. V. Henry 2004, 31).
An Oxfam official indicates that her organization, in concert with six other
INGOs, has explored the effectiveness of alternative staffing models concerning the impact of short-term assignments. Among other problems, short stays
tend to undercut one's career planning and development efforts. Richardson
explains,

Career development is seen as a way of increasing staff and organisational capacities, and also as a reward for undertaking humanitarian work. Experience of [sic] managing emergencies may be regarded as a key skill for aspiring Country Directors. Humanitarian
assignments . . . also provide an opportunity for national staff to
gain the international experience needed to join an internal roster
or emergency corps, or to apply for a more senior post. Improved

career planning, including assisting staff to move to new assignments, has enabled some INGOs to employ more programme
managers and technical staff on long-term contracts. (Richardson
2006, 339)

Although NGO leaders cannot always control the factors that determine assignment length, they can initiate candid feedback and conversation that keeps
workers apprised of the variables affecting their missions (Vale 2010, 9–10).

Second, most volunteer workers in humanitarian NGOs are not "volunteers" in the purest sense of the term—that is, provided no monetary outlay at
all for their efforts—but in fact receive "limited remuneration based on local
costs, or an allowance based on local costs at home, with an element for local subsistence costs while on a mission" within a broader package of benefits
including travel, insurance, and perhaps other expenses (J. V. Henry 2004,
21). However, in some cases, agencies actually draft contracts of employment
for volunteers, often to accommodate national laws that entitle employees to
certain benefits or rights (p. 22). The 2004 recruitment survey elaborates on
the intrinsic nature of rewards for committed volunteers willing to undertake
hardship out of loyalty for an NGO's mission. Some organizations take deliberate steps to recruit volunteers as a principal source of labor, such as (not
surprisingly) Médecins Sans Frontières.

MSF has 18 operational and partner Sections which raise funds
and provide staff and volunteers for programmes. . . . The Sections
mobilise and recruit volunteers who are able to work on international programmes, and bring back to the Section their experience
and commitment. In MSF's case five of the Sections are operational
and mount programmes in their own right, and the remaining 13
support them, but are not themselves operational. (J. V. Henry
2004, 21)

Beyond matters of monetary accommodation, NGO leaders should take
measures to reinforce volunteers' sense of commitment amid condescending
attitudes of salaried colleagues who discredit the efforts of the nonpaid. Research on volunteerism in the British NGO Voluntary Service Overseas (VSO)
in Phnom Penh, Cambodia, addresses the frustrating irony that committed
and well-qualified volunteers are subject to indignities by salaried workers who
associate their paid status with superiority. One volunteer's comments amply
illustrate the problem:

> I have had people working with me who think they should be
> working on top of me—so to speak. They have no more qualifica-
> tions or experience than I have. In fact, in one or two cases they've
> had less. And I've had to make that very clear. That I'm not here to
> be someone's minion or dogsbody. . . . They've brought with them
> the baggage of the world's presumption that if somebody's paid a
> lot of money they must be a lot better qualified. (Watts 2002, 63)

Adept human resources management could cast volunteers' self-actualization dilemmas in terms of Herzberg's (1966) work on job satisfaction that
distinguishes motivators from hygienic (i.e., dissatisfying) factors. However,
Watts asserts that nonpaid volunteer work may be perceived as simultaneously
satisfying and unsatisfying:

> It mediates the indirect satisfaction of allowing greater empathy
> with the local community and the dissatisfactions [expressed in the
> previous quote]. It is not altogether unlike giving up chocolate for
> Lent—not a particularly nice thing to do in itself, but apparently
> good for you. And, of course, like Lent, a VSO posting does not
> last forever. (Watts 2002, 64)

In effect, NGO leaders can assume clarifying roles that cut through the uncomfortable dissonance that volunteers encounter in their interactions with
paid coworkers. In addition to championing volunteer effort, leaders can
endorse volunteers' unique opportunities to "speak the unvarnished truth to
power" and occasionally use the "up yours!" response to reinvigorate self-worth
among volunteer workers (Watts 2002, 68).

Third, rights-based development organizations should be attuned to the
human resources needs of workers serving in remote field locations. On the
basis of his interviews with 109 field-workers in various-sized NGOs in Bangladesh, Ahmad reports that many serving in the field suffer severe financial
hardships, as do those in communities served, and as a result may not be able
to afford to have their families accompany them in their distant assignments.
It is not unusual for these workers to ask for loan advances in negotiating
compensation with NGO employers (2002, 187). In addition, the contributions of fieldwork staffs are often overlooked for a variety of reasons relating
to disconnects between their ongoing work and formally stated NGO goals,
competing organizational priorities, poor selection and training practices, and
tendencies to promote good field-workers into management positions (Heyns

1996, 55–56). But, as discussed in chapter 5, it is the field-worker who is expected to perform in such a way as to "make good" on the outcome indicators incorporated in the logframe planning document. Ahmad comments,

> I found that NGOs in Bangladesh are obsessed with the performance of their staff in delivering services like micro-credit, education, health-awareness programmes, etc. Donors give funds for certain activities and evaluate the impact of that "aid" against certain criteria (whether these are accessible to the target population, improvements in school dropout rates, enrolment, girls' enrolment, repayment of credit, etc.). So, to ensure regular supplies of funds, NGOs have to ask their fieldworkers to maintain performance and show the donors what success they have achieved against these criteria. (2002, 182)

Indeed, Ahmad speaks to the pivotal role of field-workers in development, calling them social pioneers (using Goetz's [1995] term) "because they are bringing changes to the lives of their clients and breaking age-old social conventions by working in the rural areas, riding bicycles and motorcycles, and working in remote regions where government bureaucrats or their staff would never go." Although keeping these social pioneers motivated is critical, it is nonetheless difficult. Promotion opportunities for field-workers are limited given their lack of college training, which is required of other NGO employees, and, in some cases, given the corrupt organizational practices driving promotion decisions (Ahmad 2002, 188). Thus, NGOs that depend on fieldworkers to implement development programs are obliged to devise particular human resources development strategies that meet the specific needs of women and men engaged in field work and offer fitting rewards for their efforts.

Fourth, humanitarian agencies that recruit internationally may offer candidates for similar positions differently worded contracts that accommodate the legal contexts of respective countries of origin. These differences could adversely affect workplace morale in that "agencies must compromise in their search for equality or equity, because the multinational agencies are too complicated for everyone to be treated the same as everyone else" (J. V. Henry 2004, 33). Furthermore, the 2004 recruitment survey indicates that variations in national income tax requirements can account for as much as 40% of differences in employees' net compensation. In this regard, some INGOs (e.g., the International Federation of Red Cross and Red Crescent Societies) delegate employee compensation matters to their in-country affiliates (p. 33).

Training and Development

Typically, the roles of training and employee development in most any type of organization are more often characterized as *means* than *ends*—that can be expressed generally (e.g., to ensure that employees do their work at an acceptable level) or specifically (e.g., to improve financial reporting for accountability purposes). To an extent, the means orientation of *training* distinguishes it from the related issue of *organization learning* (the focus of chapter 6) that relates to ends (in the sense that a "learning organization" is a valued asset in development and rights-advocacy work) and to means (e.g., of analyzing complex issues). As means to ends, training interventions can vary with regard to context and purpose, training methods and target cadres (or groups), duration of the training intervention, and funding realities.

Regarding purpose, the training rationale may be to provide specialists even more technical knowledge or to heighten sensitivity to value-based practices (such as interactive education with participation) throughout the organization. In some cases, the demands of external stakeholders (e.g., for more professionalized governance) could provide the impetus for training. In others, NGOs may depend on postemployment training to compensate for documented shortages of skilled personnel in the development sector (see Richardson 2006). Methods of training vary (internal course work, workshops, self-study, temporary assignments, etc.) as directed toward different groups (senior or top managers, technical specialists, administrative support personnel) in the organization (Fowler 2002, 452–53). Training interventions may be brief in duration (e.g., a two-day workshop) or extended as an integral component in long-term career development. With regard to funding and resource availability, training that is specific to a particular project could be underwritten by donor support (and subject to corresponding donor mandates) or, in response to resource scarcity, supported collaboratively through NGO networks that offer training opportunities to member organizations (see J. V. Henry 2004, 59).

NGOs with well-developed HR management systems can approach training, particularly for new staff, as a socialization experience that builds capacity in the organization. Referring to this socialization as *induction*, Padaki comments,

> Selecting somebody who is presumed to be suitable for a certain kind of work and bringing that person into a productive relationship with the position are two entirely different propositions. . . . Unfortunately, induction is the most neglected aspect of HR in most NGOs. Many NGOs are not even aware of such a procedure.

Its importance is rarely recognised. When one considers the nature of work in development programmes, the manpower supply, and the types of role stress that people experience, induction may well be the HR procedure that most needs to be systematically followed in NGOs. (Padaki 2007, 72–73)

In some instances, induction could inform new employees of immediate concerns vital to their occupational well-being, such as those related to personal security (Tate 2005, 60) or cultural norms that must be observed (Lahiri-Dutt 2006, 219). However, from a broader career-development standpoint, induction could consist of an individual's long-term career plans, staff mentoring roles, and the "big picture" of the agency's vision and values and extend over a one-year period (Padaki 2007, 73). According to Alan Fowler, induction provides entrants the opportunity to familiarize themselves with background information related to "documentation on the NGO as a whole," current program strategies, personnel and related policies, and explanations of the NGO's development (and rights-advocacy) approaches (2002, 451). Furthermore, he concludes that "an important outcome of the induction period is that the new staff member understands the NGO as a development agency, identifies with what the organization stands for and is trying to achieve, and can explain this when relating to the outside world" (p. 454). Thus, induction can impart institutional sense-making that transmits agency values and, assuming that they are internalized, builds capacity in the organization.

For the rights-oriented NGO, induction through training engenders strategic opportunities to "frame the nature of the problem [the NGO] seeks to address and the levers of change [that can be employed]" in apprising new staff of the intellectual versatility necessary to (re)conceptualize problems of rights deprivation and tactics to address them (Uvin 2004, 160–62). Induction can serve as the triggering device that reorients one to visualize and analyze complex issues through the eyes of a change agent, who reacts by formulating a stream of probing questions that "identify the factors that limit the promotion, protection, and provision of specific groups' rights" (p. 161). While the costs associated with human resources management are formidable for NGOs, a sophisticated HR development program offers a viable platform for cultivating intellectually agile change-agents for empowerment.

Staff Advancement and Promotion

Although career advancement and promotion prospects are recognized as key ingredients for employee morale in most organizations (Watson 2002, 44), these topics often surface as problematic issues in NGO settings. As discussed, scarcities of unrestricted funds to support coherent HR development programs account for the inconsistent and haphazard implementation of promotion and staff care practices (Vale 2010, 15). Exceptions can be found among a few large INGOs, such as the International Federation of Red Cross and Red Crescent Societies, capable of investing in proactive promotion systems (J. V. Henry 2004, 21). Although many if not most of those who work in humanitarian settings cannot be (or do not care to be) retained, NGO leaders need to know who to keep and promote. However, the effectiveness of this selective approach to career advancement is contingent on establishing a viable human resources development program. Some commentaries on promotion and advancement raise the lamentable specter of inequity and discrimination regarding particular groupings, for example, field-workers who perceive their efforts to be underappreciated in NGOs and women professionals who bear the brunt of gender discrimination blocking their advancement potential (see chapter 7). Clearly, career advancement and promotion loom as vexing challenges for NGO leaders.

From an ideological perspective, it is worth noting that in the context of development work, concern about advancement and promotion can be inimical to the altruism associated with empowering the poor. For example, in *Whose Reality Counts?* Robert Chambers refers to "the professional prison" that confines experts from participating with local communities:

> In the words of one: "For me as a trained economist the easiest way to get promot[ed] is to stay in my office and play with my computer, and not go out." To get on, you have to stay in. So professional values and methods set a trap. Status, promotion, and power come less from direct contact with the confusing complexity of people, communities, livelihoods, and farming systems, and more from isolation that permits safe and sophisticated analysis of statistics. (Chambers 1997, 54)

In evaluating the apparent failure of a UNICEF-sponsored health-care project in Ecuador, Moser and Sollis comment on community perceptions of aloof professionals who cared less about community needs and more about personal career advancement. They comment,

> Such motives are blatantly obvious and are countered with a large degree of cynicism. . . . The common view was that the big fight

over who was to become programme director had less to do with
the objectives of the programme, and more to do with the financial
reward. (Moser and Sollis 1991, 30)

That commentary prompted one reader, a leader of a women's action organization in India, to respond:

> I think the structure of payments should have been built the other
> way round, i.e. the health workers should have been paid encour-
> aging salaries . . . and the professionals and the technical team
> should have taken up the project with an altruistic, philosophi-
> cal attitude, and accepted payment at below their usual minimum
> wages. (Pathak 1992, 61)

In a perfect world, NGO workers would find a reasonable balance between
their personal aspirations and their ethics of concern. But for now, NGO leaders must grapple with the realities of reconciling professional motivations and
agency missions with limited resources.

Conclusion

Human resources management poses a fundamental dilemma for NGOs with
development, humanitarian, and/or rights-advocacy missions: on one hand,
there is a pressing need for these organizations to develop and maintain proactive human resources development strategies, but on the other hand, most
lack the financial resources to support a strong HR management component.
As suggested in chapter 5, *competency* emerges more often than not as the
"cutting-edge" performance criterion in development and empowerment
work. The changing contexts of interstate and intrastate power, conflict, and
the meaning of humanitarianism underscore the need for analytical competence to make sense out of the political, economic, and cultural complexities
surrounding human distress and rights deprivation in the twenty-first century.
To paraphrase authors of a classic essay on organization theory (Emery and
Trist 1965), sometimes contexts are so complex that "the ground is in motion,"
such that NGOs that misread the complexity can inadvertently exacerbate (as
did World Vision in Sudan) the problems they intend to alleviate. As embodied
within the organization, Uvin's rights-based perspective (2004, 122–66)—premised on the human competencies of political analysis, reconceptualization,

and reframing—calls for human resources strategies of a long-term, developmental nature that cannot "be done on the cheap."

Human resources managers face tough staffing challenges related to (1) recruiting skilled applicants in a competitive labor market, (2) maintaining mission effectiveness despite high rates of employee turnover, and (3) mitigating sources of dissatisfaction that push employees to leave the organization. In addition, HR officials need to tailor specific compensation strategies for various employee groups (e.g., full-time, temporary, and volunteer personnel), as well as address particular lifestyle and work-related problems experienced by some (such as field-workers serving in remote locations). Nonmonetary compensation strategies can be based on informal understandings, or psychological contracts, that promote job satisfaction and career development. Effective human resources management approaches the training function as a principal means of building organization capacity and as an induction opportunity to convey a sense of what the NGO values and is attempting to achieve. Severe resource limitations require NGOs to design selective promotion and advancement strategies for retaining a small pool of professionals whose continued tenure appears closely linked to future mission effectiveness.

Discussion Issues

1. As a business-support administrator in a humanitarian organization, you have to develop a presentation to persuade donors to increase funding support for human resources management. Identify four "talking points" you would incorporate in the presentation. Anticipate donor reactions to each.

2. As a recently hired NGO employee, you are unsure whether you intend to pursue a long-term career in humanitarian service or to simply have a short-term (two- or three-year) experience. What factors would be likely to influence your decision? Is it advantageous to make that decision early on? Why or why not?

3. Assume (referring to the previous question) that you decide to embark on a long-term career directed toward eventually securing a high-level position in NGO leadership. Identify four important elements of a long-term career development strategy.

4. Draft five questions that could be included in screening interviews for prospective volunteers to provide continuing adult education in poor, rural India.

5. Human resources specialists need to know which individuals, even among a generally competent workforce, should be identified as especially important to retain. Identify one or two character traits, skills, or competencies that stand out as critical determinants. Explain their significance.

Note

1. The position of human resources administrator was advertised on the Oxfam GB website at www.i-grasp.com/fe/tpl_oxfam.asp?newms=jj&id=33260&rss=1, accessed July 29, 2010.

9

Conclusion
Rights-Based Leadership in NGOs

Learning seldom if ever occurs in a vacuum. So it is not surprising that F. H. Abed and Dr. Helene Gayle—the two "learning NGO leaders" (see Hailey and James 2002) profiled in chapter 1—benefitted from learning experiences within their previous institutional experiences, business (in Abed's case, with Shell Oil) and government (in Gayle's, the US Centers for Disease Control and Prevention). One can quibble over exactly how morally autonomous individuals can be within organizations, but most would concede that we learn much about life within our work environments (see Gini 2000; Dienhart 2002). Indeed the assertions that (at least to some extent) we "find ourselves" in the institutional workplace, that (as leaders) we help others do the same, and that "work is a fundamental part of our humanity" (Dienhart 2002, 384) all do much to dispel the Rousseauian myth that human virtue flows from a pure (presumably noninstitutional) state of nature.

When an NGO leader characterizes himself "as an incorrigible introvert [such that] in the Christmas pageant of life, the characters I admire most—and the only roles for which I would ever consider auditioning—are the ox and the donkey" (see Kristof 2008, A14), he casts doubts on his learning capacities within the organization. To be sure, calling attention to a leader's limitations and shortcomings does not undo his accomplishments—in Greg Mortenson's case, efforts providing Afghan and Pakistani girls school facilities and educational opportunities. But Nicholas Kristof's (2011) speculation that Mortenson's subsequent problems (see chapter 1) can be attributed to "disorganization" invites further conjecture about the incompatibility of idiosyncratic personalities with institutions wherein people learn from each other and collectively adapt to external environments.

With due regard to Kristof's commitment to human rights and command of global affairs, it may be the case that journalists are ill equipped to pass judgment on the essence of organizational leadership. In fact, they may be inclined to gloss over the institutional concerns about how leaders cope with situational factors, preferring instead to bestow celebrity status on those with quirky dispositions. Hayward, Rindova, and Pollock maintain that in order to appeal to audiences' tastes, journalists attribute organization performance to a leader's distinctive disposition: "Put another way, people embrace leadership as a simple, vivid explanation for organizational actions rather than engage in the distressing task of trying to come to grips with the multitude of variables that shape organizations" (Hayward, Rindova, and Pollock 2004, 642, quoting Staw and Sutton 1992, 356). Furthermore, these researchers advance the proposition that *"the greater the availability of information about a CEO's idiosyncratic personal behaviors, the greater the likelihood that journalists will attribute an [organization's] strategic actions to its CEO"* (Hayward, Rindova, and Pollock 2004, 643; italics theirs)—although they make no specific mention of leaders who make information available through their own autobiographical accounts. But Hayward, Rindova, and Pollock do address the consequences of celebrity (or of "believing one's own press") in ominous terms: leaders become even further detached from the institutional realities of their situations. "The more that others provide an individual with attributional accounts, the more likely it is that the individual will adopt the view expressed by others. In other words, [leaders] as well as other actors that surround them become less likely to attribute outcomes to their situation" (p. 644). To paraphrase Smillie and Hailey, those who become distracted by their own press are more likely to "lose themselves at sea" than to manage the "dangerous sea" of the organization's institutional environments (2002, 17).

The intent of this book has been to assist those with career aspirations working in development, humanitarian, and rights-advocacy organizations to "come to grips" with the *challenging* (but hopefully not "distressing") task of understanding the institutional nature of NGOs and the "multitude of variables that shape them." In this regard, the preceding chapters have examined a variety of institutional issues that address situational contingencies that characterize NGO leadership responsibilities. The first chapter directed the reader's attention to four fundamental questions related to (1) specific management environments that affect NGOs' ability to leverage their influence to promote human rights, (2) the obstacles likely encountered in those efforts, (3) the specific management competencies needed to advance human rights agendas, and (4) realistic career development strategies that might guide those aspiring to work in rights-focused NGOs. It is fitting to conclude by revisiting those questions.

Management Environments and Rights-Leveraging Capabilities

Lacking any type of statutory authority or inherent power, NGOs are able to advance human rights generally to the extent they can leverage networks, governments, corporations, or other actors to change behaviors in ways that alleviate conditions of disempowerment. The previous chapters call attention to four management environments that affect (and in many cases complicate) NGO efforts to leverage human rights interests: the institutional power, accountability, information, and human resources environments. The term *institutional power environment* refers primarily to Northern global institutions that provide NGO funding; shape policies that articulate the meaning of "development," "humanitarianism," or "human rights"; or do both. This environment tends to deflate rights causes by first *embracing them* only to reframe (or redefine) them in terms that reinforce their ideological understanding of the world. In such cases, institutional success in reframing rights advocacy usually amounts to reducing the provocative "cutting-edge" challenge of rights claiming to a "taken for grantedness" that justifies the status quo.

The accountability environment is appropriately understood as a broad array of stakeholders who are affected by an NGO's actions, but often it is characterized more narrowly as donor agency expectations that NGOs can demonstrate tangible results and replicate local successes on a broader scale. These demands would make sense if NGOs could be likened to manufacturers seeking to market products. And in large part, Western culture promotes a rationalist view that humanitarian and rights-advocacy NGOs *are indeed* product oriented and are therefore subject to the same rules and expectations placed on producer organizations (see Meyer 1994). Stated in the vernacular, this rationalization narrative proceeds as follows: (1) anything "good" (say, humanitarian efforts to assist displaced refugees) must be "worth something" in terms of dollars and cents; (2) thus, there is a need to *count* (or account for; see Scott and Lyman 1968) how many people "do good" and how much "good" they do; and (3) organizations graft on a variety of structures and processes that assume this counting function. Meyer comments,

> Both aspects of Western rationalization—the construction of processes and the construction of entities—lead to orgies of counting.

On the one side, there is much counting of persons, workers, occupational members, organizations, processes, and resources. On
the other side, there is the counting of flows of value from costs and
investments to productive value and profits. (Meyer 1994, 127)

As a cultural force, this rationality of "monetarization" sets expectations
for the NGO sector as a whole; thus, individual agencies seek structures and
processes that appear legitimate. All of this said, rights leveraging addresses the
intangible nature of the human condition and rights-depriving situations that
are by nature *local* and as such are affected by particular political, economic,
and cultural circumstances. Thus, the accountability environment tends to encumber rights leveraging by tying it down (like Gulliver) to planning, management, and evaluation cycle protocols (particularly, the logical framework) that
characterize improving the human condition as a rational, linear, and repli-
cable process. However, the competent institutional leader recognizes the symbolic value of accountability as an opportunity to enhance the organization's
image and conserve legitimacy. Thus, NGOs that assume proactive postures
in managing their accountability environments, specifically by prioritizing the
expectations of various stakeholders, become well positioned to leverage their
credibility on behalf of human rights.

The information environment encompasses three dilemmas that affect
how well NGOs can leverage knowledge-based action promoting human rights.
First, organization memory often suffers because staff members neglect to
document the experiential knowledge acquired through their work; this problem is especially critical given the high rate of staff turnover in many NGOs.
Second, although the supply of information flowing from research, program
experiences, information clearinghouses, and a variety of other sources appears
boundless ("water, water everywhere"), NGOs confront difficulties acquiring
knowledge-based information that can inform strategies and tactics to leverage
human rights. The need for usable information becomes evident, for example,
in efforts to document gender inequalities in service provision in the absence
of collected data disaggregated by gender. But in more general terms, the information at hand is often embodied in formats (such as in academic journals
and technical reports) that cannot be readily converted into knowledge that
energizes NGO action strategies and tactics. Third, enlightened NGOs depend on external information to promote "double-loop learning"—that is, a
self-critical assessment of how the organization functions—but, in doing so,
risk succumbing to information biases or agendas that could divert attention
from rights issues. But from an institutional perspective, organization learning

and knowledge management activities represent inherent cognitive processes whereby people (re)define their identities and shared roles. For Richard Scott, a (North American) football analogy is appropriate:

> We are not surprised to hear that the quarterback of the football game handled the pass from center. . . . Social life is predictable and orderly because of shared role definitions and expectations, the authority of which rests in shared expectations of social reality— a complex of taken-for-granted assumptions—rather than in the promise of rewards or the fear of sanctions. (Scott 1994, 66)

Finally, the human resources environment pits a surplus of people (who are in one way or another motivated by humanitarian concerns) against scarce dollars to invest in "people development." Since few funding agencies support significant capacity-building investments in the human organization, NGO officials tend to downplay human resources concerns or in some cases discredit them as a diversion of resources away from worthwhile program activities. The contentious nature of the human resources environment leads to perverse outcomes wherein NGO personnel in closest contact with beneficiaries or clients, notably field-workers and volunteers, often suffer the disproportionate brunt of an unwillingness to invest in people. Although it is unlikely that the NGO community can stem tremendous rates of staff turnover in its organizations, rights-sensitive leaders bear obligations (1) to themselves to identify those persons especially well suited for future leadership and (2) to employees and volunteers in extending decent treatment and guidance for career development. On a cognitive level, leaders need to demonstrate concern for the dignity of those serving the agency—as volunteers, field-workers, women staffers, potential careerists, and others—as vital to (and isomorphic with) their concern for rights-focused missions.

Surmounting Obstacles to Making Hope "Real" and Intentional

Among all (government, business, NGO) sectors, most leaders strive to make a significant difference for their organizations. In seeking out the common attributes of 12 distinguished leaders in US government, Doig and Hargrove conclude that all can be regarded as *entrepreneurs* with two common traits. First, all 12 in their study share the characteristic of what Joseph Schumpeter (1934) called "uncommon rationality" that resists using established routines in favor of creating new traditions (Doig and Hargrove 1987, 10–12). Such a trait may be all the more vital in the NGO context where leadership needs to reconceptualize agency missions to focus on the pivotal *political issues* that deprive people of dignity. Presumably, Peter Uvin alludes to something close to uncommon rationality in describing the entrepreneurial trust of a rights-based perspective:

> One of the main advantages of the rights-based approach is that it can bring people to reframe the nature of the problems they seek to address and the levers for change they can employ. . . . Human rights act here as a heuristic device, broadening the definition of the problems to be addressed as well as, consequently, the range of actions required to affect them. (Uvin 2004, 160)

Again in reference to their 12 government leaders, Doig and Hargrove (1987) identify another commonality: "the ability to see the political logic in an emerging historical situation and to act on that insight." They associate this capability with the cognitive processes of institutional leadership, pointing out that "a leader who would use such insight must also persuade others to accept his definitions of the situation and must set forth plausible strategies of action" (p. 11).

Thus, Doig and Hargrove rank their 12 governmental leaders along a second dimension of entrepreneurial success: *coalition-building skills*. Stating it somewhat differently, Postma identifies partnership-building and networking skills as leadership requisites for "making it real and making it intentional" in his study of NGO partnerships and institutional development in Niger and Mali (1994, 448). Coalition and network leadership draws heavily on cognitive processes, as is apparent in Keck and Sikkink's discussion of transnational advocacy networks as the "*communicative structure* for political exchange . . . ; their main collective currency is information" (1998, 217–18; italics theirs). But as discussed in chapter 6, meaningful information finds its way into "tacit knowledge" that is perceived as relevant. Thus, it follows that the currency for *leadership* within networks is actually that of *perception*—in the context of this book, perceptions that are sensitized to questions of human (in)dignity and deprivation or empowerment.

In their essay "Managing Perceptions in Networks," Termeer and Koppenjan probe the cognitive intricacies involved in leading networks of diverse participants with varying attitudes toward the substantive discourse on the table and toward each other. Although they refer generally to policy networks, these Dutch scholars characterize the leadership challenge in terms relevant to reconceptualizing the overall aims of rights-oriented NGOs, allies, and adversaries. In this regard, Termeer and Koppenjan maintain that leaders need to dissolve the

> blockages [that] are not only caused by conflicts of interest and power relations, but equally by the *perceptions of the situation* of the actors involved. Actors have their own definition of the world that surrounds them, which consists of their definition of the problem, their image of other actors in the network, the nature of their dependency on others and vice versa, and the advantages and disadvantages of working together. (Termeer and Koppenjan 1997, 79; italics theirs)

In other words, the leader's cognitive task is to employ effective strategies that can bring about a mutual adjustment of perceptions necessary to establish network consensus; in large part, this undertaking mimics the organization-learning dynamic that occurs within competence-based NGOs. In attempting to dissolve blockages, leaders must cope with participants' fixations that resist accommodation. Termeer and Koppenjan argue that discourses can become "dialogues of the deaf" whereby

> actors talk at cross-purposes, arguments are constantly repeated in a ritual way and none of the participants is willing to reflect on their own arguments. . . . Fixations arise when the actors involved take their own perceptions so much for granted that they no longer reflect on them. Conflicting perceptions and, what is more, the reluctance of contestants to adapt their interpretations of the problem situation, can be seen as the main cause of blockages. (Termeer and Koppenjan 1997, 80–81)

Termeer and Koppenjan account for the tenaciousness of perceptions not only in the cognitive (taken-for-granted) realm but also in the social milieus of participants who share perceptions vis-à-vis others. Therefore, a network leader must marshal a two-pronged approach that interjects cognitive variation toward expanding (rather than contracting) substantive interpretations and social variation that adds members and/or promotes more inclusive interaction (rather than exclusion and isolation among members) in the network. Correspondingly, these scholars recommend particular leadership strategies directed toward each. In summary form, Termeer and Koppenjan's "strategies aimed at the cognitive dimension" include

- furthering a common language,
- preventing the exclusion of ideas,
- promoting the introduction of new ideas, and
- furthering reflection (pp. 92–95).

Their "strategies aimed at the social dimension" involve

- developing new procedures (that indirectly create social variation),
- preventing the exclusion of actors, and
- introducing new actors (pp. 89–91).

Ultimately, Termeer and Koppenjan's ideas about "managing perceptions in networks" corroborate the assertion that institutional maintenance depends on the active efforts of leaders (Scott 1995, 49). In government, institutional leaders rely on formal (regulative) authority and informal (cognitive and indirectly regulative) influence to conserve the normative essences of public service missions (see Terry 1995). But especially in contexts of joint action within networks, partnerships, and coalitions, NGO leaders become reliant on cognitive processes that, if used ethically to bring about consensus on rights-based initiatives, help stabilize collaborative associations.

Thus, much in the preceding chapters lends support for the proposition about institutional leadership presented in chapter 1: *NGO leadership is distinguishable by its prevalent reliance on cognitive processes to transform altruistic aspirations into operational realities "on the ground."* In its focus on the "slippery" terminology prevalent in development and human rights discourses, chapter 2 calls on leaders to cultivate rhetorical skills needed to (re)interpret and (re)frame ambiguous and contestable buzzwords—such as *poverty, empowerment,* and *participation*—in terms that advance the human condition. Moreover, NGO leaders must use those skills in challenging ideological representations of "reality" embedded within various development narratives of transformative change (see chapter 3). In large part, NGO leaders live in dialectical worlds (characterized in chapter 4) where it is necessary to protect the informal adhocracy of committed competence from the regulatory structures of formal governance and to mediate the cultural differences within the workforce and among external stakeholders. In particular, the informal organization depends on a shared sense of mission reinforced by frequent learning and assessment rituals. Programmatically, NGO professionals strive to make sense of performance-related disconnects between qualitative competency and quantitative output (or "hard results") and of diverse stakeholder accountability expectations. As discussed in chapter 5, it is apparent that NGO leaders must attend to the institutional challenge of accountability with finesse in juggling these expectations in a manner that satisfies the regulative mind-sets of donors and host nations but promotes the normative foundations of human dignity (see Romzek and Dubnick 1985; Radin 2002).

In regard to organization learning (see chapter 6), NGO administrators can demonstrate the learning ideal by modeling what being a "learning leader" entails (Hailey and James 2002) and by managing information environments by channeling (tacit) knowledge acquisition toward usable and contextually pertinent information. Chapter 7 associates analytical competence with an understanding of how various types of development or humanitarian programs affect gender relationships. Furthermore, it illustrates how NGOs (e.g., To-stan) can convey alternative ideas of rights empowerment adopted elsewhere to motivate people in particular settings to rearrange gender relationships in ways that benefit not only women but also the whole of society. Internally, agency leaders need to facilitate communicative processes intent on dissolving inter-personal blockages that account for gender inequities within the deep structure of the organization. Chapter 8 argues that NGOs should invest more heavily in human resources management to demonstrate the legitimacy of their commitment to human concern for those serving *inside the agency* and for external constituencies. Clearly, initiatives to advance human rights embrace *normative* claims of human entitlements and dignity. *However, norms and standards cannot speak for themselves to define, interpret, or demonstrate what they require, nor can they defend themselves from discourse communities that would dilute the moral authority of their claims or co-opt them in order to establish moral high ground.* Therefore, it is incumbent on rights-directed professionals to draw heavily on the cognitive elements of organization to infuse meaning into rights advocacy and actions on their behalf. As discussed, the various chapters characterize leadership roles that in various ways articulate what a human rights commitment requires in the midst of institutional challenges of resource dependency and competing agendas in the political environment. Whether these presentations support the proposition that *NGO leadership is distinguishable by its prevalent reliance on cognitive processes* can be left to the reader's scrutiny.

Critical Managerial Competencies in Rights-Focused NGOs

Organizations that assist people in establishing agency over their lives need not only to *be led* and to *lead others* toward empowerment but to *develop leadership* capabilities in those they serve as well. Thus, leadership and its requisite managerial competencies should reside throughout the rights-focused NGO rather than with one individual formally designated as the top executive or with an exclusive cadre of leaders. In chapter 1, effective NGO leadership was characterized in terms of how particular managerial competencies fit significant management environments. In addition, that first chapter introduced a variety of technical, ethical, and leadership competencies that, although recognized as critical for effective public service (see Bowman, West, and Beck 2010), appear equally important in the work of NGOs intent on advancing human rights. Table 9.1 identifies particular management competencies that become important in facilitating rights work in each of the four (institutional power, accountability, information, and human resources) management environments identified earlier. The discussions in chapter 2 on strategically crafted rhetoric suggest that NGO professionals need to develop an additional competency (beyond those identified by Bowman, West, and Beck) to understand the rhetorical narratives put forward by governments and powerful institutional actors and to challenge them when necessary (shown in table 9.1 as "rhetorical interpretation and argumentation"*).* Rhetorical skills are especially critical in the NGO sector where effective leadership depends on making use of cognitive processes in ways that transform rights aspirations to organizational and social realities. The balance of this section offers brief commentaries on particular competencies related to each of the four environments, with emphasis on those identified (in bold typeface in table 9.1) as especially significant.

The institutional power environment is characterized as encompassing those powerful actors (e.g., government regimes and bi- or multilateral funding agencies) that are influential in formulating policies and shaping discourses about what "development," "human rights," or "humanitarianism" presumably mean. Along with an ethical competency related to values management (i.e., in discerning ethical priorities and committing to them), the ability to interpret rhetorical narratives and put forth argumentation to affect that rhetoric rises as especially important in dealing within this power-laden environment. In some cases, this capability depends on understanding pertinent legal systems (e.g., in dealing with governmental regimes) and leadership attentiveness to agency goal setting.

Table 9.1

Critical Managerial Competencies by NGO Management Environments

NGO Management Environments	Managerial Competency Types		
	Technical	Ethical	Leadership
Institutional power	Legal knowledge	**Values management**	*Rhetorical interpretation and argumentation* Political/negotiation Assessment/goal setting
Accountability	Legal knowledge Specialized knowledge Program management Resource management	**Values management** Moral reasoning	*Rhetorical interpretation and argumentation* "Hard" management "Soft" management **Political/negotiation** **Evaluation**
Information	Specialized knowledge	**Values management**	"Soft" management Assessment/goal setting
Human resources	Specialized knowledge Program management Resource management	**Values management** Moral reasoning **Organizational ethics**	"Hard" management "Soft" management

Source. Bowman, James S., Jonathan P. West, and Marcia A. Beck. *Achieving Competencies in the Public Service: The Professional Edge.* Armonk, NY: M. E. Sharpe, 2010. Text in bold typeface indicates emphasis. Italics text indicates a competency not discussed in Bowman et al.

Although the accountability environment may force the NGO into a reactive posture of having to "answer" for its use of resources and structure of governance, it also provides opportunities for NGO leaders to manage the diverse expectations placed on them by a multiplicity of stakeholders. Certainly, the technical capabilities related to knowing the law and sound financial management practices (e.g., accounting and the preparation of financial reports) come into play in answering to host governments or fund donors. But the ability to manage (and perhaps prioritize) among a diversity of stakeholder expectations—and, more important, to argue the case for priority orderings or approaches to reconciling demands among the stakeholders— depends on the political ability to negotiate effectively within a framework of moral reasoning.

The information environment affects how proficiently NGOs can (1) engage in "double-loop" learning that critically examines existing values, organization structures, and management systems and (2) manage knowledge (or "know what they know") based on information generated internally and externally. Given high rates of staff turnover in most NGOs, leaders need to apply their soft management competencies (or "people skills") to urge employees to document the lessons they learn in order to conserve institutional memory. On a technical level, NGO professionals should be able to discriminate between research that can *directly support strategic or tactical action* and research that is perhaps "interesting" but is in an unusable format. In this regard, a specialized knowledge of where to find action-oriented research such as that published online by NGO-related institutes and clearinghouses is especially helpful in negotiating the information environment. Last, NGO leaders need to rely on their value commitments and goal priorities to identify underlying ideological agendas of externally available research and to interpret the findings and recommendations in the context of those biases.

The human resources environment challenges NGO leaders to confront the realities of high staff turnover, limited funds to invest in personnel development, and (in some cases) the marginalization of vulnerable employee groups. Ethical competencies (such as values management, moral reasoning, and organizational ethics) emerge as critical in mounting a collective will to recognize how people (e.g., women, field-workers, or volunteers) may be marginalized within the agency and then to commit to appropriate remedial strategies. Clearly, NGO leaders need to apply the soft people skills in probing these sensitive issues. By contrast, the harder management competencies, together with technical knowledge related to human resources planning, must be marshaled to craft long-term program strategies that provide for future staffing needs and afford decent treatment to employees.

Realistic Career Planning

Career paths typically evolve as cascading combinations of experiences, unexpected events or situations, and interpersonal encounters. Nonetheless, students and others aspiring to ultimate leadership positions in a rights-oriented NGO could target their planning efforts toward strategic questions concerning

(1) entry into NGO employment and (2) appropriate academic preparation to support NGO leadership. Although the websites of well-known NGOs usually post position openings and accept online applications, the odds of a job offer may be less than encouraging. It is more likely that offers will be extended to those who have interned (perhaps as students) with an agency or who maintain contacts with a network of individuals serving in NGOs. Through his website posting, a political science professor quotes "A Special Note on Working in NGOs" published by Yale University's undergraduate career service to advise his students at the California State University at Los Angeles:[1]

- NGOs almost never recruit on campus.
- NGOs rarely post positions online; most of the positions are found through networking or internships. Because of that, working with an NGO during your undergraduate time is one of the best things you can do.
- Working with an international NGO may require a work permit or visa. This process can be very complex, so it is important to be prepared.

This counsel corroborates the importance of NGO intern experiences in finding employment in these agencies.

Although advancement to leadership comes with appropriate experiences, a formal education *can* provide the requisite intellectual grounding associated with effective leadership. Accredited graduate programs in business administration and public management must require specific course work covering specific skill development areas mandated by accreditation agencies. In regard to public sector leadership training, the accrediting body (the National Association of Schools of Public Affairs and Administration [NASPAA]) articulates the following "universal competencies" that master's programs in public administration (or affairs) must address in one or more required courses, related to the ability

- to lead and manage in ~~public~~ ^{NGO} governance;
- to participate in and contribute to the policy process;
- to analyze, synthesize, think critically, solve problems, and make decisions;
- to articulate and apply a ~~public sector~~ $^{rights-based}$ perspective; and
- to communicate and interact productively with a diverse and changing workforce and citizenry (NASPAA 2009, 7).

With a couple of edits (as indicated previously), these five educational competencies can help students identify academic course work that supports the core conceptual competencies associated with a rights-based perspective to leadership in NGO settings. Consider how these competencies relate to some of the major themes addressed in the previous chapters:

- *To lead and manage in NGO governance.* NGO leaders need to manage their agencies in accordance with the governance expectations of stakeholders (most notably donor agencies and host governments) even though the organization may value informal, collegial working relationships. It therefore becomes incumbent on leaders to stand accountable to these governance expectations through formal financial and performance reporting procedures.
- *To participate in and contribute to the policy process.* NGO leaders must act as competent policymakers to leverage agency influence on behalf of human rights. In some cases, argumentation skills—especially as used in reframing institutional rhetoric and "change for the better" narratives—serve as subtle but powerful personal resources in affecting development or other rights-related policies. Leaders need as well to orchestrate policy negotiations among stakeholders to manage respective accountability demands in ways that prioritize human empowerment.
- *To analyze, synthesize, think critically, solve problems, and make decisions.* Put succinctly, *astute political analysis* (in the widest sense of the term) *is critical* in effective rights work. Since nearly all rights violations (like politics) are "local," NGO professionals need to anticipate the likely impacts of institutional "policy talk" and subsequent actions with respect to particular social, economical, and cultural settings, as well as *within the NGO itself* (with regard to gender inequalities and other marginalizing circumstances). Moreover, individual and collective capacities for critical thinking are essential if organization learning is to succeed in scrutinizing existing NGO values, practices, structures, and management systems.
- *To articulate and apply a rights-based perspective.* Even NGOs that conscientiously adopt a human rights orientation may encounter situations (e.g., in interacting with other organizations, satisfying accountability expectations, or following routine management practices *within* the agency) that could compromise

that rights commitment. NGO leaders need to act as vigilant conservators to protect that commitment from "being hijacked" by actors both outside and within the NGO.

- *To communicate and interact productively with a diverse and changing workforce and citizenry.* NGO managers often mediate two faces of the organization, the first representing its formal governance structure, and the second encompassing its actual work arrangement that may appear as an adhocracy lacking structure. Beyond interacting productively with the organization at work, leaders may need to buffer it from the direct pressures exerted by external stakeholders (particularly those that evaluate the agency in terms of formal governance standards). In addition, leaders must be culturally sensitive to the communities served and to the work-related expectations of in-country employees. Finally, NGO leaders can do much to facilitate communications and interactions in a diverse workforce by developing a coherent human resources program designed to meet the personal and career-development needs of employees who serve in various capacities. A rights-based organization is obliged to afford its workers—whether short term or long term, female or male, field-workers or headquartered staff, volunteers or salaried personnel—decent treatment and guidance for the future.

In sum, it is reasonable to suggest that one can indeed *realistically prepare* for a career in human-rights-related work with the intent to advance into a position of leadership within an NGO. By making prudent choices in academic course work (at both the undergraduate and the graduate levels), individuals aspiring to leadership can demonstrate their scholarly engagement in core leadership competency areas as preparation for prospective service within an NGO.

Note

1. See "Professor Lim's CourseSite" at http://instructional1.calstatela.edu/tclim/careers.htm, accessed October 15, 2010.

Bibliography

Aagaard-Hansen, Jens, and Annette Olsen. "Research Into Practice: A Comprehensive Approach." *Development in Practice* 19 (2009): 381–85.

Adams, Guy B., and Danny L. Balfour. *Unmasking Administrative Evil.* Thousand Oaks, CA: Sage, 1998.

Afshar, Haleh. "Gendering the Millennium: Globalising Women." *Developmemt in Practice* 10, no. 3–4 (2000): 527–34.

Agosín, Manuel R., and David E. Bloom. "Making Globalization and Liberalization Work for People." In *Reinventing Government for the Twenty-First Century*, edited by Dennis A. Rondinelli and G. Shabbir Cheema, 61–82. Bloomfield, CT: Kumarian Press, 2003.

Ahmad, Mokbul Morshed. "Who Cares? The Personal and Professional Problems of NGO Fieldworkers in Bangladesh." *Development in Practice* 12, no. 2 (2002): 177–91.

Ahmed, Sara. "Engendering Organisational Practice in NGOs: The Case of Utthan." *Development in Practice* 12, no. 3–4 (2002): 298–311.

Alim, Abdul. "Changes in Villagers' Knowledge, Perceptions, and Attitudes Concerning Gender Roles and Relations in Bangladesh." *Development in Practice* 19, no. 3 (2009): 300–10.

Allen, Adriana. "Urban Sustainability Under Threat: The Restructuring of the Fishing Industry in Mar Del Plata, Argentina." *Development in Practice* 11, no. 2–3 (2001): 152–73.

Alvesson, Matts. "Organizations as Rhetoric: Knowledge-Intensive Firms and the Struggle With Ambiguity." *Journal of Management Studies* 30 (1993): 997–1015.

Anderson, G. Norman. *Sudan in Crisis: The Failure of Democracy.* Gainesville: University Press of Florida, 1999.

Anderson, Ian. "Northern NGO Advocacy: Perceptions, Reality, and the Challenge." *Development in Practice* 10, no. 3–4 (2000): 445–52.

Anderson, Kenneth. "What NGO Accountability Means: And Does Not Mean." *American Journal of International Law* 103 (2009): 170–78.

Anderson, Mary B. *Do No Harm: How Aid Can Support Peace—Or War.* Boulder, CO: Lynne Rienner, 1999.

Andersson, Neil, and Melissa Roche. "Gender and Evidence-Based Planning: The CIET Methods." *Development in Practice* 16, no. 2 (2006): 141–52.

Andreassen, Bård A., and Stephen P. Marks, eds. *Development as a Human Right.* Cambridge, MA: Harvard University Press, 2006.

Anner, Mark, and Peter Evans. "Building Bridges Across a Double Divide: Alliances Between US and Latin American Labour and NGOs." *Development in Practice* 14, no. 1–2 (2004): 34–47.

Antlöv, Hans, Rustam Ibrahim, and Peter van Tuijl. "NGO Governance and Accountability in Indonesia: Challenges in a Newly Democratizing Country." In *NGO Accountability: Politics, Principles and Innovation*, edited by Lisa Jordan and Peter van Tuijl, 147–66. London: Earthscan, 2007.

Anyonge, T. M., C. Holding, K. K. Kareko, and J. W. Kimani. "Scaling Up Participatory Agroforestry Extension in Kenya: From Pilot Projects to Extension Policy." *Development in Practice* 11, no. 4 (2001): 449–59.

Appleford, Gabrielle. "Women's Groups for Whom? The Colonisation of Women's Groups in Papua New Guinea." *Development in Practice* 10, no. 1 (2000): 82–89.

Argote, Linda. "Organizational Memory." In *Knowledge Management and Organizational Learning*, edited by Laurence Prusak and Eric Matson, 148–72. New York: Oxford University Press, 2006.

Argyris, Chris. "Double-Loop Learning, Teaching, and Research." *Academy of Management Learning and Education* 1, no. 2 (2002): 206–18.

———. "Initiating Change That Perseveres." *Journal of Public Administration Research and Theory: J-PART* 4, no. 3 (1994): 343–55.

Arneson, Richard J. "Self-Ownership and World Ownership: Against Left-Libertarianism." *Social Philosophy and Policy* 27 (2010): 168–94.

Asllani, Arben, and Fred Luthans. "What Knowledge Managers Really Do: An Empirical and Comparative Analysis." *Journal of Knowledge Management* 7, no. 3 (2003): 53–66.

Aune, Jens B. "Logical Framework Approach and PRA: Mutually Exclusive or Complementary Tools for Project Planning?" *Development in Practice* 10, no. 5 (2000): 687–90.

Barnett, Michael. "Evolution Without Progress? Humanitarianism in a World of Hurt." *International Organization* 63 (2009): 621–63.

———. "Humanitarianism Transformed." *Perspectives on Politics* 3, no. 4 (2005): 723–34.

Barrientos, Stephanie, Sharon McClenaghan, and Liz Orton. "Stakeholder Participation, Gender, and Codes of Conduct in South Africa." *Development in Practice* 11, no. 5 (2001): 575–86.

Bartlett, Sheridan. "Children and Development Assistance: The Need to Re-orient Priorities and Programmes." *Development in Practice* 11, no. 1 (2001): 62–72.

Batchelor, S., P. Norrish, N. Scott, and M. Webb. "Analysis and Overview of Case Studies—Research Report." *Sustainable Initiatives* (January 2003). Accessed April 16, 2010. http://www.sustainableicts.org/fulloverview.htm.

Batliwala, Srilatha. "Taking the Power out of Empowerment: An Experiential Account." *Development in Practice* 17, no. 4–5 (2007): 557–65.

Baumgartner, Frank R. *Conflict and Rhetoric in French Policy Making*. Pittsburgh, PA: University of Pittsburgh Press, 1989.

Becker, Lawrence C. *Property Rights: Philosophic Foundations*. London: Routledge, 1977.

Beckwith, Colin, Kent Glenzer, and Alan Fowler. "Leading Learning and Change From the Middle: Reconceptualising Strategy's Purpose, Content, and Measures." *Development in Practice* 12, no. 3–4 (2002): 409–23.

Beitz, Charles R. "Human Rights as a Common Concern." *American Political Science Review* 95 (2001): 269–82.

———. "What Human Rights Mean." *Daedalus* 132 (2003): 36–46.

Bendel, Jem, and Phyllida Cox. "The Donor Accountability Agenda." In *NGO Accountability: Politics, Principles and Innovation,* edited by Lisa Jordan and Peter van Tuijl, 109–28. London: Earthscan, 2007.

Bennett, Milton J., and Mitchell R. Hammer. *The Intercultural Development Inventory (IDI): Individual Profile.* Portland, OR: Intercultural Communication Institute, 2002. Accessed August 31, 2010. http://www.languageandculture.com/en_us/idi_sample.pdf.

Bhandari, Bhupesh. "The Man Behind GE's India Success." *Rediff India Abroad* (May 29, 2007). Accessed August 31, 2010. www.rediff.com/money/2007/may/29bay.htm.

Bhardwaj, Meeta, and John Monin. "Tacit to Explicit: An Interplay Shaping Organization Knowledge." *Journal of Knowledge Management* 10, no. 3 (2006): 72–85.

Biggs, Stephen D., and Arthur D. Neame. "Negotiating Room to Maneuver: Reflections Concerning NGO Autonomy and Accountability Within the New Policy Agenda." In *Beyond the Magic Bullet,* edited by Michael Edwards and David Hulme, 40–52. West Hartford, CT: Kumarian Press, 1996.

Bökkerink, Sasja, and Ted van Hees. "Eurodad's Campaign on Multilateral Debt: The 1996 HIPC Debt Initiative and Beyond." *Development in Practice* 8, no. 3 (1998): 323–34.

Boonstra, Albert, David Boddy, and Moira Fischbacher. "The Limited Acceptance of an Electronic Prescription System by General Practitioners: Reasons and Practical Implications." *New Technology, Work and Employment* 19, no. 2 (2004): 128–44.

Bornstein, David. *The Price of a Dream.* New York: Simon & Schuster, 1996.

Bowman, James S., Jonathan P. West, and Marcia A. Beck. *Achieving Competencies in the Public Service: The Professional Edge.* Armonk, NY: M. E. Sharpe, 2010.

Breen, Claire. "The Role of NGOs in the Formulation of and Compliance With the Optional Protocol to the Convention on the Rights of the Child on Involvement of Children in Armed Conflict." *Human Rights Quarterly* 25, no. 2 (2003): 453–81.

Brinkerhoff, Jennifer M. "Digital Diasporas and Governance in Semi-authoritarian States: The Case of the Egyptian Copts." *Public Administration and Development* 25, no. 3 (2005): 193–204.

Broad, Robin. "'Knowledge Management': A Case Study of the World Bank's Research Department." *Development in Practice* 17, no. 4–5 (2007): 700–8.

Bryant, Antony. "Wiki and the Agora: 'It's Organising, Jim, but Not as We Know It.'" *Development in Practice* 16, no. 6 (2006): 559–69.

Bryld, Erik. "The Technocratic Discourse: Technical Means to Political Problems." *Development in Practice* 10, no. 5 (2000): 700–5.

Cammack, John. "Finance: Friend or Foe?" *Development in Practice* 7, no. 1 (1997): 79–81.

CARE. *Defining Characteristics of the Rights-Based Approach (by Andrew Jones).* Atlanta, GA: CARE, 2001.

Cassiday, Patricia A. "Expatriate Leadership: An Organizational Resource for Collaboration." *International Journal of Intercultural Relations* 29, no. 4 (2005): 391–408.

Cavill, Sue, and M. Sohail. "Increasing Strategic Accountability: A Framework for International NGOs." *Development in Practice* 17, no. 2 (2007): 231–48.

Cecchini, Simone, and Christopher Scott. "Can Information and Communications Technology Applications Contribute to Poverty Reduction? Lessons From Rural India." *Information Technology for Development* 10, no. 2 (2003): 73–84.

Centre for Electronic Governance. *An Evaluation of Gyandoot.* Ahmedabad: Indian Institute of Management, 2002. Accessed April 15, 2010. http://unpan1.un.org/intradoc/groups/public/documents/APCITY/UNPAN015131.pdf.

Centre for International Development and Training. *A Guide for Developing a Logical Framework*. Wolverhampton, UK: University of Wolverhampton, n.d.

Chambers, Robert. "Rapid Rural Appraisal: Rationale and Repertoire." *Public Administration and Development* 2, no. 2 (1981): 95–106.

———. *Rural Development? Putting the Last First*. London: IT Publications, 1983.

———. *Whose Reality Counts? Putting the Last First*. Warwickshire, UK: Practical Action, 1997.

Chandhoke, Neera. "Civil Society." *Development in Practice* 17, no. 4–5 (2007): 607–14.

Chapman, Jennifer, and Thomas Fisher. "The Effectiveness of NGO Campaigning: Lessons From Practice." *Development in Practice* 10, no. 2 (2000): 151–65.

Charny, Joel R. "Upholding Humanitarian Principles in an Effective Integrated Response." *Ethics and International Affairs* 18 (2004): 13–20.

Cingöz-Ulu, Banu, and Richard N. Lalonde. "The Role of Culture and Relational Context in Interpersonal Conflict: Do Turks and Canadians Use Different Conflict Management Strategies?" *International Journal of Intercultural Relations* 31, no. 4 (2007): 443–58.

Clark, John. *Democratizing Development: The Role of Voluntary Organizations*. West Hartford, CT: Kumarian Press, 1991.

Clarke, Matthew. "Achieving Behaviour Change: Three Generations of HIV/AIDS Programming and Jargon in Thailand." *Development in Practice* 12, no. 5 (2002): 625–36.

Clay, Joy A. "Public Institutional Processes: Beyond Conventional Wisdom About Management Processes." *Administration and Society* 26 (1994): 236–51.

Cleaver, Frances. "Paradoxes of Participation: Questioning Participatory Approaches to Development." In *The Earthscan Reader on NGO Management*, edited by Michael Edwards and Alan Fowler, 225–40. London: Earthscan, 2002.

Coates, Barry, and Rosalind David. "Learning for Change: The Art of Assessing the Impact of Advocacy Work." *Development in Practice* 12, no. 3–4 (2002): 530–41.

Cohen, Cynthia P., Stuart N. Hart, and Susan M. Kosloske. "Monitoring the United Nations Convention on the Rights of the Child: The Challenge of Information Management." *Human Rights Quarterly* 18, no. 2 (1996): 439–71.

Cohen, G. A. *Rescuing Justice and Equality*. Cambridge, MA: Harvard University Press, 2008.

Cohn, Mike. *User Stories Applied*. Boston: Addison-Wesley, 2004.

Collison, Chris, and Geoff Parcell. *Learning to Fly: Practical Knowledge Management From Leading and Learning Organizations*. West Sussex, UK: Capstone, 2004.

Constantino-David, Karina. "Unsustainable Development: The Philippine Experience." *Development in Practice* 11, no. 2–3 (2001): 232–41.

Cooper, Christopher, and Robert Block. *Disaster: Hurricane Katrina and the Failure of Homeland Security*. New York: Henry Holt, 2006.

Cornell, Tricia, Kate Kelsch, and Nicole Palasz. *New Tactics in Human Rights: A Resource for Practitioners*. Minneapolis, MN: Center for Victims of Torture, 2004.

Cornwall, Andrea. "Buzzwords and Fuzzwords: Deconstructing Development Discourse." *Development in Practice* 17, no. 4–5 (2007): 471–84.

Cornwall, Andrea, and Karen Brock. *Beyond Buzzwords: "Poverty Reduction," "Participation" and "Empowerment" in Development Policy* (Programme Paper No. 10). Geneva: UN Research Institute for Development, 2005.

Cornwall, Andrea, Elizabeth Harrison, and Ann Whitehead. *Gender Myths and Feminist Fables: The Struggle for Interpretive Power in Gender and Development*. Oxford: Wiley Blackwell, 2008.

Corrin, Chris. "Developing Policy on Integration and Re/Construction in Kosova." *Development in Practice* 13, no. 2–3 (2003): 189–207.

Courville, Sasha, and Nicole Piper. "Harnessing Hope Through NGO Activism." *Annals of the American Academy of Political and Social Science* 592, no. 1 (2004): 39–61.

Covey, Jane G. "Accountability and Effectiveness in NGO Policy Alliances." In *Beyond the Magic Bullet*, edited by Michael Edwards and David Hulme, 53–64. West Hartford, CT: Kumarian Press, 1996.

Coward, Tim, and James Fathers. "A Critique of Design Methodologies Appropriate to Private-Sector Activity in Development." *Development in Practice* 15, no. 3–4 (2005): 451–62.

Craig, David, and Doug Porter. "Framing Participation: Development Projects, Professionals, and Organizations." *Development in Practice* 7, no. 3 (1997): 229–36.

Crawford, David, Michael Mambo, Zainab Mdimi, Harriet Mkilya, Anna Mwambuzi, Matthias Mwiko, and Sekiete Sekasua, with Dorcas Robinson. "A Day in the Life of a Development Manager." *Development in Practice* 9, no. 1–2 (1999): 170–75.

Crenshaw Williams, Kimberlé. "Background Paper for the CERD Expert Meeting on the Gender-Related Aspects of Race Discrimination." Paper presented at the CERD Expert Meeting, Zagreb, Croatia, November 14–21, 2000.

———. "Mapping the Margins: Intersectionality, Identity Politics, and Violence Against Women of Color." *Stanford Law Review* 43 (1991): 1241–99.

Cross, Rob, Andrew Parker, Laurence Prusak, and Stephen P. Borgatti. "Knowing What We Know: Supporting Knowledge Creation and Sharing in Social Networks." In *Knowledge Management and Organizational Learning*, edited by Laurence Prusak and Eric Matson, 270–96. New York: Oxford University Press, 2006.

Currie, Graeme, and Stephen Proctor. "Impact of MIS/IT Upon Middle Managers: Some Evidence From the NHS." *New Technology, Work and Employment* 17, no. 2 (2002): 102–18.

Cushner, Kenneth. "Conflict, Negotiation, and Mediation Across Cultures." *International Journal of Intercultural Relations* 29, no. 6 (2005): 635–38.

Cutter, Susan L., and Christopher T. Emrich. "Face of Vulnerability Along the Hurricane Coasts." *Annals of the American Academy of Political and Social Science* 604, no. 1 (2006): 102–12.

Dale, Reidar. "The Logical Framework: An Easy Escape, a Straitjacket, or a Useful Planning Tool?" *Development in Practice* 13, no. 1 (2003): 57–70.

Daly, Gerald. "Working Under Pressure: How People and Organizations Can Achieve More." *Development in Practice* 8, no. 3 (1998): 362–66.

D'Andrade, Roy G. "Cultural Meaning Systems." In *Culture Theory: Essays on Mind, Self, and Emotion*, edited by Richard A. Shweder and Robert A. LeVine, 88–119. Cambridge: Cambridge University Press, 1984.

Davenport, Thomas H., and Laurence Prusak. *Working Knowledge: How Organizations Manage What They Know.* Boston: Harvard Business School Press, 1998.

Davidheiser, Mark. "Culture and Mediation: A Contemporary Processual Analysis From Southwestern Gambia." *International Journal of Intercultural Relations* 29, no. 6 (2005): 713–38.

Dawson, Elsa. "Strategic Gender Mainstreaming in Oxfam GB." *Gender and Development* 13, no. 2 (2005): 80–89.

Dearden, Philip N., and Bob Kowalski. "Programme and Project Cycle Management (PPCM): Lessons From South and North." *Development in Practice* 13, no. 5 (2003): 501–14.

Debebe, Gelaye. "Guest Learning and Adaptation in the Field: A Navajo Case Study." *Development in Practice* 12, no. 3–4 (2002): 355–69.

de Bono, Edward. *Six Thinking Hats.* Boston: Back Bay Books, 1999.

Deneulin, Séverine. *An Introduction to the Human Development and Capability Approach.* London: Earthscan, 2009.

Denning, Steve. "How Stories Embody Tacit Knowledge: Zen and the Art of Motorcycle Maintenance." 2000. Accessed August 16, 2011. http://www.stevedenning.com/Business-Narrative/storytelling-to-capture-tacit-knowledge.aspx.

Desai, Vandana. "NGOs, Gender Mainstreaming, and Urban Poor Communities in Mumbai." *Gender and Development* 13, no. 2 (2005): 90–98.

de Torrenté, Nicolas. "Humanitarianism Sacrificed: Integration's False Promise." *Ethics and International Affairs* 18 (2004): 3–12.

de Waal, Maretha, "Evaluating Gender Mainstreaming in Development Projects." *Development in Practice* 16, no. 2 (2006): 209–14.

Dienhart, John W. "Review: Working Definitions of the Self and the Emergence of Ethical Efficiency." *Business Ethics Quarterly* 12 (2002): 383–401.

Dobel, J. Patrick. *Public Integrity.* Baltimore, MD: Johns Hopkins University Press, 1999.

Doig, Jameson W., and Erwin C. Hargrove. *Leadership and Innovation.* Baltimore, MD: Johns Hopkins University Press, 1987.

Donini, Antonio. "An Elusive Quest: Integration in the Response to the Afghan Crisis." *Ethics and International Affairs* 18 (2004): 21–27.

Donnelly, Jack. "Human Rights and Human Dignity: An Analytic Critique of Non-Western Conceptions of Human Rights." *American Political Science Review* 76 (1982): 303–16.

Drèze, Jean, and Amartya Sen. *Hunger and Public Action.* Oxford: Clarendon Press, 1989.

Drucker, Peter. *Managing the Non-Profit Organisation: Principles and Practices.* New York: HarperCollins, 1990.

Dubnick, Melvin J. "Accountability and the Promise of Performance: In Search of the Mechanisms." *Public Performance and Management Review* 28, no. 3 (2005): 376–417.

Dubnick, Melvin J., and Kaifeng Yang. "Accountability Research: The History, the Future, and the Challenge." Presented at the Annual Conference sponsored by the American Society for Public Administration, Miami, Florida, 2009.

Duffield, Mark. *Global Governance and the New Wars: The Merging of Development and Security.* London: Zed Books, 2001.

Dworkin, Ronald. *Taking Rights Seriously.* Cambridge, MA: Harvard University Press, 1977.

Eade, Deborah. "Capacity Building: Who Builds Whose Capacity?" *Development in Practice* 17, no. 4–5 (2007): 630–39.

———. "Change and Continuity: The Challenge of Transition." *Development in Practice* 7, no. 4 (1997): 500–4.

———. "Editorial." *Development in Practice* 9, no. 1–2 (1999): 5–6.

———. "Editorial." *Development in Practice* 10, no. 2 (2000): 149–50.

———. "Editorial." *Development in Practice* 17, no. 4–5 (2007): 467–70.

———. "Introductory Remarks." *Development in Practice* 13, no. 2–3 (2003): 147–48.

Earl, Sarah, and Fred Carden. "Learning From Complexity: The International Development Research Centre's Experience With Outcome Mapping." *Development in Practice* 12, no. 3–4 (2002): 518–24.

Earl, Sarah, Fred Carden, Terry Smutylo, and Michael Quinn Patten. *Outcome Mapping: Building Learning and Reflection Into Development Programs*. Ottawa: International Development Research Centre, 2001.

Easton, Peter, Karen Monkman, and Rebecca Miles. "Social Policy From the Bottom Up: Abandoning FGC in Sub-Saharan Africa." *Development in Practice* 13, no. 5 (2003): 445–58.

Edwards, Michael. "'Does the Doormat Influence the Boot?' Critical Thoughts on UK NGOs and International Advocacy." *Development in Practice* 3, no. 3 (1993): 163–75.

Edwards, Michael, and Alan Fowler. "Introduction: Changing Challenges for NGDO Management." In *The Earthscan Reader on NGO Management*, edited by Michael Edwards and Alan Fowler, 1–11. London: Earthscan, 2002.

Edwards, Michael, and David Hulme. "Making a Difference: Scaling-up the Development Impact on NGOs—Concept and Experiences." In *The Earthscan Reader on NGO Management*, edited by Michael Edwards and Alan Fowler, 53–73. London: Earthscan, 2002.

———. "NGO Performance and Accountability." In *Beyond the Magic Bullet*, edited by Michael Edwards and David Hulme, 1–20. West Hartford, CT: Kumarian Press, 1996.

Ellerman, David. "Should Development Agencies Have Official Views?" *Development in Practice* 12, no. 3–4 (2002): 285–97.

Emery, Fred E., and Eric L. Trist. "The Causal Texture of Organizational Environments." *Human Relations* 1 (1965): 21–32.

Epstein, Paul D. "Redeeming the Promise of Performance Measurement: Issues and Obstacles for Governments in the United States." In *Organizational Performance and Measurement in the Public Sector*, edited by Arie Halachmi and Geert Bouckaert, 51–76. Westport, CT: Quorum Books, 1996.

Ergeneli, Azize, Raheel Gohar, and Zhanar Temirbekova. "Transformational Leadership: Its Relationship to Culture Value Dimensions." *International Journal of Intercultural Relations* 31, no. 6 (2007): 703–24.

Esteva, Gistavo. "Development." In *The Development Dictionary: A Guide to Knowledge as Power*, edited by Wolfgang Sachs, 1–23. New York: Zed Books, 1993.

Esteva, Gustavo, and Madhu Suri Prakash. "Beyond Development, What?" *Development in Practice* 8, no. 3 (1998): 280–96.

Estimo, Roberta F. *The Curse of the MWSS Water Utility Privatization in the Philippines: Private Mismanagement and Worker's Woes*. Transnational Institute, May 2007. Accessed March 24, 2012. http://www.tni.org/sites/www.tni.org/archives/water-docs/adbestimo.pdf.

Feek, Warren. "Best of Practices?" *Development in Practice* 17, no. 4–5 (2007): 653–55.

Feldman, Martha. *Order Without Design: Information Production and Policy Making*. Stanford, CA: Stanford University Press, 1989.

Feldman, Shelley. "Paradoxes of Institutionalisation: The Depoliticisation of Bangladeshi NGOs." *Development in Practice* 13, no. 1 (2003): 5–26.

Fernando, Jude L., and Alan W. Heston. "Introduction: NGOs Between States, Markets, and Civil Society." *Annals of the American Academy of Political and Social Science* 554 (1997): 8–20.

Festinger, Leon. *A Theory of Cognitive Dissonance*. Stanford, CA: Stanford University Press, 1957.

Finnemore, Martha, and Kathryn Sikkink. "International Norm Dynamics and Political Change." *International Organizations* 52, no. 4 (1998): 887–917.

Fischer, Frank. "Policy Discourse and the Politics of Washington Think Tanks." In *The Argumentative Turn in Policy Analysis*, edited by Frank Fischer and John Forester, 21–42. Durham, NC: Duke University Press, 1993.

Fligstein, Neil. "The Structural Transformation of American Industry: An Institutional Account of the Causes of Diversification in the Largest Firms, 1919–1979." In *The New Institutionalism in Organizational Analysis*, edited by Walter W. Powell and Paul J. DiMaggio. Chicago: University of Chicago Press, 1991.

Foster, Kenneth W. "Improving Municipal Governance, Increasing Local Democracy: Reflections on Recent Initiatives in China." In *Proceedings of 2005 International Conference on Public Administration*, edited by Zhu Xiao-ning, 90–100. Chengdu, China: UESTC Press, 2005.

Fountain, Jane E. *Building the Virtual State: Information Technology and Institutional Change.* Washington, DC: Brookings Institution, 2001.

Fowler, Alan. "Demonstrating NGO Performance: Problems and Possibilities." *Development in Practice* 6, no. 1 (1996): 58–65.

———. "Human Resource Management." In *The Earthscan Reader on NGO Management*, edited by Michael Edwards and Alan Fowler, 441–55. London: Earthscan, 2002.

———. "Relevance in the Twenty-First Century: The Case for Devolution and Global Association of International NGOs." *Development in Practice* 9, no. 1–2 (1999): 143–51.

———. *Striking a Balance: A Guide to Enhancing the Effectiveness of NGOs in International Development.* London: Earthscan, 1997.

Fox, Jonathan. "Advocacy Research and the World Bank: Propositions for Discussion." *Development in Practice* 13, no. 5 (2003): 519–27.

———. "Lessons From Action-Research Partnerships: LASA/Oxfam America 2004 Martin Diskin Memorial Lecture." *Development in Practice* 16, no. 1 (2006): 27–38.

———. "The Uncertain Relationship Between Transparency and Accountability." *Development in Practice* 17, no. 4–5 (2007): 663–71.

Frederckson, H. George, and Todd R. LaPorte. "Airport Security, High Reliability, and the Problem of Rationality." Special issue, *Public Administration Review* 62 (2002): 33–43.

Frederckson, H. George, and Kevin B. Smith. *The Public Administration Theory Primer.* Boulder, CO: Westview, 2003.

Freire, Paulo. *The Pedagogy of the Oppressed.* New York: Continuum, 1970.

Galvani, Flavia, and Stephen Morse. "Institutional Sustainability: At What Price? UNDP and the New Cost-Sharing Model in Brazil." *Development in Practice* 14, no. 3 (2004): 311–27.

Gaventa, John. "Crossing the Great Divide: Building Links and Learning Between NGOs and Community-Based Organizations in the North and South." In *The Earthscan Reader on NGO Management*, edited by Michael Edwards and Alan Fowler, 256–74. London: Earthscan, 2002.

Giddens, Anthony. *The Construction of Society: Outline of the Theory of Structuralization.* Berkeley: University of California Press, 1984.

Gilligan, Carol. *In a Different Voice: Psychological Theory and Women's Development.* New York: Oxford University Press, 1982.

Gini, Al. *My Job, My Self: Work and the Creation of the Modern Individual.* New York: Routledge, 2000.

Goetz, Anne Marie. *Employment Experiences of Women Development Agents in Rural Credit Programmes in Bangladesh: Working Towards Leadership in Women's Interests.* Brighton: IDS, 1995.

———. "Getting Institutions Right for Women in Development." In *The Earthscan Reader on NGO Management,* edited by Michael Edwards and Alan Fowler, 389–405. London: Earthscan, 2002.

———. "Managing Organisational Change: The 'Gendered' Organisation of Space and Time." *Gender and Development* 5, no. 1 (1997): 17–27.

Golub, Stephen. "NGO Accountability and the Philippine Council for NGO Certification: Evolving Roles and Issues." In *NGO Accountability: Politics, Principles and Innovation,* edited by Lisa Jordan and Peter van Tuijl, 93–108. London: Earthscan, 2007.

Gormley, William T., and Steven J. Balla. *Bureaucracy and Democracy: Accountability and Performance.* Washington, DC: CQ Press, 2004.

Gotschi, Elisabeth, Jemimah Njuki, and Robert Delve. "Gender Equity and Social Capital in Smallholder Farmer Groups in Central Mozambique." *Development in Practice* 18, no. 4–5 (2008): 650–57.

Greiner, John M. "Positioning Performance Measurement for the Twenty-First Century." In *Organizational Performance and Measurement in the Public Sector,* edited by Arie Halachmi and Geert Bouckaert, 11–50. Westport, CT: Quorum Books, 1996.

Grove, Natalie J., and Anthony B. Zwi. "Beyond the Log Frame: A New Tool for Examining Health and Peacebuilding Initiatives." *Development in Practice* 18, no. 1 (2008): 66–81.

Guangzhou Municipal Government Legal Affairs Office. "Guangzhou Municipal Provisions on Open Government Information." *Government Information Quarterly* 23, no. 1 (2006a): 18–27.

———. "Introduction to Open Government Information Work by the Guangzhou Municipal Government." *Government Information Quarterly* 23, no. 1 (2006b): 11–17.

Gupta, Anil, and Vijay Govindarajan. "Knowledge Management's Social Dimension: Lessons From Nucor Steel." In *Knowledge Management and Organizational Learning,* edited by Laurence Prusak and Eric Matson, 229–42. New York: Oxford University Press, 2006.

Hailey, John. "Indicators of Identity: NGOs and the Strategic Imperative of Assessing Core Values." 10th anniversary issue, *Development in Practice* 10, no. 3–4 (2000): 402–7.

Hailey, John, and Rick James. "Learning Leaders: The Key to Learning Organisations." *Development in Practice* 12, no. 3–4 (2002): 398–408.

Hajer, Maarten A. "Discourse Coalitions and the Institutionalization of Practice." In *The Argumentative Turn in Policy Analysis,* edited by Frank Fischer and John Forester, 43–76. Durham, NC: Duke University Press, 1993.

Hale, Angela. "Trade Liberalisation in the Garment Industry: Who Is Really Benefiting?" *Development in Practice* 12, no. 1 (2002): 33–44.

Hallberg, Kristin. *A Market-Oriented Strategy for Small and Medium Scale Enterprises* (International Finance Corporation Discussion Paper No. 40). Washington, DC: International Finance Corporation, 2000.

Hammer, Mitchell R. "The Intercultural Conflict Style Inventory: A Conceptual Framework and Measure of Intercultural Conflict Resolution Approaches." *International Journal of Intercultural Relations* 29, no. 6 (2005): 675–95.

Hankivsky, Olena. "Gender vs. Diversity Mainstreaming: A Preliminary Explanation of the Role and Transformative Potential of Feminist Theory." *Canadian Journal of Political Science* 38 (2005): 977–1001.

Harris-Curtis, Emma. "Rights-Based Approaches: Issues for NGOs." *Development in Practice* 13, no. 5 (2003): 558–64.

Hashemi, Syed M. "NGO Accountability in Bangladesh: Beneficiaries, Donors, and the State." In *Beyond the Magic Bullet*, edited by Michael Edwards and David Hulme, 123–31. West Hartford, CT: Kumarian Press, 1996.

Hayward, Mathew L. A., Violina P. Rindova, and Timothy G. Pollock. "Believing One's Own Press: The Causes and Consequences of CEO Celebrity." *Strategic Management Journal* 25 (2004): 637–53.

Heimann, Deborah. "Supporting Communication for Development With Horizontal Dialogue and a Level Playing Field: The Communication Initiative." *Development in Practice* 16, no. 6 (2006): 603–10.

Henry, James V. *Understanding HR in the Humanitarian Sector*. London: People in Aid, 2004.

Henry, Nicholas. *Public Administration and Public Affairs*. Upper Saddle River, NJ: Pearson/ Prentice Hall, 2004.

Herzberg, Frederick. *Work and the Nature of Man*. Cleveland, OH: World Publishing, 1966.

Heyns, Stephen. "Organisational Capacity-Building, and the 'Quick and Dirty' Consultant." *Development in Practice* 6, no. 1 (1996): 54–57.

Hirschman, Albert. *Development Projects Observed*. Washington, DC: Brookings Institution, 1967.

Hirschmann, David. "'Implementing an Indicator': Operationalising USAID's 'Advocacy Index' in Zimbabwe." *Development in Practice* 12, no. 1 (2002): 20–32.

———. "Keeping 'the Last' in Mind: Incorporating Chambers in Consulting." *Development in Practice* 13, no. 5 (2003): 487–500.

Hofstede, Gert. *Culture's Consequences*. Newbury Park, CA: Sage, 1984.

Holt, Jennifer L., and Cynthia James DeVore. "Culture, Gender, Organizational Role, and Styles of Conflict Resolution: A Meta-Analysis." *International Journal of Intercultural Relations* 29, no. 2 (2005): 165–96.

Howard, Patricia L. "Beyond the 'Grim Resisters': Towards More Effective Gender Mainstreaming Through Stakeholder Participation." *Development in Practice* 12, no. 2 (2002): 164–76.

Howard, Rhonda E., and Jack Donnelly. "Human Dignity, Human Rights, and Political Regimes." *American Political Science Review* 80 (1986): 801–17.

Hummel, Ralph P. *The Bureaucratic Experience*. New York: St. Martin's Press, 1977.

Husselbee, David. "NGOs as Development Partners to the Corporates: Child Football Stitchers in Pakistan." 10th anniversary issue, *Development in Practice* 10, no. 3–4 (2000): 377–89.

International Federation of Red Cross and Red Crescent Societies. *World Disasters Report*. Bloomfield, CT: Kumarian Press, 2005.

International Health Exchange/People in Aid. *The Human Face of Aid*. London: International Health Exchange and People in Action, 1997.

Jackson, Paul. "Square Pegs and Round Holes: Participatory Methodologies Among Entrepreneurs in Zimbabwe." *Development in Practice* 10, no. 5 (2000): 712–15.

Jayapadma, R. V. "Dimensions, Manifestations, and Perceptions of Gender Equity: The Experiences of Gram Vikas." *Development in Practice* 12, no. 2 (2009): 148–59.

Jennings, Bruce. "Counsel and Consensus: Norms of Argument in Health Policy." In *The Argumentative Turn in Policy Analysis*, edited by Frank Fischer and John Forester, 101–16. Durham, NC: Duke University Press, 1993.

Johnson, Deb. "Insights on Poverty." *Development in Practice* 12, no. 2 (2002): 127–37.

Johnson, Douglas A. "The Need for New Tactics." In *New Tactics in Human Rights*, edited by Tricia Cornell, Kate Kelsch, and Nicole Palasz, 12–18. Minneapolis, MN: Center for Victims of Torture, 2004.

Johnson, Hazel, and Gordon Wilson. "Institutional Sustainability as Learning." *Development in Practice* 9, no. 1–2 (1999): 43–55.

Jordan, Ann. "Women and Conflict Transformation: Influences, Roles, and Experiences." *Development in Practice* 13, no. 2–3 (2003): 239–51.

Jordan, Lisa, and Peter van Tuijl. "Rights and Responsibilities in the Political Landscape of NGO Accountability: Introduction and Overview." In *NGO Accountability: Politics, Principles and Innovation*, edited by Lisa Jordan and Peter van Tuijl, 3–20. London: Earthscan, 2007.

Kanter, Rosebeth Moss. *The Measurement of Organisational Effectiveness, Productivity, Performance and Success: Issues and Dilemmas in Service and Non-Profit Organisations*. PONPO Working Paper No. 8, Yale University, Institution for Social and Policy Studies. Boston: Institute of Development Research, 1979.

Kaplan, Allan. "Leadership and Management." In *The Earthscan Reader on NGO Management*, edited by Michael Edwards and Alan Fowler, 423–40. London: Earthscan, 2002.

Karim, Mahbubul. "NGOs in Bangladesh: Issues of Legitimacy and Accountability." In *Beyond the Magic Bullet*, edited by Michael Edwards and David Hulme, 132–41. West Hartford, CT: Kumarian Press, 1996.

Katz, Jonathan M. "With Cheap Food Imports, Haiti Can't Feed Itself." *Washington Post*, March 20, 2010. Accessed August 31, 2010. http://www.washingtonpost.com/wp-dyn/content/article/2010/03/20/AR2010032001329.html.

Kaufman, Herbert. *The Administrative Behavior of Federal Bureau Chiefs*. Washington, DC: Brookings Institution, 1981.

Keck, Margaret E., and Kathryn Sikkink. "Transnational Advocacy Networks in the Movement Society." In *The Social Movement Society: Contentious Politics for a New Century*, edited by David S. Meyer and Sidney Tarrow, 217–38. Lanham, MD: Rowman and Littlefield, 1998.

Keet, Dot. "The International Anti-debt Campaign: A Southern Activist View for Activists in 'the North' . . . and 'the South.'" *Development in Practice* 10, no. 3–4 (2000): 461–77.

Kelly, Linda, Patrick Kilby, and Nalini Kasynathan. "Impact Measurement for NGOs: Experiences From India and Sri Lanka." *Development in Practice* 14, no. 5 (2004): 696–702.

Kelly, Robert E. "No 'Return to the State': Dependency and Developmentalism Against Neo-Liberalism." *Development in Practice* 18, no. 3 (2008): 319–32.

Keniston, K. "IT for the Common Man: Lessons From India, MN Srinivas Memorial Lecture. Bangalore: National Institute of Advanced Studies, India Institute of Science." 2002. Accessed April 16, 2010. http://web.mit.edu/%7Ekken/Public/PAPERS/EPW_paper.html.

Kgamphe, Lerato. *Using Government Budgets as a Monitoring Tool*. Minneapolis, MN: Center for Victims of Torture, 2004.

Kim, W. Chan, and Renée Mauborgne. "Fair Process: Managing in the Knowledge Economy." In *Knowledge Management and Organizational Learning*, edited by Laurence Prusak and Eric Matson, 243–58. New York: Oxford University Press, 2006.

Korten, David C. "Community Organization and Rural Development: A Learning Approach." *Public Administration Review* 40, no. 5 (1980): 480–511.

———. "The Life Game: Survival Strategies in Ethiopian Folktales." *Journal of Cross-Cultural Psychology* 2, no. 3 (1971): 209–24.

———. "Strategic Organization for People-Centered Development." *Public Administration Review* 44, no. 4 (1984): 341–52.

———. *When Corporations Rule the World*. London: Earthscan, 1995.

Kransdorff, Arnold, and Russell Williams. "Swing Doors and Musical Chairs." In *Knowledge Management and Organizational Learning*, edited by Laurence Prusak and Eric Matson, 139–47. New York: Oxford University Press, 2006.

Kristof, Nicholas D. "It Takes a School, Not Missiles." *New York Times*, July 13, 2008, A14.

———. "'Three Cups of Tea,' Spilled." *New York Times*. April 20, 2011, A27.

Kusakabe, Kyoko. "Women's Involvement in Small-Scale Aquaculture in Northeast Thailand." *Development in Practice* 13, no. 4 (2003): 333–45.

Lahiri-Dutt, Kuntala. "Mainstreaming Gender in the Mines: Results From an Indonesian Colliery." *Development in Practice* 16, no. 2 (2006): 215–21.

Landolt, Laura K. "(Mis)Constructing the Third World? Constructivist Analysis of Norms Diffusion." *Third World Quarterly* 25 (2004): 579–91.

Laszlo, Kathia Castro, and Alexander Laszlo. "Evolving Knowledge for Development: The Role of Knowledge Management in a Changing World." *Journal of Knowledge Management* 6, no. 4 (2002): 400–12.

Leach, Fiona, and Shashikala Sitaram. "Microfinance and Women's Empowerment: A Lesson From India." *Development in Practice* 12, no. 5 (2002): 575–88.

Leal, Pablo Alejandro. "Participation: The Ascendancy of a Buzzword in the Neo-Liberal Era." *Development in Practice* 17, no. 4–5 (2007): 539–48.

Leipold, Gerd. "Campaigning: A Fashion or the Best Way to Change the Global Agenda?" *Development in Practice* 10, no. 3–4 (2000): 453–60.

Lélé, S. M. "Sustainable Development: A Critical Review." *World Development* 19, no. 6 (1991): 607–22.

Leonard, Dorothy, and Walter Swap. "Generating Creative Options." In *Knowledge Management and Organizational Learning*, edited by Laurence Prusak and Eric Matson, 94–124. New York: Oxford University Press, 2006.

Lewis, David E. "Nongovernmental Organizations and Caribbean Development." *Annals of the American Academy of Political and Social Science* 533 (1994): 125–38.

———. "Organization Culture, and Institutional Sustainability." *Annals of the American Academy of Political and Social Science* 590 (2003): 212–26.

Lofredo, Gino. "Help Yourself by Helping the Poor." *Development in Practice* 5, no. 4 (1995): 342–45.

Longwe, Sara Hlupekile. "The Evaporation of Gender Policies in the Patriarchal Cooking Pot." *Development in Practice* 7, no. 2 (1997): 148–56.

Macrae, Joanna. "Understanding Integration From Rwanda to Iraq." *Ethics and International Affairs* 18 (2004): 29–35.

Magazine, Roger. "An Innovative Combination of Neoliberalism and State Corporatism: The Case of a Locally Based NGO in Mexico City." *Annals of the American Academy of Political and Social Science* 590 (2003): 243–56.

Mahadevia, Darshini. "Sustainable Urban Development in India: An Inclusive Perspective." *Development in Practice* 11, no. 2–3 (2001): 242–59.

Maina, Wachira. "Kenya: The State, Donors and the Politics of Democratization." In *Civil Society and the Aid Industry*, edited by Alison Van Rooy, 134–67. Sterling, VA: Earthscan, 2000.

Makhoul, Jihad, and Lindsey Harrison. "Development Perspectives: Views From Rural Lebanon." *Development in Practice* 12, no. 5 (2002): 613–24.

Malešević, Siniša. "Globalism and Nationalism: Which One Is Bad?" *Development in Practice* 9, no. 5 (1999): 579–83.

Mallick, Ross. "Implementing and Evaluating Microcredit in Bangladesh." *Development in Practice* 12, no. 2 (2002): 153–63.

Marchand, Louise. "Statement-Item 5 of the Substantive Session of the United Nations Economic and Social Council (ECOSOC)." Foreign Affairs and International Trade Canada. 2003. Accessed August 23, 2011. http://www.international.gc.ca/humanitarian-humanitaire/ecosoc_2003.aspx?lang=eng&view=d/.

Marcuello, Carmen, and Chaime Marcuello. "Northern Words, Southern Readings." *Development in Practice* 9, no. 1–2 (1999): 151–58.

Marcuello Servos, Chaime, and Carmen Marcuello. "NGOs, Corporate Social Responsibility, and Social Accountability: Inditex vs. Clean Clothes." *Development in Practice* 17 (2007): 393–403.

Marsella, Anthony J. "Culture and Conflict: Understanding, Negotiating, and Reconciling Conflicting Constructions of Reality." *International Journal of Intercultural Relations* 29, no. 6 (2005): 651–73.

Martínez, Luz María. "Recovering the Future: Grandmothers Campaigning for Human Rights." *Development in Practice* 6, no. 4 (1996): 362–63.

May, John D'Arcy. "Human Dignity, Human Rights, and Religious Pluralism: Buddhist and Christian Perspectives." *Buddhist-Christian Studies* 26 (2006): 51–60.

Mayoux, Linda. "Women's Empowerment and Micro-Finance Programmes: Strategies for Increasing Impact." *Development in Practice* 8, no. 2 (1998): 235–41.

McPherson, Thomas. "The Moral Patient." *Philosophy* 59 (1984): 171–83.

Merali, Isfahan. "Advancing Women's Reproductive and Sexual Health Rights: Using the International Human Rights System." *Development in Practice* 10, no. 5 (2000): 609–24.

Meyer, John W. "Social Environments and Organizational Accounting." In *Institutional Environments and Organizations*, edited by W. Richard Scott, John W. Meyer, and Associates, 121–36. Thousand Oaks, CA: Sage, 1994.

Minear, Larry. "Informing the Integration Debate With Recent Experience." *Ethics and International Affairs* 18 (2004): 53–58.

Mintzberg, Henry. "Developing Leaders? Developing Countries?" *Development in Practice* 16, no. 1 (2006): 4–14.

———. "Managing Exceptionally." *Organization Science* 12, no. 6 (2001): 759–71.

———. *Structure in Fives: Designing Effective Organizations*. Englewood Cliffs, NJ: Prentice Hall, 1993.

Miszvlivetz, Ferenc, and Katalin Ertsey. "Hungary: Civil Society in the Post-Socialist World." In *Civil Society and the Aid Industry*, edited by Alison Van Rooy, 71–103. Sterling, VA: Earthscan, 2000.

Mkandawire, Thandike. "'Good Governance': The Itinerary of an Idea." *Development in Practice* 17, no. 4–5 (2007): 679–81.

Mkenda-Mugittu, Vera F. "Measuring the Invisibles: Gender Mainstreaming and Monitoring Experience From a Dairy Development Project in Tanzania." *Development in Practice* 13, no. 5 (2003): 459–73.

Mompati, Tlamelo, and Gerard Prinsen. "Ethnicity and Participatory Development Methods in Botswana: Some Participants Are to Be Seen and Not Heard." *Development in Practice* 10, no. 5 (2000): 625–37.

Moore, Mick, and Sheelagh Stewart. "Corporate Governance for NGOs?" *Development in Practice* 8, no. 3 (1998): 335–42.

Morgan, Gareth. *Images of Organization: The Executive Edition.* San Francisco: Berrett-Koehler, 1998.

Mortenson, Greg. *Stones Into Schools: Promoting Peace With Books, Not Bombs, in Afghanistan and Pakistan.* New York: Viking, 2009.

———. *Three Cups of Tea: One Man's Mission to Promote Peace—One School at a Time.* New York: Penguin, 2007.

Moser, Caroline, and Annalise Moser. "Gender Mainstreaming Since Beijing: A Review of Success and Limitations in International Institutions." *Gender and Development* 13, no. 2 (2005): 11–22.

Moser, Caroline, and Peter Sollis. "Did the Project Fail? A Community Perspective on a Participatory Primary Health Care Project in Ecuador." *Development in Practice* 1, no. 1 (1991): 19–33.

Mulder, Ursala, and Alma Whiteley. "Emerging and Capturing Tacit Knowledge: A Methodology for a Bounded Environment." *Journal of Knowledge Management* 11, no. 1 (2007): 68–83.

Musyoki, Samuel. "Can Bilateral Programmes Become Learning Organisations? Experiences From Institutionalising Participation in Keiyo Marakwet in Kenya." *Development in Practice* 12, no. 3–4 (2002): 370–82.

Narayan, Deepa. "Can Anyone Hear Us? Voices From 47 Countries." *Voices of the Poor.* Vol. 1. New York: Poverty Group (PREM) World Bank, 1999.

National Association of Schools of Public Affairs and Administration. "Accreditation Standards for Master's Degree Programs." In *NASPAA Standards 2009.* Washington, DC: National Association of Schools of Public Affairs and Administration, 2009.

Nelson, Paul. "Heroism and Ambiguity: NGO Advocacy in International Policy." 10th anniversary issue, *Development in Practice* 10, no. 3–4 (2000): 478–90.

Nevile, Ann. *Policy Choices in a Globalized World.* Huntington, NY: Nova Science, 2002.

Nonaka, Ikujiro, and Hiro Takeuchi. *The Knowledge-Creating Company.* New York: Oxford University Press, 1995.

Nosek, John T. "Group Cognition as a Basis for Supporting Group Knowledge Creation and Sharing." *Journal of Knowledge Management* 8, no. 4 (2004): 54–64.

Nussbaum, Martha C. *Creating Capabilities.* Cambridge, MA: Harvard University Press, 2011.

Nyamugasira, Warren. "NGOs and Advocacy: How Well Are the Poor Represented?" *Development in Practice* 8, no. 3 (1998): 297–308.

Olufemi, Olusola. "Women and the Burden of Unsustainable Development: Practice and Policy Contradictions." *Development in Practice* 14, no. 3 (2004): 428–32.

Osborne, David, and Ted Gaebler. *Reinventing Government: How the Entrepreneurial Spirit Is Transforming the Public Sector.* New York: Penguin, 1993.

Padaki, Vijay. "Coming to Grips With Organisational Values." 10th anniversary issue, *Development in Practice* 10, no. 3–4 (2000): 420–35.

———. "The Human Organization: Challenges in NGOs and Development Programmes." *Development in Practice* 17, no. 1 (2007): 65–77.

———. "Making the Organisation Learn: Demystification and Management Action." *Development in Practice* 12, no. 3–4 (2002): 321–37.

Panayiotopoulos, Prodromos. "Anthropology Consultancy in the UK and Community Development in the Third World: A Difficult Dialogue." *Development in Practice* 12, no. 1 (2002): 45–58.

Paterson, Ruth. "Women's Empowerment in Challenging Environments: A Case Study From Balochistan." *Development in Practice* 18, no. 3 (2008): 333–44.

Pathak, Ila. "Feedback." *Development in Practice* 2, no. 1 (1992): 61.

Patra, Sanjay. "Governance of NPOs." *Civil Society Voices* (March–June 2007): 23–25.

Patrón, Pepi. "Peru: Civil Society and the Autocratic Challenge." In *Civil Society and the Aid Industry*, edited by Alison Van Rooy, 168–96. Sterling, VA: Earthscan, 2000.

Payne, Geoffrey. "Lowering the Ladder: Regulatory Frameworks for Sustainable Development." *Development in Practice* 11, no. 2–3 (2001): 308–18.

Payne, Lina, and Ines Smyth. "The Need for Reliable Systems: Gendered Work in Oxfam's Uganda Programme." *Development in Practice* 9, no. 1–2 (1999): 175–78.

Pearson, Ruth. "The Rise and Rise of Gender and Development." In *A Radical History of Development Studies: Individuals, Institutions and Ideologies*, edited by Uma Kothari, 157–69. London: Zed Books, 2006.

People in Action. *Code of Good Practice in the Management and Support of Aid Personnel.* London: People in Aid, 2003.

Perrow, Charles. "Hospitals: Technology, Structure and Goals." In *Handbook of Organizations*, edited by J. G. March, 910–71. Chicago: Rand McNally, 1965.

Peruzzotti, Enrique. "Civil Society, Representation, and Accountability: Restating Current Debates on Representativeness and Accountability in Civic Associations." In *NGO Accountability: Politics, Principles and Innovation*, edited by Lisa Jordan and Peter van Tuijl, 43–60. London: Earthscan, 2007.

Pijnenburg, Bart, and Isilda Nhantumbo. "Participatory Development Interventions in Mozambique." *Development in Practice* 12, no. 2 (2002): 192–99.

Pitanguy, Jacqueline. "Reconceptualizing Human Rights Language: Gender and Violence." *Health and Human Rights* 2, no. 3 (1997): 27–30.

Plantenga, Dorine. "Gender, Identity, and Diversity: Learning From Insights Gained in Transformative Gender Training." *Gender and Development* 12 (2004): 40–46.

Plowman, Penny. "Organisational Change From Two Perspectives: Gender and Organisational Development." *Development in Practice* 10, no. 2 (2000): 189–203.

Postma, William. "NGO Partnership and Institutional Development: Making It Real and Making It Intentional." *Canadian Journal of African Studies* 28 (1994): 447–71.

Povey, Elaheh Rostami. "Women in Afghanistan: Passive Victims of the Borga or Active Social Participants?" *Development in Practice* 13, no. 2–3 (2003): 266–77.

Powell, Mike. "Which Knowledge? Whose Reality? An Overview of Knowledge Used in the Development Sector." *Development in Practice* 16, no. 6 (2006): 518–32.

Powell, Walter W., and Paul J. DiMaggio. *The New Institutionalism in Organizational Analysis.* Chicago: University of Chicago Press, 1991.

Power, Grant, Matthew Maury, and Susan Maury. "Operationalising Bottom-Up Learning in International NGOs: Barriers and Alternatives." *Development in Practice* 12, no. 3–4 (2002): 272–84.

Pressman, Jeffrey L., and Aaron Wildavsky. *Implementation: How Great Expectations in Washington Are Dashed in Oakland*. Berkeley: University of California Press, 1973.

Prusak, Laurence, and Eric Matson, eds. *Knowledge Management and Organizational Learning*. New York: Oxford University Press, 2006.

Pupavac, Vanessa. "The Politics of Emergency and the Demise of the Developing State: Problems for Humanitarian Advocacy." *Development in Practice* 16, no. 3–4 (2006): 255–69.

Qiao, Zhigang. "Exploration and Practice in Promoting Shanghai Municipal Open Government Information." *Government Information Quarterly* 23, no. 1 (2006): 28–35.

Raab, Michaela. "Could Cognitive Theory Enhance Development Practice?" *Development in Practice* 18, no. 3 (2008): 430–34.

Radin, Beryl. *The Accountable Juggler*. Washington, DC: CQ Press, 2002.

Rahman, Aminur. "Micro-Credit Initiatives for Equitable and Sustainable Development: Who Pays?" *World Development* 27, no. 1 (1999): 67–82.

Rahnema, Majid. "Participation." In *Development Dictionary: A Guide to Knowledge and Power*, edited by Wolfgang Sachs, 116–31. London: Zed Books, 1993a.

———. "Participatory Action Research: The 'Last Temptation of Saint Development.'" *Alternatives* 15 (1990): 199–226.

———. "Poverty." In *Development Dictionary: A Guide to Knowledge and Power*, edited by Wolfgang Sachs, 158–76. London: Zed Books, 1993b.

Ramalingam, Ben. *Tools for Knowledge and Learning: A Guide for Development and Humanitarian Organisations*. London: Overseas Development Institute, 2005.

Rao, Aruna, and David Kelleher. "Gender Lost and Gender Found: BRAC's Gender Quality Action-Learning Programme." *Development in Practice* 8, no. 2 (1998): 173–85.

———. "What Is Gender at Work's Approach to Gender Equity and Institutional Change?" *Gender at Work*. n.d. Accessed June 1, 2010. http://www.genderatwork.org/sites/gender atwork.org/files/resources/Gender_at_Works_Approach.pdf.

Raymond-McKay, Maureen, and Malcolm MacLachlan. "Critical Incidents in Emergency Relief Work." *Development in Practice* 10, no. 5 (2000): 674–86.

Reason, Peter. "Three Approaches to Participative Inquiry." In *Handbook of Qualitative Research*, edited by Norman K. Denzin and Yvonna S. Lincoln. Thousand Oaks, CA: Sage, 1994.

Rein, Martin, and Donald Schön. "Reframing Policy Discourse." In *The Argumentative Turn in Policy Analysis*, edited by Frank Fischer and John Forester, 145–66. Durham, NC: Duke University Press, 1993.

Results. *The Micro-Credit Summit: Declaration and Plan of Action*. Washington, DC: RESULTS, 1997.

Riak, Abikök. "The Local Capacities for Peace Project: The Sudan Experience." *Development in Practice* 10, no. 3–4 (2000): 501–5.

Riccucci, Norma M. "Dr. Helene Gayle and the AIDS Epidemic." In *Public Administration: Concepts and Cases*, edited by Richard J. Stillman II, 86–103. Boston: Houghton Mifflin, 2005.

Richardson, Frances. "Meeting the Demand for Skilled and Experienced Humanitarian Workers." *Development in Practice* 16, no. 3–4 (2006): 334–41.

Ridde, Valéry. "Performance-Based Partnership Agreements for the Reconstruction of the Health System in Afghanistan." *Development in Practice* 15, no. 1 (2005): 4–15.

Riley, Kevin. "Street-Smart Officers Have Bright Ideas for Downtown." *Dayton Daily News.* November 22, 2009, A26.

Risse, Thomas, Stephen C. Ropp, and Kathryn Sikkink. *The Power of Human Rights: International Norms and Domestic Change.* New York: Cambridge University Press, 1999.

Rist, Gilbert. "Development as a Buzzword." *Development in Practice* 17, no. 4–5 (2007): 485–91.

Roberts, Martin, and Finbar Lillis. "Accredited Learning Frameworks and NGO Capacity-Building Programmes in Nigeria." *Development in Practice* 11, no. 1 (2001): 96–101.

Robertson, David. *A Dictionary of Human Rights.* London: Routledge, 2004.

Robinson, Dorcas. "The Development Management Task and Reform of 'Public' Social Services." *Development in Practice* 9, no. 1–2 (1999): 78–87.

Roche, Chris. "Impact Assessment: Seeing the Wood and the Trees." 10th anniversary issue, *Development in Practice* 10, no. 3–4 (2000): 543–55.

Rodríguez-Carmona, Antonio. "Development NGOs, Local Learning, and Social Capital: The Experience of CARE Bolivia in Villa Serrano." *Development in Practice* 14, no. 3 (2004): 354–65.

Romzek, Barbara S. *"Accountability and Contracting in a Networked Policy Arena: The Case of Welfare Reform."* In *Accountable Governance: Problems and Promises,* edited by Melvin J. Dubnick and H. George Frederickson, 22–41. Armonk, NY: M. E. Sharpe, 2011.

Romzek, Barbara S., and Melvin J. Dubnick. "Accountability in the Public Sector: Lessons From the Challenger Tragedy." *Public Administration Review* 47, no. 3 (1987): 227–38.

Rondinelli, Dennis A. "Partnering for Development: Government-Private Sector Cooperation in Service Provision." In *Reinventing Government for the Twenty-First Century,* edited by Dennis A. Rondinelli and G. Shabbir Cheema, 219–42. Bloomfield, CT: Kumarian Press, 2003a.

———. "Promoting National Competitiveness in a Global Economy." In *Reinventing Government for the Twenty-First Century,* edited by Dennis A. Rondinelli and G. Shabbir Cheema, 33–60. Bloomfield, CT: Kumarian Press, 2003b.

Rousseau, Denise. *Psychological Contracts in Organizations: Understanding Written and Unwritten Agreements.* Thousand Oaks, CA: Sage, 1995.

Rowlands, Jo. "Empowerment Examined." *Development in Practice* 5, no. 2 (1995): 101–7.

Russell, Grahame. "All Rights Guaranteed, All Actors Accountable: Poverty Is a Violation of Human Rights." *Development in Practice* 8, no. 3 (1998): 353–57.

Sachs, Wolfgang. *Development Dictionary: A Guide to Knowledge and Power.* London: Zed Books, 1992.

Schick, Allan. "The Road to PPB: The Stages of Budget Reform." In *Classics of Public Administration,* edited by Jay M. Shafritz and Albert C. Hyde, 260–77. Pacific Grove, CA: Brooks/Cole, 1992. First published 1966.

Schumpeter, Joseph A. *The Theory of Economic Development.* Cambridge, MA: Harvard University Press, 1934.

Schunk, Javier. "The Role of the External Practitioner." *Development in Practice* 13, no. 4 (2003): 377–80.

Scoones, Ian. "Sustainability." *Development in Practice* 17, no. 4–5 (2007): 589–96.

Scott, Marvin B., and Stanford M. Lyman. "Accounts." *American Sociological Review* 33 (1968): 46–62.

Scott, W. Richard. *Institutions and Organizations.* Thousand Oaks, CA: Sage, 1995.

———. *"Institutions and Organizations: Toward a Theoretical Synthesis."* In *Institutional Environments and Organizations*, edited by W. Richard Scott, John W. Meyer, and Associates, 55–80. Thousand Oaks, CA: Sage, 1994.

Scott-Villiers, Patta. "The Struggle for Organisational Change: How the ActionAid Accountability, Learning and Planning System Emerged." *Development in Practice* 12, no. 3–4 (2002): 424–35.

Seeley, Janet, and Iqbal Alam Khan. "Building Skills in Qualitative Research to Inform Pro-Poor Policy: Experience From a Bangladeshi NGO." *Development in Practice* 16, no. 2 (2006): 153–68.

Selman, Paul. "Local Agenda 21: Substance or Spin?" *Journal of Environmental Planning and Management* 45, no. 5 (1998): 533–53.

Selznick, Philip. *Leadership in Administration: A Sociological Interpretation.* Evanston, IL: Row Patterson, 1957.

Sen, Amartya. *Development as Freedom.* New York: Anchor Books, 1999.

Senge, Peter. *The Fifth Discipline: The Art and Practice of the Learning Organization.* London: Century Business Books, 1990.

Shamir, Ronen. "Meet the Gap: The Commodification of Corporate Social Responsibility." *Symbolic Interaction* 28 (2005): 229–53.

Shanghai Municipal People's Government. "Shanghai Municipal Provisions on Open Government Information." *Government Information Quarterly* 23, no. 1 (2006): 36–47.

Shariq, Syed Z. "Sense Making and Artifacts: An Exploration Into the Role of Tools in Knowledge Management." *Journal of Knowledge Management* 2, no. 2 (1998): 10–20.

Shue, Henry. *Basic Rights: Subsistence, Affluence, and U.S. Foreign Policy.* Princeton, NJ: Princeton University Press, 1980.

Simmons, P. J. "Learning to Live With NGOs." *Foreign Policy* 112 (1998): 82–96.

Slim, Hugo. "Dissolving the Difference Between Humanitarianism and Development: The Mixing of a Rights-Based Solution." 10th anniversary issue, *Development in Practice* 10, no. 3–4 (2000): 491–94.

———. "Doing the Right Thing: Relief Agencies, Moral Dilemmas, and Moral Responsibility in Political Emergencies and War." *Disasters* 21, no. 3 (1997): 244–57.

———. "What Is Development?" *Development in Practice* 5, no. 2 (1995): 143–48.

Smillie, Ian, and John Hailey. *Managing for Change: Leadership, Strategy, and Management in Asian NGOs.* London: Earthscan, 2002.

Smyth, Ines. "Talking of Gender: Words and Meanings in Development Organisations." *Development in Practice* 17, no. 4–5 (2007): 582–88.

Snyder, William, and Thomas Cummings. "Organisation Learning Disorders: Conceptual Model and Intervention Hypotheses." *Human Relations* 51, no. 7 (1998): 873–95.

Soal, Sue. "NGOs on the Line." *Community Development Resources Association Annual Report 2001/2002.* 2002. Accessed August 31, 2010. http://www.cdra.org.za/index.php?option=com_content&view=article&id=28%3Angos-on-the-line&Itemid=2.

Sorel, Georges. *Reflections on Violence.* New York: Peter Smith, 1941.

Sperling, Valerie, Myra Marx Ferree, and Barbara Risman. "Constructing Global Feminism: Transnational Advocacy Networks and Russian Women's Activism." *Signs* 26, no. 4 (2001): 1155–86.

Spitzeck, Heiko. "Organizational Moral Learning: What, If Anything, Do Corporations Learn From NGO Critique?" *Journal of Business Ethics* 88 (2009): 157–73.

Sprenger, Ellen. "Organizational Gender Diagnosis." In *The Earthscan Reader on NGO Management*, edited by Michael Edwards and Alan Fowler, 413–22. London: Earthscan, 2002.

Staw, B. M., and R. I. Sutton. "Macro-Organizational Psychology." In *Social Psychology and Organizations: Advances in Theory and Research*, 350–84, edited by J. K. Murnigham. Englewood Cliffs, NJ: Prentice Hall, 1992.

Stone, Deborah. *Policy Paradox: The Art of Political Decision Making.* New York: W. W. Norton, 2002.

Storey, Andy. "The World Bank, Neo-Liberalism, and Power: Discourse Analysis and Implications for Campaigners." *Development in Practice* 10, no. 3–4 (2000): 361–70.

Sydow, Jorg, and Arnold Windeler. "Organizing and Evaluating Interfirm Networks: A Structurationist Perspective on Network Processes and Effectiveness." *Organization Science* 9 (1998): 265–84.

Takahashi, Chie. "Partnerships, Learning, and Development: A Case Study From Ghana." *Development in Practice* 16, no. 1 (2006): 39–50.

Tallontire, Anne, Catherine Dolan, Sally Smith, and Stephanie Barrientos. "Reaching the Marginalised? Gender Value Chains and Ethical Trade in African Horticulture." *Development in Practice* 15, no. 3–4 (2005): 559–71.

Tandon, Rajesh. "'Board Games': Governance and Accountability in NGOs." In *Beyond the Magic Bullet*, edited by Michael Edwards and David Hulme, 53–64. West Hartford, CT: Kumarian Press, 2002.

Tate, Janice. "Aiding and Abetting the Politicians?" *Development in Practice* 15, no. 1 (2005): 60–63.

Termeer, C. J. A. M., and J. F. M. Koppenjan. "Managing Perceptions in Networks." In *Managing Complex Networks*, edited by Walter J. M. Kickert, Erik-Hans Klijn, and Joop F. M. Koppenjan, 79–97. London: Sage, 1997.

Terry, Geraldine. "Poverty Reduction and Violence Against Women: Exploring Links, Assessing Impact." *Development in Practice* 14, no. 4 (2004): 469–80.

Terry, Larry. *Leadership of Public Bureaucracies: The Administrator as Conservator.* Thousand Oaks, CA: Sage, 1995.

Thaw, Davine. "Stepping Into a River of Change." In *The Earthscan Reader on NGO Management*, edited by Michael Edwards and Alan Fowler, 146–63. London: Earthscan, 2002.

Thomas, Alan. "What Makes Good Development Management?" *Development in Practice* 9, no. 1–2 (1999): 9–17.

Thomas-Slayter, Barbara, and Genese Sodikoff. "Sustainable Investments: Women's Contributions to Natural Resource Management Projects in Africa." *Development in Practice* 11, no. 1 (2001): 45–61.

Thurston, Wilfreda E., Pip J. Farrar, Ann L. Casebeer, and Judith C. Grossman. "Hearing Silenced Voices: Developing Community With an Advisory Committee." *Development in Practice* 14, no. 4 (2004): 481–94.

Tostan. *Five-Year Strategic Plan: 2006–2011.* 2006. Accessed March 24, 2012. http://www.tostan.org/data/files/tostan%20five%20year%20strategic%20plan.pdf.

———. *Tostan: Community-led Development.* 2007. Accessed April 27, 2010. http://www.tostan.org/.

Trist, E. L. *The Evolution of Socio-technical Systems: A Conceptual Framework and an Action Research Program* (Occasional Paper No. 2). Toronto: Ontario Quality of Working Life Centre, 1981.

Tyndale, Wendy. "Faith and Economics in 'Development': A Bridge Across the Chasm?" *Development in Practice* 10, no. 1 (2000): 9–18.

UN Office for the Coordination of Humanitarian Affairs. *Fact Sheet*. Policy Studies and Development Branch, March 2011a.

———. *To Stay and Deliver: Good Practices for Humanitarianism in Complex Security Environments*. Policy Studies and Development Branch, 2011b.

United Nations. *Report of the Economic and Social Council for 1997*. General Assembly: Fifty-Second Session, September 18, 1997. New York: United Nations, 1997.

Uny, Isabelle Wazo. "Factors and Motivations Contributing to Community Volunteers' Participation in a Nursery Feeding Project in Malawi." *Development in Practice* 18, no. 3 (2008): 437–45.

Uphoff, Norman. "Why NGOs Are Not a Third Sector: A Sectoral Analysis With Some Thoughts on Accountability, Sustainability, and Evaluation." In *Beyond the Magic Bullet*, edited by Michael Edwards and David Hulme, 23–39. West Hartford, CT: Kumarian Press, 1996.

Uvin, Peter. *Aiding Violence: The Development Enterprise in Rwanda*. Bloomfield, CT: Kumarian Press, 1998.

———. "From the Right to Development to the Rights-Based Approach: How 'Human Rights' Entered Development." *Development in Practice* 17, no. 4–5 (2007): 597–606.

———. *Human Rights and Development*. Bloomfield, CT: Kumarian Press, 2004.

Vale, Ian. *Addressing Staff Retention in the Horn of Africa*. London: People in Aid, 2010.

Vandemoortele, Jan. "The MDG Conundrum: Meeting the Targets Without Missing the Point." *Development Policy Review* 27, no. 4 (2009): 355–71.

Van Reisen, Mirjam. *EU 'Global Player': North–South Policy of the European Union*. Brussels: International Books, 1999.

Van Rooy, Alison. *Civil Society and the Aid Industry*. Sterling, VA: Earthscan, 2000.

Vasan, Sudha. "NGOs as Employers: Need for Accountability." *Economic and Political Weekly*. May 29, 2004, 2197–98.

Von Dach, Suzanne Wymann. "Integrated Mountain Development: A Question of Gender Mainstreaming." *Mountain Research and Development* 22, no. 3 (2002): 236–39.

Waal, Maretha de. "Evaluating Gender Mainstreaming in Development Projects." *Development in Practice* 16, no. 2 (2006): 209–14.

Wallace, Tina. *The Aid Chain*. Warwickshire, UK: Practical Action Publishing, 2007.

Wallace, T., C. Crowther, and A. Shepherd. *Standardizing Development: Influences on UK NGOs' Policies and Procedures*. Oxford: Worldview Press, 1997.

Walsh, Eoghan, and Helena Lenihan. "Accountability and Effectiveness of NGOs: Adapting Business Tools Successfully." *Development in Practice* 16, no. 5 (2006): 412–24.

Watson, Robert P. *Public Administration: Cases in Managerial Role-Playing*. New York: Addison-Wesley Longman, 2002.

Watts, Michael. "Should They Be Committed? Motivating Volunteers in Phnom Penh, Cambodia." *Development in Practice* 12, no. 1 (2002): 59–70.

Weiss, Leigh, and Laurence Prusak. "Seeing Knowledge Plain: How to Make Knowledge Visible." In *Knowledge Management and Organizational Learning*, edited by Laurence Prusak and Eric Matson, 323–33. New York: Oxford University Press, 2006.

Wells, Duncan. "Introducing Computers Into Development Programmes: Some Problems and Suggested Solutions." *Development in Practice* 3, no. 1 (1993): 36–43.

Wells, Rob. "Ensuring NGO Independence in the New Funding Environment." *Development in Practice* 11, no. 1 (2001): 73–77.

Whaites, Alan. "Let's Get Civil Society Straight: NGOs and Political Theory." *Development in Practice* 6, no. 3 (1996): 240–44.

———. "NGOs, Civil Society and the State: Avoiding Theoretical Extremes in Real World Issues." *Development in Practice* 8, no. 3 (1998): 343–49.

———. "NGOs, Disasters, and Advocacy: Caught Between the Prophet and the Shepherd Boy." 10th anniversary issue, *Development in Practice* 10, no. 3–4 (2000): 506–16.

Wheat, Sue. "What Are NGOs Doing Here?" *The Courier* 181 (2000): 55–57.

Whetten, David A. "Organization Growth and Decline Processes." *American Review of Sociology* 13 (1987): 335–58.

White, Sarah C. "Depoliticising Development: The Uses and Abuses of Participation." *Development in Practice* 6, no. 1 (1996): 6–15.

Wildavsky, Aaron. *The Nursing Father: Moses as a Political Leader.* Tuscaloosa: University of Alabama Press, 1984.

Willetts, Julia, and Paul Crawford. "The Most Significant Lessons About the Most Significant Change Technique." *Development in Practice* 19, no. 6 (2007): 367–79.

Williams, Cindy. *Strengthening Homeland Security: Reforming Planning and Resource Allocation.* Washington, DC: IBM Center for the Business of Government, 2008.

Wilson-Grau, Ricardo. "The Risk Approach to Strategic Management in Development NGOs." *Development in Practice* 13, no. 5 (2003): 533–36.

Wiseberg, Laurie S. "Protecting Human Rights Activists and NGOs: What More Can Be Done?" *Human Rights Quarterly* 13, no. 4 (1991): 525–44.

Witter, Sophie, and Jenifer Bukokhe. "Children's Perceptions of Poverty, Participation, and Local Governance in Uganda." *Development in Practice* 14, no. 5 (2004): 645–59.

Worchel, Stephen. "Culture's Role in Conflict and Conflict Management: Some Suggestions, Many Questions." *International Journal of Intercultural Relations* 29, no. 6 (2005): 739–57.

World Bank. *Thailand-Rural Information Empowerment Project* (P071185). 2001. Accessed August 31, 2010. http://www-wds.worldbank.org/external/default/WDSContentServer/WDSP/IB/2001/04/14/000094946_01041102152842/Rendered/PDF/multi0page.pdf.

———. *World Development Report 1997.* Washington, DC: World Bank, 1997.

Yang, Kaifeng. "Emergent Accountability and Structuration Theory: Implications." In *Accountable Governance: Problems and Promises,* edited by Melvin J. Dubnick and H. George Frederickson, 269–81. Armonk, NY: M. E. Sharpe, 2011.

Young, Dennis R., Bonnie L. Koening, Adil Najam, and Julie Fisher. "Strategy and Structure in Managing Global Associations." In *The Earthscan Reader on NGO Management,* edited by Michael Edwards and Alan Fowler, 164–86. London: Earthscan, 2002.

Young, Oran R. *The Effectiveness of International Environmental Regimes: Causal Connections and Behavioral Mechanisms.* Cambridge, MA: MIT Press, 1999.

Zadek, Simon, and Murdoch Gatward. "Transforming the Transnational NGOs: Social Auditing or Bust?" In *Beyond the Magic Bullet,* edited by Michael Edwards and David Hulme, 226–40. West Hartford, CT: Kumarian Press, 1996.

Index

Also available from Kumarian Press

Sustainable Capitalism: A Matter of Common Sense
John Ikerd

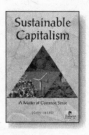

"For years, John Ikerd's writings and speeches have provided precious insights into the economics of this nation's food system, exploding the myth that factory farms are economically imperative. In this brilliant book, he makes a powerful case for a new capitalistic economy: one that is environmentally sound, socially just, and economically sustainable." —*Robert F. Kennedy, Jr.*

The Myth of the Free Market: The Role of the State in a Capitalist Economy
Mark A. Martinez

"In this thoughtful and erudite book, Mark Martinez forces us to re-examine the myth of the 'natural' free market order. Using very intelligently a wide range of fascinating historical and contemporary examples, he takes us through many important economic, political, and philosophical reflections about the true nature of the market system and its important but limited role in the construction of a civilized society." —*Ha-Joon Chang, University of Cambridge, author of* Kicking Away the Ladder *and* Bad Samaritans

"Explains the role of political processes in creating and supporting capitalist markets." —*Publishers Weekly*

The Great Turning: From Empire to Earth Community
David C. Korten

"A work of amazing scope and depth that shows we can create cultures where our enormous human capacities for joy, caring, and cooperation are realized." —*Riane Eisler, author of* The Chalice and the Blade

Kumarian Press
An Imprint of Stylus Publishing

22883 Quicksilver Drive
Sterling, VA 20166-2102

Subscribe to our e-mail alerts: www.kpbooks.com

Kumarian Press, located in Sterling, Virginia, is a forward-looking, scholarly press that promotes active international engagement and an awareness of global connectedness.